LPC CASE STUDY:
CRIMINAL LITIGATION

LPC CASE STUDY: CRIMINAL LITIGATION

Professor Hugh Brayne, Solicitor

Head of Kingston Law School, Kingston University

and

Philip Plowden, Solicitor

Principal Lecturer, University of Northumbria

First published in Great Britain 1994 by Blackstone Press Limited, Aldine Place, London W12 8AA.
Telephone: 0181-740 2277

© H. Brayne, 1994
H. Brayne, P. Plowden, 1997

First edition, 1994
Second edition, 1995
Third edition, 1996
Fourth edition, 1997

ISBN: 1 85431 696 6

British Library Cataloguing in Publication Data
A CIP catalogue record for this book is available from the British Library.

Typeset by Montage Studios Limited, Tonbridge, Kent
Printed by Ashford Colour Press, Gosport, Hampshire

All rights reserved. No part of this book may be reproduced or transmitted in any form or by any means, electronic or mechanical, including photocopying, recording, or any information storage or retrieval system without prior permission from the publisher.

CONTENTS

Preface ix

Acknowledgments xi

Acknowledgments to previous editions xiii

Introduction xv

Criminal Case Study: *R v Rushkin* 1

The documents contained in the case study are as follows:

Date	Event/document		Document No.
19.4.97	Arrest of Steven		
PART A:	THE POLICE STATION		1
	Notices to detainee given to Steven	Doc 1	3
	Custody record opened at Oldcastle Police Station	Doc 2	10
	Defence solicitor attends police station		
	Defence solicitor's notes of interview	Doc 3	20
	Notice to person whose interview has been tape recorded	Doc 3A	23
	Record of authority granted by a superintendent	Doc 4	25
	Steven is charged with driving whilst disqualified	Docs 5A and 5B	27–28
	Solicitor's attendance note of events at police station	Doc 6	29
	Steven is released on police bail to return 3.5.97		
21.4.97	Steven sees his solicitor and signs a green form	Doc 7	33
	Green form key card no. 27	Doc 8	34
22.4.97	Solicitor interviews alibi witness P. Gramsci and writes statement	Doc 9	35
2.5.97	Return to police station, identification parade held	Docs 10A–10C	38–47
	Steven charged with attempted burglary, bail refused	Doc 11	50
	Solicitor's attendance note of second police station visit	Doc 12	51
7.5.97	Solicitor submits report to Legal Aid Board for payment for advice at police station (DSPS 1)	Doc 13	53–54
PART B:	MAGISTRATES' COURT		55
3.5.97	Steven appears at Oldcastle Magistrates' Court		
	Mode of trial decision adjourned for advance information		
	Application for bail refused		
	Legal aid application submitted in Form 1 and Form 5	Doc 14	57–67
	Notice of refusal of bail	Doc 15	70
	Solicitor's attendance notes for first court hearing	Doc 16	71
	Refusal of legal aid	Doc 17	73

v

CONTENTS

7.5.97	Application for review of refusal	Doc 18	74
	Letter in support	Doc 19	76
16.5.97	Notification of grant of legal aid by Area Committee of Legal Aid Board	Doc 20	78
	Initial client statement prepared	Doc 21	79
7.5.97	Letter to client including client care issues	Doc 22	81
	Witness interviewed and statement prepared	Doc 23	83
	Letter to CPS requesting advance information	Doc 24	85
8.5.97	Defendant's details received from police	Doc 25	87
	Printout of convictions	Doc 26	88
	Solicitor's attendance note	Doc 27	89
	Full argument certificate following refusal of bail	Doc 28	90
	Defence application to Crown Court for bail	Doc 29	92
	Written grounds for Crown Court application	Doc 30	94
12.5.97	Attendance note for bail application	Doc 31	95
20.5.97	CPS send out advance information:		
	accompanying letter	Doc 32	96
	statements of prosecution witnesses	Docs 33 to 39	97–103
	record of taped interviews	Docs 40 to 43	104–107
	Steven gives further instructions	Doc 44	108
22.5.97	Solicitor's attendance note	Doc 45	112
	Legal aid granted	Doc 46	113
	Crim 10 used to obtain medical report	Doc 47	115
3.6.97	Defence request transcript of police interviews	Doc 48	117
17.6.97	CPS letter regarding committal	Doc 49	119
	draft indictment	Doc 50	120
	section 41 request	Doc 51A	120
	schedule for s. 41 matter	Doc 51B	121
	list of prosecution witnesses and list of exhibits	Doc 52	121
	notice of record of interview	Doc 53	122
	Right to object to written evidence	Doc 53A	123
18.6.97	Solicitor advises Steven not to object to committal to Crown Court	Doc 54	125
3.7.97	Solicitor's attendance note	Doc 55	126
	Committal certificate	Doc 56	127
	Defence legal aid claim submitted (Crim 13)	Doc 57	129
PART C:	**CROWN COURT**		**131**
	Witness requirements: letter to CPS	Doc 58A	132
	Notification of witness requirements	Doc 58B	132
	Defence seek authority (Crim 10) for legal aid costs of transcript of police interview	Doc 59	134
7.7.97	Primary prosecution disclosure: letter	Doc 60A	136
	Disclosure schedule	Doc 60B	138
	Rights and duties of accused persons	Doc 60C	139
	Witness statement: misused material	Doc 60D	141
14.7.97	Defence statement sent to CPS	Doc 61A	143
	Defence statement	Doc 61B	144
	Draft judge's questionnaire for plea and directions hearing prepared	Doc 62	148
	Proofs of evidence prepared	Docs 63 to 65	151–154
	Counsel is briefed for the plea and directions hearing	Doc 66	155
22.7.97	Transcripts of police interviews received	Docs 67 to 68	159–163
24.7.97	PDH at Oldcastle Crown Court, Steven pleads not guilty		
29.7.97	Secondary prosecution disclosure	Doc 69	165
1.8.97	Defence seek formal admissions from CPS	Doc 70	167

8.8.97	Defence receive formal admissions from CPS	Doc 71	167
11.8.97	CPS send further witness statement to defence with plan of scene of crime exhibited	Docs 72A to 72C	168–170
14.8.97	Defence write to object to statement	Doc 73	171
	Medical report received (with covering letter)	Docs 74A to 74B	172–174
15.8.97	Letter sent to CPS disclosing report	Doc 75	174
14.8.97	Statement of expert witness under CJA 1967, s. 9	Doc 76	175
20.8.97	Witness Summons	Doc 77	176
21.8.97	Counsel briefed for trial	Doc 78	177
12.9.97	Steven is convicted and remanded in custody for reports		
29.9.97	Pre-sentence report prepared	Doc 79	182
6.10.97	Steven sent to prison		
	Counsel is instructed to advise on appeal	Doc 80	185
	Specimen notice of appeal	Doc 81	187
14.10.97	Defence submit claim for standard costs to Crown Court	Doc 82	193

PREFACE

Why have a Case Study?

Any subject studied in the abstract loses its appeal, and this is particularly the case with criminal litigation, with its often intimidating partner, criminal evidence. Yet in reality a criminal practioner's work is often entertaining, and almost always exhilerating (although 2 a.m. visits to the police station do sometimes lose something of that early thrill!). The purpose of this case study is to take criminal litigation out of the classroom and to place it in its real context, the criminal case itself.

This case study therefore follows a typical case from the arrest through to trial, and (as is the depressing way with case studies) through to sentencing and appeal. We have tried to illustrate not simply the paperwork, but also the practicalities of a case. The case study looks at the typical documentation that the solicitor or trainee will face, and at the range of standard letters, forms, applications and hearings that arise in a case, but it also looks at the tactical decisions that need to be taken in every case, and at the realities of fixed fees and legal aid which inevitably underlie all our work.

Alongside every stage of the case, and accompanying every document, you will find an explanation of what is happening and why and, where appropriate, what tactical decisions are being made. If we have done our work well, you will find the case study useful not only when you are studying litigation, but as an early *aide memoire* when you first enter into practice.

The case study does not replace the LPC course text. It looks at how the law works in the context of one particular case. It does not try to cover every element of procedure and every rule of evidence. For that you need a litigation textbook and we recommend Craig Osborne's *LPC Guide: Criminal Litigation 1997/98* (Blackstone Press). You will also need to get in the habit of using a practitioner text, such as *Blackstone's Criminal Practice* or *Stone's Justices' Manual*. The preparatory work which is done on the case in the case study continues to show how essential such work is in the context of the case as a whole.

Finally, the case study is not simply intended to illustrate criminal litigation and evidence. It also aims to illustrate a variety of different drafting styles, whether in letters, documents or briefs. It shows examples of good practice and, in the case of some of the official documents which are reproduced, bad practice as well.

Changes to the Case Study

Since Hugh first wrote this case study, four years ago, there has been a vast amount of new legislation. Criminal practice has changed considerably. Last year students and practitioners alike had to struggle with developments in the law on the right of silence, the inferences that can now be drawn in certain circumstances from a failure to answer police questions or a failure to give evidence. This year the bulk of the Criminal Procedure and Investigations Act 1996 was implemented as of 1 April 1997, and that has not only changed committals again, but has introduced a vast new statutory framework for the disclosure of material by the prosecution and, for the first time, by the defence.

PREFACE

These new developments are difficult to understand in the abstract, not least because their impact is never entirely certain. If you exercise your right of silence and fail to put forward defence facts, an inference *may* be drawn if it is reasonable to do so — but equally possibly, it may not. What will a jury think is reasonable — and it seems that it is purely a matter for the jury (see *Argent*, *The Times*, 19 December 1996) — and how does that affect your advice in the police station in a particular case? How much detail must be included in a defence statment to avoid an inference at trial (under s. 11, Criminal Procedure and Investigations Act 1996) and what would that inference be in any case?

This case study is the ideal way of seeking how these changes impact on a solicitor's work in practice. Thus, while this case study has evolved every year to take account of all the new developments, this year I have focussed on the two key areas of the practitioner's work which have most been affected by the recent changes in the law: police station work and post-committal preparations.

In the first part of the book you will find that there is a greater focus on Jane's work in the police station. This does not simply reflect the recent changes in the law (especially the limitations on the right of silence) but also the increasing concerns about the role of the solicitor in the police station. Watching Jane deal with non-disclosure and the need to advise on the interview should give you a sense of how the right of silence now works in its practical context. Similarly, once the case has reached court, you will find that more time is spent in the book considering the need for an early preparation of matters in order to fit in with the tight new timetable for post-committal defence disclosure and the new possibility of binding pre-trial rulings (under s. 40, Criminal Procedure and Investigations Act 1996) at plea and directions hearings.

There is no sign that the pace of change will slow down in the next year, which will bring with it the implementation of the Police Act 1997 and possibly the Crime (Sentences) Act 1997. It is, however, the sign of a good case study that it evolves almost effortlessly to illustrate new and unanticipated developments, and the basic story of Steven Rushkin and the burglary at MegaWin remains largely unchanged from Hugh's original account. By next year, of course, Steve Rushkin may be worried about the possibility of a mandatory sentence and may be less inclined to come quietly!

Philip Plowden
May 1997

I am enormously grateful to Philip Plowden for giving this case study a new lease of life. His updating, and reshaping of substantial parts of the text has, I think, produced a text that is clear, authoratative, useful and readable.

Hugh Brayne
Kingston, May 1997

ACKNOWLEDGMENTS

I must acknowledge my indebtedness to all those mentioned by Hugh in his acknowledgments, and in particular acknowledge the continuing permissions to use forms and other documentation. The assistance of all those mentioned has continued to ensure that this case study is as accurate and realistic as possible.

I am extremely grateful to the Newcastle Area Office of the Legal Aid Board for their prompt assistance with the up-dated forms. And I am also indebted to Peter Tatham of Northumbria Police for his help in ensuring that the police station materials continue to be accurate. I have to acknowledge that I have kept the standard form custody record and charge sheet, rather than adopting Northumbria Police's new computerised versions, since I am conscious that full computerisation of these documents is not yet widespread across the country, but I am certain that this will come in time.

This year, however, when there have been so many new documents to deal with I must acknowledge the very generous assistance of the Crown Prosecution Service Operational Practice Division, and in particular the assistance of Alan Kirkwood, Stephen Hopwood and Deborah Steele. The Criminal Procedure and Investigations Act 1996 has brought many changes for us all, and it has only been with their help that I have been able to ensure that this case study reflects the new regime.

I am of course indebted to Paula Doolan and the team at Blackstone Press for all their hard work and to Hugh Brayne, whose case study this is, and whose original hard work and vision has made my job of up-dating so much easier. For once the phrase 'without whom this would not have been possible' is entirely accurate.

Notwithstanding all the assistance I have received from the above, any errors or omissions are of course entirely my own.

ACKNOWLEDGMENTS TO PREVIOUS EDITIONS

Nigel Barnes gave enormous help in the criminal case study, in helping to shape the factual scenario and advising on defence solicitors' tactics. He also helped check the contents. If I am ever in trouble with the police, Nigel will be my brief!

Andy Cope, also an experienced defence solicitor, helped by reading the entire case study through and providing very helpful comments.

I am grateful to Michelle Robson, who has written the companion *LPC Case Study: Civil Litigation*, for her help and advice.

Materials for a book like this could not be created by a lawyer alone. It contains materials that only experts and specialists in their own fields can produce. Superintendant John Stoddart of Northumbria Police has given generous help in obtaining and helping me to complete police documents, and I am grateful for his force's permission to use sample documents. Chris Livesley and Phil Hindson of South Tyneside Magistrates were similarly helpful in providing sample documents.

Thanks to Dr Jill Millar for producing a medical report on Mr Rushkin (without being able to examine him!) and to Colin Hunter for his guidance on the pre-sentence report.

If there are any mistakes, they are my fault, and if any kind reader points them out, I will attend to them in the next edition.

Permissions to use the following forms are gratefully acknowledged:

Documents illustrated by kind permission of Northumbria Police are Notice to Detained Person (page 3), Custody Record (page 10), Notice to Person whose Interview has been Tape Recorded (page 20), Record of Authority granted by Superintendent (page 25), Charge Sheets (page 27), Identification Parade Forms (pages 38–47), and Defendant Details from Police (page 87).

Documents reproduced by kind permission of the Legal Aid Board are the Green Form and Key Card (pages 33 and 34), Advice at Police Stations Report (page 53), Claim for Lower Standard Fee (page 129) and Application for Prior Authority Expenditure in Criminal Proceedings (page 134).

The Notice of Application Relating to Bail to be made to the Crown Court (page 92), Judge's Questionnaire (page 148), Notice and Grounds of Appeal (page 187), and Claim for Crown Court Costs (page 193) are reproduced by kind permission of HMSO.

The Refusal of Bail form is reproduced by kind permission of Kalamazoo System Print plc.

I thank David Evans and colleagues at the CPS for permission to copy the wording of CPS documents, checking that the ones I use are up-to-date, and advice on the Criminal Procedure and Investigations Act 1996.

ACKNOWLEDGMENTS TO PREVIOUS EDITIONS

Derek Oakey, of the Lord Chancellor's Department, gave very helpful information on pleas and directions hearings, and kindly supplied the new judge's questionnaire (page 148). Catherine Lee at the Home Office kindly supplied information on the Criminal Proceedure and Investigations Bill at a time when what I needed was not yet published.

All other documents are created for this case study, modelled on those found in practice or specified in regulations. References to Oldcastle Police, CPS, magistrates' court and Crown Court are fictitious, as are the characters who appear in the study.

INTRODUCTION

In this case you will follow the defendant Steven Rushkin from arrest to his preparation for trial at Crown Court, and advice on appeal against sentence.

The case is almost entirely presented through material in the defence file. Some documents, however, have been omitted. In particular, I have not set out every letter and every attendance note; many of these are entirely routine and would only obscure the main storyline of the case. At some points (and in particular to illustrate the effects of a refusal of legal aid) I depart from the story and digress for a few pages in order to include documents that will often be relevant in criminal cases.

At the time of writing the bulk of the Criminal Procedure and Investigations Act 1996 has been implemented with effect from 1 April 1997 (one hopes the date is not an omen), although some provisions (indications of plea at mode of trial; new arrangements for third party disclosure) have not yet been brought into force. Although there are at present effectively two regimes in place — the 'old' regime and the new CPIA regime — by the time of publication only very long-running investigations will fall under the pre-CPIA rules and I have therefore concentrated on the effects of the new regime.

The law is stated as of 1 May 1997.

CRIMINAL LITIGATION CASE STUDY
R v RUSHKIN

PART A — THE POLICE STATION

The Initial Phone Call: Saturday morning: 19 April 1997: 7.14 a.m.

Jane Watkins is a partner in the criminal department of Watkins O'Dwyer. On 19 April 1997 she receives a call from Central Police Station, advising her that Steven Rushkin has been detained on suspicion of attempted burglary and that he has asked for her to attend. The custody officer informs her that the investigating officer wants to interview Steven about the attempted burglary, and that he will in any event be charged with driving while disqualified.

Watkins O'Dwyer has acted for Steven on a number of previous occasions. In 1995 he pleaded guilty to actual bodily harm following a dispute with his neighbour, and in 1996 he again pleaded guilty, this time to burglary of derelict premises. In this latter case he was also convicted of the offence of absconding for failing to answer his bail. Jane also knows that the civil litigation department in the firm is currently acting for Steven in relation to a road traffic accident in 1996.

Attending the police station

Jane is being asked to attend the police station as an 'own solicitor'. In other words, she is attending as Steven's solicitor, rather than because she is the Duty Solicitor on the Duty Solicitor Rota for that morning.

Most firms that do a significant amount of criminal work will have organised their own 'internal' rota for police station work at night and over the weekends. Jane might therefore choose to ring up a colleague (who could be another solicitor in the firm, or a trainee, or a 'clerk' — a person employed part-time by the firm to do police station and other work) in order to ask them to attend. However, she has always dealt with Steven in the past and she knows he will not be pleased if someone else arrives. She therefore decides to attend herself.

(Note: non-qualified staff, including trainee solicitors (from February 1997), are now required to complete an accreditation process if they are to attend police stations as fee earners. This requires a number of supervised visits, the submission of a portfolio of police station work, and a critical incidents test.)

Does Jane need to attend now?

Jane asks the custody officer when the police intend to interview and is told that it won't be before 8.30 a.m. She checks with the officer:

(a) the grounds and circumstances of the arrest and detention;

(b) the time of arrival at the police station;

(c) what, if anything, Steven has already said to the police;

(d) what evidence the police have, and what they wish to obtain;

(e) whether there is any ground for concern, such as a medical condition.

The custody officer tells Jane that Steven was arrested just after midnight and has been detained since about 00.45 this morning. The delay was to give Steven a rest period and to enable the police to interview witnesses.

Jane then asks to speak to Steven. She tells him that she will be coming down to the police station. She stresses that Steven should not answer any questions until she arrives. Jane makes sure that she tells the custody officer that she intends to attend for interview and that Steven should not be interviewed before she arrives. This ensures that the custody officer is aware of what is going on, but also prevents any suggestion that Steven has now had his 'independent legal advice' (see below) and can be interviewed without a solicitor present.

Jane's attendance note (Document 6, page 29) sets out her record of the events.

The power to detain and question

Steven Rushkin's arrest, detention and questioning occur within the framework set out in the Police and Criminal Evidence Act 1984 (PACE 1984) and its Codes of Practice. PACE Code C deals with the 'Detention, Treatment and Questioning of Persons by Police Officers'.

In this case study I have provided summaries of the relevant provisions rather than lengthy extracts so as not to hold up the progress of the case, but there is no better way of getting a sense of the PACE regime than reading the Code itself. It is generally written in (relatively) clear English!

When Jane arrives at the police station she will want to check:

(a) that there was a power to arrest Steven;

(b) that there was a power to detain Steven;

(c) that Steven has been properly treated while detained;

(d) that Steven has been informed of his rights and, where appropriate, allowed to exercise those rights.

What are Steven's rights as a detainee in the police station?

Code C provides:

3.1 When a person is brought to a police station under arrest or is arrested at the police station having attended there voluntarily, the custody officer must tell him clearly of the following rights and of the fact that they are continuing rights which may be exercised during the period in custody.

(i) the right to have someone informed of his arrest ...;

(ii) the right to consult privately with a solicitor and the fact that independent legal advice is available free of charge; and

(iii) the right to consult these codes of practice.

Code C, para. 3.2 provides that the custody officer must give the suspect a written notice setting out these three rights. A copy of the notice used by Northumbria Police is set out below (Document 1).

Document 1

Northumbria Police

Notice to Detained Person

The section in capital letters is to be read to the detained person by the Custody Officer before giving the notice to the detained person.

If you are asked questions about a suspected offence, you do not have to say anything, but it may harm your defence if you do not mention when questioned, something which you later rely on in court. Anything you do say may be given in evidence.

YOU HAVE THE RIGHT TO:
1. SPEAK TO AN INDEPENDENT SOLICITOR FREE OF CHARGE.
2. HAVE SOMEONE TOLD THAT YOU HAVE BEEN ARRESTED.
3. CONSULT A COPY OF THE CODES OF PRACTICE COVERING POLICE POWERS AND PROCEDURES

YOU MAY DO ANY OF THESE THINGS NOW, BUT IF YOU DO NOT, YOU MAY STILL DO SO AT ANY OTHER TIME WHILST DETAINED AT THE POLICE STATION.

More information is given below.

Free Legal Advice

You can speak to a solicitor at the police station at any time, day or night. It will cost you nothing.

Access to legal advice can only be delayed in certain exceptional circumstances (see Annex B of Code of Practice C).

If you do not know a solicitor, or you can not contact your own solicitor, ask for the duty solicitor. He or she is nothing to do with the police. Or you can ask to see a list of local solicitors.

You can talk to the solicitor in private on the telephone, and the solicitor may come to see you at the police station.

If the police want to question you, you can ask for the solicitor to be there.
If there is a delay, ask the police to contact the solicitor again. Normally the police must not question you until you have spoken to the solicitor. However, there are certain circumstances in which the police may question you without a solicitor being present.(See paragraph 6.6 of the Code of Practice C).

If you want to see a solicitor, tell the Custody Officer at once. You can ask for Legal advice at any time during your detention. Even if you tell the police you don't want a solicitor at first, you can change your mind at any time.

Your right to legal advice does not entitle you to delay procedures under the Road Traffic Act 1988 which require the provision of breath, blood or urine specimens.

THE LAW SOCIETY

The right to have someone informed of your detention.

You may on request have one person known to you, or who is likely to take an interest in your welfare, informed at public expense as soon as practicable of your whereabouts. If the person you name cannot be contacted you may choose up to two alternatives. If they too cannot be contacted the Custody Officer has discretion to allow further attempts until the information has been conveyed. This right can only be delayed in exceptional circumstances (see Annex B of Code of Practice C).

PACE 11 (2.96)

The right to consult the Codes of Practice.

The Codes of Practice will be made available to you on request. These codes govern police procedures. The right to consult the Codes of Practice does not entitle you to delay unreasonably any necessary investigative and administrative action, neither does it allow procedures under the Road Traffic Act 1988 requiring the provision of breath, blood or urine specimens to be delayed.

The right to a copy of the Custody Record.

A record of your detention will be kept by the Custody Officer. When you leave police detention or are taken before a Court, you or your legal representative or the appropriate adult shall be supplied on request with a copy of the Custody Record as soon as practicable. This entitlement lasts for 12 months after your release from police detention.

R v RUSHKIN

Person attending voluntarily at a Police Station and not under arrest

Free Legal Advice

You are not under arrest and may leave the police station at any time, unless you are placed under arrest.

If the police wish to ask you questions about your suspected involvement in an offence they must caution you in the following terms:

> "You do not have to say anything, but it may harm your defence if you do not mention when questioned something which you later rely on in court. Anything you do say may be given in evidence".

If you have been cautioned by the police, you can speak to a solicitor at the police station at any time, day or night. It will cost you nothing. If you wish to speak to a solicitor, the police may not question you until you have done so.

If you want to speak to a solicitor, tell the police officer at once. Even if at first you tell the police you do not want a solicitor, you can change your mind at any time.

If you do not know a solicitor, or you cannot contact your own solicitor, ask for the duty solicitor. He or she is nothing to do with the police. Or you can ask to see a list of local solicitors.

You can talk to the solicitor in private on the telephone, and the solicitor may come to see you at the police station.

If the police want to question you, you can ask for the solicitor to be there. If there is a delay, ask the police to contact the solicitor again. You can ask the police to wait for the solicitor to be at the interview.

NORTHUMBRIA POLICE

NOTICE OF ENTITLEMENTS

This notice summarises provisions contained in Codes C and D of the Codes of Practice regarding your entitlements whilst in custody. The letters and numbers in brackets relate to appropriate Code and paragraph references. If you require more detailed information please ask to consult the Codes.

All persons should read parts A and B of this notice. Part C explains provisions which apply to juveniles and persons suffering from mental disorder or mental handicap and part D explains additional provisions which apply to citizens of independent commonwealth countries and nationals of foreign countries.

PART A — GENERAL ENTITLEMENTS

Whilst in police custody you are entitled to the following:

1. **Visits and contact with outside persons.**

    In addition to your rights to have someone informed of your arrest, and to legal advice, you may receive visits, at the custody officer's discretion. Unless certain conditions apply you may also make one telephone call, and be supplied with writing materials. ('C' 5.4 & 5.6).

2. **Reasonable Standards of Physical Comfort.**

    Where practicable you should have your own cell ('C' 8.1), which is clean, heated, ventilated and lit ('C' 8.2). Bedding should be clean and serviceable ('C' 8.3).

3. **Adequate Food and Drink.**

    Three meals per day. Drinks with and, upon reasonable request between meals. ('C' 8.6).

4. **Access to Toilets and Washing Facilities.** ('C' 8.4).

5. **Replacement Clothing.**

    If your own clothes are taken from you, you must be given replacements that are clean and comfortable. ('C' 8.5).

6. **Medical Attention.**

    You may ask to see the police surgeon (or other doctor at your own expense) for a medical examination, or if you require medication. You may also be allowed to take or apply your own medication at appropriate times but in the case of controlled drugs the police surgeon will normally supervise you when doing so. ('C' 9.4 - 'C' 9.6).

7. **Exercise.**

    Where practicable, brief outdoor exercise every day. ('C' 8.7).

8. **If in 'Police Detention' to make representations when your detention is reviewed.**

    When the grounds for your detention are periodically reviewed, you have a statutory right to say why you think you should be released, unless you are unfit to do so because of your condition or behaviour. ('C' 15.1).

PART B — CONDUCT OF INTERVIEWS

1. Interview rooms should be adequately heated, lit and ventilated. ('C' 12.4).

2. Persons being interviewed should not be required to stand. ('C' 12.5).

3. Unless certain conditions apply, in any 24 hour period you must be allowed at least eight hours rest, normally at night. ('C' 12.2).

4. Breaks should be made at recognised meal times, and short breaks for refreshments should normally be made at intervals of approximately two hours. ('C' 12.7).

5. Interviewing officers should identify themselves by name and rank (or by warrant or other identification number in terrorism cases). ('C' 12.6).

PACE 11a (3.95)

PART C — APPROPRIATE ADULTS

If you are under 17 years of age or suffering from a mental disorder or mental handicap, you should be assisted by an "appropriate adult" as explained in Code C, paragraph 1.7. A solicitor or lay visitor present at the station in that professional capacity may not act as the appropriate adult ('C' note 1F). The appropriate adult will be present when you are:

1. informed of and served with notices explaining the rights of detained persons, and when informed of the grounds for detention   ('C' 3.11);

2. interviewed (except in urgent cases), or provide or sign a written statement   ('C' 11.14);

3. intimately or strip searched   ('C' Annex A, Paragraphs 5 and 11(c));

4. cautioned   ('C' 10.6);

5. given information, asked to sign documentation, or asked to give consent regarding any identification procedure   ('D' 1.11, 1.12, 1.13); or

6. charged   ('C' 16.1); or

7. when the grounds for detention are periodically reviewed   ('C' 15.1).

   You should always be given the opportunity, where an appropriate adult is called to the Police Station, to speak privately to a solicitor in the absence of the appropriate adult should you wish to do so.

PART D — FOREIGN NATIONALS/COMMONWEALTH CITIZENS

If you are a citizen of a foreign or commonwealth country, you are entitled to the following:

1. To communicate at any time with your High Commission, Embassy or Consulate, and have them told of your whereabouts and the grounds for your detention   ('C' 7.1).

2. To private visits from a consular officer to talk, or to arrange for legal advice   ('C' 7.3).

The most important right for Steven at this stage is his right to the 'independent legal advice'.

Right to legal advice

Section 58 of PACE 1984 states:

> *(1) A person arrested and held in custody in a police station or other premises shall be entitled, <u>if he so requests</u>, to consult <u>a solicitor privately</u> at any time. (my emphasis)*

'if he so requests'

Steven does not have to see a solicitor. He could have chosen not to exercise this right. There have in the past been concerns that some officers have tried to persuade suspects not to ask for a solicitor, arguing that it will only cause a further delay or will in some way complicate matters. However, now that inferences can be drawn from a suspect's silence at interview (s. 34, Criminal Justice and Public Order Act 1994, discussed below), most officers would rather have a solicitor present in order to ensure that the interview cannot be criticised and ruled inadmissible at trial.

Code C provides:

> *6.1 Subject to the provisos in Annex B (right to delay where authorised in serious arrestable offences) all people in police detention must be informed that they may at any time consult and communicate privately, whether in person, in writing or by telephone with a solicitor, and that independent legal advice is available free of charge from the duty solicitor.*

Section 58 of PACE 1984 states:

> *6.4 No police officer shall at any time do or say anything with the intention of dissuading a person in detention from obtaining legal advice.*

> *6.5 ... If on being informed or reminded of the right to legal advice, the person declines to speak to a solicitor in person, the officer shall point out that the right to legal advice includes the right to speak with a solicitor on the telephone and ask him if he wishes to do so. If the person continues to waive his right to legal advice the officer shall ask him the reasons for doing so, and any reasons shall be recorded on the custody record or the interview record as appropriate....*

'solicitor'

Solicitor is defined by Code C, para. 6.12 and it includes solicitors with practising certificates (such as Jane), trainee solicitors, duty solicitor representatives or accredited representatives.

'privately'

Note that although Jane makes sure that she speaks to Steven on the telephone to ensure that he knows she will be coming, she does not discuss the case with him or ask for his version of events at this stage. If Steven had started to talk about the case, Jane would have stopped him. Most telephones will be in the custody suite of the police station and are unlikely to be private. There have been concerns that many phone calls are listened in on, or are tape-recorded. Any discussion should therefore wait until a private conversation can take place.

Can Steven be interviewed before Jane arrives?

Generally, no. Code C provides:

> *6.6 A person who wants legal advice may not be interviewed or continue to be interviewed until he has received it ...*

However, Code C, para. 6.6 goes on to set out four exceptions to the principle. The first is that the right to legal advice has been delayed by virtue of Annex B (this permits the police to delay the suspect access to legal advice in certain circumstances; this is discussed below).

Secondly, Steven could be interviewed if an officer of at least the rank of superintendent has reasonable grounds for believing that either the delay will involve 'an immediate risk' of harm to persons or of serious loss or damage to property, or where a solicitor has agreed to attend but that waiting for his arrival would cause unreasonable delay to the progress of the investigation.

Thirdly, the interview could go ahead where the client's nominated solicitor either cannot be contacted or will not attend and the suspect refuses to use the Duty Solicitor (or the Duty Solicitor is also unavailable).

Finally, the interview could go ahead if Steven changed his mind about wanting legal advice — but in this case an officer of at least the rank of Inspector would have to ask him why he had changed his mind and would need to give authorisation for the interview.

There have, however, been suggestions that once a suspect has spoken to his solicitor on the phone, he has now had his right to legal advice and the interview can then go ahead. This is why Jane is careful to tell the custody officer that she wishes to attend. Code C states:

> 6.8 Where a person has been permitted to consult a solicitor and the solicitor is available (i.e., present at the station or on his way to the station or easily contactable by telephone) at the time the interview begins or is in progress, the solicitor must be allowed to be present while he is interviewed.

When can the right to legal advice be delayed?

Exceptionally the right to legal advice can be delayed under Annex B to Code C. In summary this provides that the offence must be a 'serious arrestable offence' *and* that an officer of at least the rank of superintendent has reasonable grounds for believing that the exercise of the right to legal advice will lead to interference or harm to evidence or physical injury to other people, or that it will lead to the alerting of other suspects who have not yet been arrested, or it will hinder the recovery of property.

Steven has been arrested on suspicion of attempted burglary. He is also suspected of driving while disqualified. Burglary is an offence carrying a maximum sentence of 14 years' imprisonment if tried on indictment (i.e., in the Crown Court); it is therefore an 'arrestable offence' within the definition in s. 24(1)(b), PACE 1984 (and an attempt is treated similarly by virtue of s. 24(3)(b), PACE 1984). In contrast, driving while disqualified carries a *power* of arrest (s. 103(3), Road Traffic Act 1988), but is not an 'arrestable offence' within the PACE definition. Only arrestable offences can be 'serious arrestable offences', and so only the attempted burglary needs to be considered.

Steven's right of access to Jane could therefore be delayed if the burglary is classed as a 'serious' arrestable offence. Serious arrestable offences are defined by s. 116, PACE 1984. If you look at this section, you will see that burglary or attempted burglary are not automatically serious arrestable offences. The offence will only be 'serious' if it leads to a s. 116(6) consequence — here either substantial financial gain or serious financial loss (the seriousness of the loss depends on whether it is serious to the person who suffers it). It might therefore be possible for the attempted burglary to be classified as a serious arrestable offence, depending on the facts of the case. If so, a senior officer would then need to have a reasonable belief that allowing Steven access to his solicitor would lead to one of the serious consequences set out above before he could authorise a delay.

If you look at the custody record (Document 2, page 10) you will see that no delay has been authorised in this case.

Arrival at the Police Station: Saturday morning: 19 April 1997: 9.00 a.m.

Jane arrives at the police station. Her job is to advise Steven about the case, and the most pressing issue is to advise him on how to deal with the police interrogation. What happens at the police station is likely to be the most important single factor in the future development of the case.

In order to advise Steven, Jane needs to know what has happened so far, and what the police now intend to do. She therefore needs to:

(a) see the custody record;

(b) talk to the custody officer about the case;

(c) if possible, talk to the officer in the case (in other words the police officer who is leading the investigation).

Jane therefore introduces herself to the custody officer and produces proof of identity. She asks to see the custody record. She must be permitted to see this as soon as practicable after her arrival: Code C, para. 2.4.

The custody officer is responsible for the accuracy of the custody record: Code C, para. 2.3. He will ensure that a separate custody record is opened as soon as practicable for each detainee (Code C, para. 2.1) and that all entries have been timed and signed by the makers (Code C, para. 2.6).

The full custody record (Document 2) is set out below. Bear in mind that at this stage, it would only be complete up to 9.00 a.m. on 19 April — in other words, up to the top of page 3 of the custody record (see page 12).

R v RUSHKIN

Document 2

CUSTODY RECORD

Custody Record No.:	OLC/97/293
Police Station:	OLDCASTLE CENTRAL
Other ref.:	

Time/Date-Arrival at Station: 19.4.97 AT 00.27
Time/Date Arrest: 19.4.97 AT 00.15
Place of Arrest: NORTH ROAD, OLDCASTLE
Brought to Station by: PC 1234 PATEL
Arrested by: PC 1234 PATEL
Officer in case: DC 2345 STUBBS
(In Cases of Terrorism show Warrant Numbers ONLY)

Condition of Person on Arrival‡ ....

Surname: RUSHKIN
(Mr., Mrs., Miss)*(Add Maiden Name where applicable)
First Names: STEVEN
Address: 12 PARK VIEW, LONGFIELD, OLDCASTLE, OL10 2AB
Occupation: UNEMPLOYED
Age: 44 D.O.B. 12.1.53 Height: 6'00 M/F*
Place of Birth: OLDCASTLE

A notice setting out my rights has been read to me and I have been provided with a copy. I have been provided with a written notice setting out my entitlements whilst in custody
Signature of person detained ....
Time 00.40 Date 19.4.97
Signature of Appropriate Adult/Interpreter ....
Time .... Date ....

I WANT a solicitor as soon as practicable
†Named solicitor ....
Signature of person detained ....
Time .... Date ....
Signature of Appropriate Adult/Interpreter ....
Time .... Date ....

I DO NOT want a solicitor at this time
Signature of person detained ....
Time 00.40 Date 19.4.97
Signature of Appropriate Adult/Interpreter ....
Time .... Date ....

At the time of Notice, notification of detention to named person, NOT REQUESTED/~~REQUESTED~~*
†Named person ....
Time .... Date ....

Security Checks	Time	Date	Officer
Address Verified	00.40	19.4.97	
P.N.C.	00.45	19.4.97	
C.I.S.	00.42	19.4.97	
Warrant	00.42	19.4.97	

Officer opening Custody Record
Signature: B. Pollard
Name: B. POLLARD Rank/No. Sgt 3456

Reasons and Grounds for arrest (show place/time/circumstances/offence)‡

Suspicion of attempted burglary at Megawin, Castle Street. Prisoner matches description given by witness, seen leaving area by car, arrested North Road 00.15. Enquiries also reveal prisoner is a disqualified driver.

Sgt. Pollard

SPECIMEN

R v RUSHKIN

Last review of detention conducted at: —		Name: STEVEN RUSHKIN
First/Next review of detention due before: 06:27		

SPECIMEN

Full details of any action/occurrence involving detained person
(Include full particulars of ALL visits/officers)
Individual entries need not be restricted to one line.
All entries to be signed by the writer (include rank and number).

Date	Time	Entry
19.4.97	00.45	Detention is authorised to secure and preserve evidence by way of questioning. Prisoner reminded of right to legal advice in accordance with Code C, s.65 and stated 'I am too tired to think straight at the moment. Can I talk to someone later.' Sgt 3456 Pollard
19.4.97	00.46	Prisoner complains of pain from existing back injury, requests painkillers. Contacted duty surgeon Dr Sangster. Sgt 3456 Pollard
19.4.97	00.50	PC Patel informs prisoner that he is arrested also on suspicion of driving whilst disqualified. Sgt 3456 Pollard
19.4.97	00.51	To cell Sgt 3456 Pollard
19.4.97	00.59	Requested cup of tea, supplied Sgt 3456 Pollard
19.4.97	1.25	Taken to medical room for examination by Dr Sangster, Police Surgeon Sgt 3456 Pollard
19.4.97	1.40	DOCTOR ENTRY I saw Steven Rushkin. He complained of severe back pain. I consider him fit to be detained and interviewed. I gave him paracetamol, two tablets to be taken every 4 hours. DKK
19.4.97	1.50	To cell Sgt 3456 Pollard
19.4.97	2.00	In cell, asleep Sgt 3456 Pollard
19.4.97	3.00	In cell, asleep Sgt 3456 Pollard
19.4.97	4.00	In cell, asleep Sgt 3456 Pollard
19.4.97	5.00	In cell, asleep Sgt 3456 Pollard
19.4.97	5.55	Custody transferred to Sgt 4567 Williams Sgt 3456 Pollard
19.4.97	6.27	Review of detention carried out. Detention authorised to secure evidence by way of questioning. Prisoner has been allowed rest period. Asleep at time of review. Will inform of review at first opportunity. Insp. 9876 Russell
19.4.97	7.00	Prisoner awake, given tea & two paracetamol. Sgt 4567 Williams
19.4.97	7.10	Prisoner informed of intention to interview him and result of review. Solicitor requested J. Watkins Sgt 4567 Williams

R v RUSHKIN

Last review of detention conducted at: 0.627
First/Next review of detention due before: 15:27

Name: STEVEN RUSHKIN

Date	Time	Full details of any action/occurrence involving detained person (Include full particulars of ALL visits/officers) Individual entries need not be restricted to one line. All entries to be signed by the writer (include rank and number). NOTE: In most cases the first entry will concern the grounds for detention which shall be made in the presence of the person arrested unless he is incapable of understanding, violent, or in urgent need of medical attention.
19.4.97	7.14	Spoke to solicitor who will attend. Sgt 4567 Williams
19.4.97	8.00	In cell, awake. Sgt 4567 Williams
19.4.97	8.10	Given breakfast Sgt 4567 Williams
19.4.97	9.00	In cell, awake Sgt 4567 Williams
19.4.97	9.10	Solicitor to interview room B. Prisoner to interview room B Sgt 4567 Williams
19.4.97	9.15	Call to prisoners wife at his request Sgt 4567 Williams
19.4.97	9.20	Custody to DC 2345 Stubbs for interviewing Sgt 4567 Williams
19.4.97	9.35	The interview with the prisoner is concluded. The prisoner has been treated in accordance with the provisions of the Police and Criminal Evidence Act 1984 and Codes of Practice. Signed: P. Stubbs Rank: Det Const. Number 2345.
19.4.97	9.37	To my custody, returned to cell Sgt 4567 Williams
19.4.97	10-07	Prisoner consents to taking of a non-intimate sample (hair from the head) + warned in accordance with code that sample may be subject of a speculative search Sgt 4567 Williams
19.4.97	10-08	I consent to providing fingerprints + hair sample from my head. S. Rushkin
19.4.97	10.17	To my custody interview room B Sgt 4567 Williams
19.4.97	10.18	Charged with driving whilst disqualified. Offence admitted Bailed to Central Magistrates Court 8.5.97. Sgt 4567 Williams
19.4.97	10.22	Bailed for attempted burglary to Central Police Station on 2.5.97 Sgt 4567 Williams
2.5.97	14.00	Responded to police bail. Attended Central police station with solicitor J. Watkins. Detention is authorised to save and preserve evidence by way of questioning if necessary following result of an identification parade Sgt 6789 Smith
2.5.97	14.05	To Interview Room B with solicitor Sgt 6789 Smith

R v RUSHKIN

| Last review of detention conducted at: | 06.27 | Name: STEVEN RUSHKIN |
| First/Next review of detention due before: | 19.05 | |

Date	Time	Full details of any action/occurrence involving detained person (Include full particulars of ALL visits/officers) Individual entries need not be restricted to one line. All entries to be signed by the writer (include rank and number).
2.5.97	14.30	To my custody for identification parade PC 5432 White
2.5.97	14.45	To my custody, interview room B with solicitor Sgt 6789 Smith
2.5.97	15.35	The interview with the prisoner is concluded. The prisoner has been treated in accordance with the provisions of the Police and Criminal Evidence Act 1984 and Codes of Practice. Signed: P Stubbs Rank: Det Const Number 2345
2.5.97	15.35	To my custody, interview room B with solicitor Sgt 6789 Smith
2.5.97	15.45	Charged with attempted burglary. After caution solicitor stated "My client, on my advice, will make no further statement. He has given a full account of his movements and other matters during interview." Bail refused on the ground that he has previously absconded repeatedly. Sgt 6789 Smith
2.5.97	15.49	Solicitor leaves Sgt 6789 Smith
2.5.97	15.50	To cell Sgt 6789 Smith
2.5.97	15.55	Tea provided Sgt 6789 Smith
2.5.97	17.00	In cell, awake Sgt 6789 Smith
2.5.97	17.15	Requested tablets for pain, given 2 paracetamol Sgt 6789 Smith
2.5.97	18.00	In cell, awake Sgt 6789 Smith
2.5.97	18.15	Meal in cell Sgt 6789 Smith
2.5.97	19.00	Review. Continued detention authorised because if released prisoner may abscond. Prisoner's representation that he would not abscond taken into consideration. Sgt 6789 Smith
2.5.97	20.00	In cell, awake Sgt 6789 Smith
2.5.97	21.00	In cell, awake Sgt 6789 Smith
2.5.97	22.00	In cell, awake Sgt 6789 Smith
2.5.97	22.40	Tea provided Sgt 6789 Smith
2.5.97	23.00	In cell, awake Sgt 6789 Smith
3.5.97	24.00	To my custody Sgt 3456 Pollard

SPECIMEN

R v RUSHKIN

Last review of detention conducted at: 06.00
First/Next review of detention due before: 19.05
Name: STEVEN RUSHKIN

Date	Time	Full details of any action/occurrence involving detained person (Include full particulars of ALL visits/officers) Individual entries need not be restricted to one line. All entries to be signed by the writer (include rank and number).
3.5.97	01.00	In cell, asleep — Sgt 3456 Pollard
3.5.97	02.00	In cell, asleep — Sgt 3456 Pollard
3.5.97	03.00	In cell, asleep — Sgt 3456 Pollard
3.5.97	04.00	In cell, asleep — Sgt 3456 Pollard
3.5.97	04.16	Painkillers requested, 2 paracetamol provided Sgt 3456 Pollard
3.5.97	05.00	In cell, awake — Sgt 3456 Pollard
3.5.97	06.00	In cell, awake — Sgt 3456 Pollard
3.5.97	06.00	Review: Continued detention is authorised because if the prisoner is released he may abscond. No representations. Prisoner informed. Sgt 3456 Pollard
3.5.97	06.30	Breakfast provided — Sgt 3456 Pollard
3.5.97	07.00	In cell, awake — Sgt 3456 Pollard
3.5.97	08.00	In cell, awake — Sgt 3456 Pollard
3.5.97	08.18	Into custody of PC 1357 Jagger for transport to Central Magistrate's Court Sgt 3456 Pollard

SPECIMEN

R v RUSHKIN

PROPERTY

Withheld by Police | Retained by Prisoner

Seal No. *123*   Cash *£38.23*

1 set keys
1 pair shoe laces
Cigarettes and matches

SPECIMEN

Reason for witholding property (if applicable) *To prevent harm or loss to self or property*

I agree that the property listed above is correct.   Signature *S. Rushkin*   Date *19.4.97*
Witness *B. Pollard*   Witness *M. Patel*

AMENDMENTS

Withheld by Police | Retained by Prisoner

Property Added/Removed* | Property Added/Removed*

Reason for amendment/witholding ....
Reseal No. .... Time .... Date ....

I certify that the property bag was opened and resealed in my presence. I agree that the property added/removed* is correct.

Signature .... Date ....
Witnessed .... Witnessed ....

AMENDMENTS

Withheld by Police | Retained by Prisoner

Property Added/Removed* | Property Added/Removed*

Reason for amendment/witholding ....
Reseal No. .... Time .... Date ....

I certify that the property bag was opened and resealed in my presence. I agree that the property added/removed* is correct.

Signature .... Date ....
Witnessed .... Witnessed ....

*Delete as necessary   (For further amendments use form PACE 10A)

DISPOSAL

How disposed of *Returned to prisoner*   Signature *S. Rushkin*   Date *19.4.97*
Witness *D. Williams*   Witness *P. Stubbs*

15

Information from the custody record

From the custody record, Jane can see that Steven was arrested at 00.15 in North Road by PC Patel. The officer in the case is DC Stubbs. Steven arrived at the station at 00.27 and there was a delay while he was waiting to be booked in. Steven has signed to say he did not want a solicitor at that stage, and has not requested that anyone be told of his arrest.

Jane will now want to check:

(a) what are the grounds for the arrest;

(b) what are the grounds on which the custody officer has authorised Steven's detention;

(c) what has happened since Steven's detention was first authorised at 00.45.

The grounds for arrest are suspicion of attempted burglary, as had been stated in the initial phone call, and Jane can see that the police have subsequently discovered that Steven is a disqualified driver. The police have then arrested him for driving while disqualified as well — see the entry at 00.50 hours. The police are required to carry out this 'second' arrest because it is a different offence: see s. 31, PACE 1984.

The reason given for detention is 'to secure and preserve evidence by way of questioning'. Under PACE detention is permitted only in certain specified circumstances. Under s. 37, Steven can either be detained long enough to charge him for the offence (if there is sufficient evidence to do so), or detention may be authorised provided:

> (2) ...the custody officer has reasonable grounds for believing that his detention without being charged is necessary to secure or preserve evidence relating to an offence for which he is under arrest or to obtain such evidence by questioning him.

Jane needs to check that detention has been properly authorised. Unfortunately, like many custody officers, Sergeant Pollard has simply recited the law. He has not explained why he has reasonable grounds for believing the detention is needed in order to secure or preserve or obtain the evidence. Jane's key consideration, however, is the limited power to detain. Under s. 37(7), as soon as the custody officer has sufficient evidence to charge Steven, he must do so. Once Steven has been charged, he cannot normally be questioned any further and he must either be produced at court as soon as possible or bailed to attend court.

The rest of the custody record shows that since the detention was authorised, Steven has been seen by a police surgeon following complaints of back pain. He has been given paracetamol but certified fit to be interviewed. Since then he has been asleep. A review of detention was properly carried out at 06.27 — just within the six hour time limit for the first review: s. 40(3), PACE 1984. Steven has asked for a solicitor when he was told he would be interviewed. Jane has then been contacted promptly. Steven has now been given breakfast and more paracetamol.

Information from the custody officer

The custody officer is now Sergeant Williams. Jane asks Sergeant Williams about the allegations against her client. He tells her that two men were seen in the rear yard of an amusement arcade just before midnight, one of them trying to force open a window with a screwdriver. The witness saw the two men take fright after the alarm had gone off. They climbed over the wall and ran off. Steven and another man, Chapman, were in a car driven by Steven which was in the area just after midnight. The car was stopped by officers since they fitted the description given by the witness. On being asked where he'd come from, Steven said he had been in a pub, the King's Arms. The car was searched and a screwdriver set with a missing screwdriver was found. No further comments were made on arrest and caution. Chapman has apparently admitted involvement in the offence.

The custody officer then asks Jane if she will act for Chapman. She declines at this stage on the basis that if Chapman is admitting the offence and if, as turns out to be the case, Steven is not, there will almost certainly be a conflict of interest. If Jane advises both clients and there then turns out to be a conflict she will generally have to cease acting for them both: para. 15.03, *Law Society Guide to Professional Conduct of Solicitors* (seventh edition).

Information from the officer in the case

Jane also speaks to DC Stubbs who is waiting in the custody suite. She asks him if he will provide her with copies of any witness statements. He refuses to do this. She then asks if she can see the statements in order to take notes so that she can get Steven's instructions. Again he refuses, but he confirms that Sergeant Williams' account is accurate. He is, however, prepared to give her details of the witness' description of the man alleged to be Steven — 'about six foot, dark hair, bald, slim build, blue jeans, trainers, anorak, glasses, scar on cheek'.

Note that Jane has no right under PACE to any disclosure of information, other than the details of the original description by any identification witness. Even this need not be given to Jane until just before any identification parade: Code D, para. 2.0. The police will often be prepared to give some information about the offence, although this must be treated with caution as they will often imply that the evidence is stronger than it later turns out to be, and they will almost always withhold details of evidence for use in the interview.

It has been argued that if there has not been disclosure by the police, the suspect cannot be expected to answer the questions at interview and that no inference can reasonably be drawn from his silence under s. 34, Criminal Justice and Public Order Act 1994. However, in *R v Argent, The Times*, 19 December 1996, the Court of Appeal concluded that non-disclosure by the police no doubt affected the solicitor's advice to his or her client, but the test for the application of s. 34 was whether the suspect's silence was reasonable and not whether the solicitor's advice was good. The advice was just one of the factors for a jury to take into account.

Confusingly, in *R v Condron and Condron* [1997] 1 CrAppR a different Court of Appeal seemed to suggest that the advice from the solicitor might be relevant, but that giving details of that advice would often waive legal privilege, allowing the defendant and the solicitor to be cross-examined about all the legal advice given, and not simply the issue of silence.

In this case, Jane has to accept that she has now got as much information as she is going to get. She now needs to talk to Steven, to find out his version of events and to advise him on how to deal with the interview.

Advising the client

You will see from the custody record that Jane has a brief discussion with Steven in one of the interview rooms. Many solicitors are concerned that there may be listening devices in interview rooms, and indeed we know from reported cases that police cells are also sometimes bugged in the hope of obtaining evidence from suspects in the cells together. Solicitor-client conversations are privileged and there have been assurances that the police would turn off any listening devices. Equally, however, concerns have been expressed that the new Police Act 1997 will allow the police to listen to such conversations in certain circumstances. The general advice would therefore be to be careful in what is said anywhere in the police station.

Jane first reminds Steven of her status in the police station — in other words, that she is here as his solicitor, to look out for his interests, and that her advice is free, completely confidential and independent. Even with experienced clients it does no harm to remind the client that you are unconnected to the investigation.

Jane then asks Steven how he is feeling. She is worried about his back and whether this will affect his performance at interview. Steven says that his back is no worse than usual (this is a pre-existing injury, and not connected with the incident or the arrest). He says that he would rather go ahead and get the interview out of the way. Jane has noted that Steven did not take advantage of his right of intimation, i.e. his right to have a third party informed of his arrest: s. 56, PACE 1984 (see the box on the front page of the custody record in Document 2). She asks if Steven's wife knows where he is. Steven confirms that he would like her informed; he is worried that she will be very concerned about him, and he is also worried that the car needs collecting. Jane makes a note to ask the custody officer to telephone with the details. Steven was apparently unaware that he had this right. Arrival at the police station is obviously stressful and often confusing; it is therefore generally worth checking that clients are aware of all their rights.

Jane then tells Steven what she knows about the case so far. This is often the best way of starting the process of taking instructions. Steven immediately confirms that he was driving while disqualified, having been banned from driving for 12 months for an excess alcohol offence in February of this year. Jane and Steven agree that he will admit this offence in interview, which will help with mitigation on the offence (he is co-operating with the investigation and saving police time) and should ensure that he will get the maximum discount under s. 48, Criminal Justice and Public Order Act 1994 for entering an early guilty plea.

Steven denies any involvement in the burglary. He agrees that he was arrested in a car in the area at the time, but states that he had recently finished his evening shift as a barman at the King's Arms. He had seen Chapman and offered him a lift. They are neighbours.

Jane goes over the evidence against him. There is the missing screwdriver; his presence at or near the scene; possible evidence from Chapman; an identification witness. Steven says that the screwdriver found at the scene is nothing to do with him. The screwdriver missing from his set went missing a long time ago. He has explained what he was doing in the area. If Chapman was involved in the burglary, he (Steven) knows nothing about it, and if Chapman says otherwise, Chapman is lying. As for the identification witness, Steven reiterates that it was not him. He points out that with his bad back and legs there is no way he could climb a wall.

Steven will therefore clearly be denying any involvement in the burglary. What now needs to be considered is whether he should answer police questions.

Whether to answer questions in interview

Steven has a right of silence. This is absolute. He is not required to answer police questions and commits no offence by refusing to do so.

However, in certain circumstances, if Steven exercises his right of silence, the court may later draw inferences from his failure to answer questions if it was reasonable to expect him to do so.

There are three provisions to consider at this stage (the fourth, failure to testify at trial (s. 35, Criminal Justice and Public Order Act 1994) will not arise until trial). In summary these provisions are:

(a) s. 34, Criminal Justice and Public Order Act 1994: failure to mention any fact that he later relies upon in his defence when questioned under caution;

(b) s. 36 Criminal Justice and Public Order Act 1994: failure to account for object, substances or marks after arrest when asked to do so (provided a special caution is given — see s. 36(4), CJPOA 1994 and Code C, para. 10.5B);

(c) s. 37, Criminal Justice and Public Order Act 1994: failure to account for presence after arrest when asked to do so (again a special caution is required).

There is still debate as to whether any of these provisions can arise 'in the street' — in other words, before arrival at the police station. Jane therefore has to consider whether there could be any suggestion that inferences have arisen from any failure to answer questions or account for presence, marks etc. so far. According to the custody officer, Steven has already explained his presence by saying he was at the King's Arms. In any event, there is no suggestion that any questions have been asked after the caution or the arrest.

What about inferences if Steven fails to answer the questions in interview? Here it is clear that the Criminal Justice and Public Order Act 1994 provisions will apply. The questioning will be under caution and after arrest, so that prima facie both the general 'failure to put forward defence facts' (s. 34) and the 'failure to account for presence/marks etc.' (ss. 36 and 37) could arise.

Is there any reason why Steven should not put forward his story in interview? The traditional view was that suspects should generally exercise their right of silence (although comparatively few ever did, even with their solicitors present!). The advice was that, if the police had sufficient evidence to charge, they should do so; if they did not, there was no reason for the suspect to assist them in obtaining that evidence. But clearly, this must now be balanced against the risk of the future inferences at trial. Jane will be concerned that if Steven gives his account at interview:

(a) the story may not stand up to detailed police questioning;

(b) if Steven puts forward his alibi at this stage, the police are likely to go and check with the witness at once, and again the story may not stand up;

(c) the evidence against Steven hinges on the identification witness; if there is no such witness, or the witness fails to identify Steven, the rest of the evidence is circumstantial and there may not be sufficient evidence to charge Steven in any event;

(d) there may be further evidence that the police are withholding and which they will produce for the first time during the interview.

Jane explains her concerns to Steven. The decision on whether to answer police questions must be his. He is adamant that he has nothing to hide. In particular, he has no worries about his alibi.

Jane now reminds Steven of how the interview will be conducted. She reminds him that the interview will be taped and that the officers will be asking him questions. He can stop the interview at any time to obtain legal advice from her, but she will only intervene to prevent improper or unfair questions. It would not be proper for her to answer the questions for him. Above all, she emphasises that he should not answer some questions and exercise his right of silence in respect of others. If he is not sure what to do, he should ask her for advice, but a 'partial comment' interview always sounds very incriminating if it is played in court.

The First Interview: Saturday morning: 19 April 1997: 9.20–9.35 a.m.

Jane and Steven are now joined in the interview room by DC Stubbs, the officer in the case. He explains the tape recording process and starts the interview.

Although the interview is being recorded, Jane does her best to keep notes. This is so that she has an independent record of what happened on and off the tape. She can use this until she gets a copy of the tape (if Steven is charged in due course) and in case a summary of the tape cannot be agreed.

Jane's notes are produced in Document 3 below. The notes are inevitably patchy since Jane has to intervene on a number of occasions (the notes were handwritten but have been typed for legibility purposes!). A full transcript of the interview is not prepared until almost six months later (see Documents 67 and 68).

R v RUSHKIN

Document 3

Present: Self, Steven Rushkin, DC Stubbs (OIC)

Start: 9.20 a.m.

Introductions.
I introduce myself. Client wishes to co-operate fully. Has nothing to hide. Will admit that he was driving while disqualified. Deeply regrets this. Nothing to do with the burglary. Has made this clear from the start.

Stubbs: You admit disqualified.

A: Yes.

Q: Why driving?

A: Wife not around. Had to get to work. Silly. Regret it etc.

Q: Serious matter.

Self: Client admits driving disqualified. Seriousness is a matter for the court. Sufficient evidence to charge on this. No purpose in further questioning.

Q: Very well. Other matter more serious.

A: Yes

Q: Your version?

A: I had nothing to do with a break in.

Q: Put a number of points to you. Answer carefully. All evidence points to you. One by one.

A: OK

Q: Screwdriver — WA1 — recognise it?

A: No.

Q: Read name on it.

A: Woolfood.

Q: Yes. More screwdrivers here. Not in bag. Know where these from?

A: (silent)

Q: Know where these from? Found few hours ago? In car?

A: Yes. My car.

Q: Names on screwdriver.

A: Woolford.

Q: So connection?

A: No.

Q: Screwdriver found at amusement arcade tonight. Someone trying to break in dropped it. Fits your set. Not just same type. One that is actually missing. Perfect match. You were there, weren't you? Bob admits it. Bob in your car. Your screwdriver at scene.

A: Screwdriver missing for ages. Your one not from my set.

Q: Unlikely. When did you buy them?

A: Couple of years ago. In car all time.

Q: One missing?

A: Don't know what happened. Long time ago. Rest still useful for car.

Q: Not convinced. Move on. Could be fingerprints on screwdriver, let us have your prints?

Self: Intervene.

Tape off: Discuss with client. No problem with prints.

Restart: Client agrees to give prints.

Q: Wearing gloves were you.

Self: Object.

Q: Move on. You with Bob. He admits it. I/d witness describes you both exactly. So where were you, when, who with, etc.?

Self: Object — one question at a time.

Q: Chapman plus one at 11.55 trying to hack open window at MegaWin. Where were you then?

A: King's Arms.

Q: 11.55 it should be shut.

A: Work there.

Q: When leave?

A: Just after midnight.

Q: Handy. How do you know? Any witness?

A: Left when finished work. Phil can tell you. He paid me off.

Q: Phil who? How much paid?

A: Don't know name. Runs the King's Arms.

Q: Check it out. Pay?

A: £5 per hour.

Q: No wage slip etc. when we picked you up?

A: Paid in cash.

R v RUSHKIN

Q: Avoid tax, benefits etc. You were in pub, but with Chapman. That's what he says. You drinking with him before going to do the arcade.

A: No. Only saw him when I was leaving the car park after work.

Q: After midnight.

A: Yes.

Q: How so sure of time?

A: Don't normally work so late. Had to work out extra time so Phil could pay me.

Q: Witness gave very good description of you and Bob.

A: Wrong. Not me. Not there.

Q: Your screwdriver. You picked up man who confesses. Witness describes it all.

A: What does Bob say?

Q: Worried? He admits he did it. Says another man with him. No name. Honour among thieves? If you say it was not you, identification parade. Will you go on parade?

A: Should I?

Self: Intervene to advise.

Tape off: Discuss with client. Adamant not him. Advise parade if sure not him.

Restart.

Q: Caution. Ready?

Self: Client will go on parade. I want to be notified.

Q: Can't take it any further.

Self: Please put allegation re: running off, climbing wall.

Q: Puts allegation.

A: Couldn't climb six foot wall. Bad car accident two years back. Permanent pain in legs and back. Can't work. Couldn't climb wall.

Q: If couldn't work, then how come at pub working?

A: Can't do normal job painting and decorating. Can do casual work.

Q: Nothing more for now unless anything you wish to add.

A: No.

Sol.: Let me know re: parade?

End interview c.9.35 a.m.

Document 3A

Northumbria Police

NOTICE TO PERSON WHOSE INTERVIEW HAS BEEN TAPE RECORDED

This notice explains how the tape recording will be used and how you or your solicitor can, if you wish, arrange to listen to it if you are prosecuted.

GENERAL

The interview has been recorded on tape. One of these tapes/sets of tapes has been sealed in your presence and will be kept securely in case it is needed in court. The other tape/set of tapes will be a working copy to which the police and you or your solicitor may listen if you wish. Both tapes/sets of tapes are protected against tampering.

IF YOU HAVE A SOLICITOR

If your solicitor wishes to obtain a copy of the tape he should apply to the Crown Prosecution Service at the address shown below.

IF YOU DO NOT HAVE A SOLICITOR

If you do not have a solicitor now you should think about whether you should seek one. If you do not want a solicitor and you are prosecuted, you will, if you wish, be able to listen to the tape recording yourself by applying to the Crown Prosecution Service at the following address.

a) **Newcastle Area.**

Cuthbert House,
All Saints Office Centre,
Newcastle upon Tyne,
NE1 2DW.

b) **North Tyneside Area.**

North Tyneside ASU,
Police Station,
Upper Pearson Street,
North Shields,
NE30 1AB.

c) **South Tyneside Area.**

Coniston House,
Washington,
NE38 7RN.

N.B. Notice to Interviewing Officer: Please delete those addresses not applicable.

IMPORTANT NOTICE:

IN CASES OF URGENCY A COPY OF THE TAPE MAY BE OBTAINED FROM THE POLICE STATION WHERE YOU WERE INTERVIEWED.

PLEASE QUOTE THE FOLLOWING REFERENCE IN ALL CORRESPONDENCE:

(STATION REFERENCE ....)

IF YOU ARE CHARGED OR INFORMED YOU WILL BE PROSECUTED YOU ARE ENTITLED TO A COPY OF THE TAPE(S).

CID 80 (5.96)

R v RUSHKIN

COMMENTARY

1. Inferences arising before the interview: the officer should put any significant comments or silences that have arisen before the interview at the start of the interview (Code C, para. 11.2A). This is to identify any disputes as early as possible. No matters are put, and it therefore looks as if Jane is right to assume there are no earlier matters to worry about.

2. Inferences from the interview: technically there cannot be any s. 36 or 37 inferences (i.e. from a failure to account for any object, substance or mark or for presence) because no 'ordinary language' caution had been given (i.e. the special s. 36/37 warning: see Code C, para. 10.5B). In any case, Steven has fully answered the case against him. Similarly, he appears to have raised all relevant defence facts so that there can be no s. 34 inference. Note how Jane specifically asked the officer to put the allegation about climbing the wall so that Steven could put forward his 'defence fact' (i.e., his bad back and legs) at this stage.

3. Fingerprints: the police can take fingerprints by consent, and in any event after charge for a 'recordable offence' (basically any offence which can carry a custodial sentence, and a few others: see Code D, Note for Guidance 3A). Equally, fingerprints can be taken without consent with a superintendent's authority if the superintendent has reasonable grounds for suspecting the person's involvement in an offence and for believing the fingerprints may confirm or disprove the involvement. Document 4 below is an example of a Record of Authority in such cases.

Fingerprinting is often not mentioned until the interview is over, and sometimes after the solicitor has gone. But in any case, knowing that there was a screwdriver left at the scene, Jane could have anticipated the request and should have advised Steven about it before the interview.

4. Identification parade: again, this is another matter Jane should have anticipated, since she knows the case hinges on identification evidence. Identification procedures are set out in PACE, Code D. Code D, para. 2.3 states that a parade 'shall' be held in disputed identification cases if the suspect agrees unless for some reason it is not practicable. Group identifications or video identifications can be used instead, but a parade is regarded as the most reliable procedure.

What if Steven did not agree to a parade — can an inference be drawn? It is often thought that an inference can be drawn from a refusal, but there is no legal basis for this. If Steven refuses a parade, the police can try a group identification or a video identification (see Code D, paras 2.7 and 2.10). As a last resort, the police can arrange a confrontation between the witness and Steven, but this is obviously the least satisfactory method.

5. Jane's interventions during the interview: Jane intervened on a number of occasions, both to advise Steven but also to object to a 'portmanteau question' — in other words, a number of questions rolled up together, so that it is hard to see which question Steven is being asked to answer. PACE, Code C, Notes for Guidance 6D states:

> *The solicitor's only role in the police station is to protect and advance the legal rights of his client. On occasions this may require the solicitor to give advice which has the effect of his client avoiding giving evidence which strengthens a prosecution case. The solicitor may intervene in order to seek clarification or to challenge an improper question to his client or the manner in which it is put, or to advise his client not to reply to particular questions, or if he wishes to give his client further legal advice. Paragraph 6.9 [the power to exclude a solicitor from an interview] will only apply if the solicitor's approach or conduct prevents or unreasonably obstructs proper questions being put to the suspect or his response being recorded. Examples of unacceptable conduct include answering questions on a suspect's behalf or providing written replies for him to quote.*

This makes clear that Jane's job is to look out for Steven's interests. She must be ready to intervene and to object in order to do this.

R v RUSHKIN

Document 4

NORTHUMBRIA POLICE

POLICE AND CRIMINAL EVIDENCE ACT 1984
CRIMINAL JUSTICE AND PUBLIC ORDER ACT 1994

Record of Authority Granted by a Superintendent

Name of Person involved (if applicable) ....

Custody Record Number (if applicable) ....

Police Station (if applicable) ....

Custody Officer (if applicable) ....

Time and Date Authority Granted ....

Officer in Charge of Case (if applicable) ....

DETAILS OF AND REASONS FOR GRANTING AUTHORITY

Relevant Section of Police and Criminal Evidence Act/Criminal Justice and Public Order Act	

Result of Authority Granted ....

....

Any other comments ....

Signature .... Rank ....

PACE 14 *(3.95)*   **Blue copy**—File with Custody Record (if applicable)   **White copy**—To remain in book

After the Interview: Saturday Morning 19th April 1997: 9.37 to 10.22 a.m.

When the interview is finished, Steven is returned to his cell.

There are now a number of matters that need sorting out:

(a) Driving disqualified: Steven has admitted this in the interview. There is clearly now sufficient evidence for him to be charged and under s. 37(7), PACE 1984 (discussed above, page 000) the custody officer must now charge him with this offence.

(b) Fingerprint evidence: Steven has consented to having his fingerprints taken and this is now done.

(c) Non-intimate samples: DC Stubbs reveals that a hat was found at the scene. He therefore wishes to take a hair sample from Steven. Section 65, PACE 1984 confirms that hair (other than pubic hair) is a 'non-intimate sample'. It can therefore be taken by consent. In certain circumstances it can be taken without consent and the police can use reasonable force to take the sample. Those circumstances are similar to the fingerprint provisions, and include a situation where a superintendent gives authority and reasonably suspects the person's involvement in a recordable offence and that the sample will tend to confirm or disprove this.

Again, Steven denies involvement and agrees to give the sample. Note, however, how this information had been kept back. Matters have a way of arising at odd points in the police station and Jane needs to make sure that she has dealt with anything that could arise before she leaves.

(d) The identification parade: this will need to be arranged. The police can of course keep Steven in detention while they do this, but the 24 hour limit on detention will continue to tick away.

(As was noted above, page 000, burglary is potentially a serious arrestable offence and the police could therefore in theory apply for extensions to the detention period to 36 hours with a superintendent's consent, and up to a total of 96 hours with the leave of the court. However, there is no evidence on the facts of this case that this burglary was intended to cause substantial gain or substantial loss, and no attempt is made to extend the detention period.)

As you will see from the custody record (Dococument 2, page 000), the samples are duly taken with Steven's consent.

The Driving Whilst Disqualified Charge: Saturday Morning: 19 April: 10.18 a.m.

Steven is then charged with driving whilst disqualified. He is bailed to attend the magistrates' court on Thursday 8 May 1997. He is also bailed in respect of the attempted burglary: here the bail is to return to the police station for the identification parade on Friday 2 May. The charge sheet is set out below as Document 5A. and the accompanying bail form in respect of the attempted burglary, set out as Document 5B.

R v RUSHKIN

Document 5A

NORTHUMBRIA POLICE
NOTICE OF OFFENCE(S) CHARGED

ORIGINAL / AMENDED / ADDITIONAL	Sheet No. 1 of 1
	Custody Record No. OLC 97/293
CRO No. R1234	OIC No. 2345	URN COMPLETED AT ASU

- Area Command: OLDCASTLE
- Section: CENTRAL
- Court: CENTRAL at 10 a.m., on THURSDAY 8/5/1997
- PERSON CHARGED: Steven Rushkin
- ADDRESS: 12 Park View, Longfield, Oldcastle
- Date of Birth: 12.1.53
- Occupation/Place of Education: Unemployed
- Male/~~Female~~

YOU ARE CHARGED WITH THE OFFENCE(S) SHOWN BELOW
You do not have to say anything unless you wish to do so, but what you say may be given in evidence.

DRIVING WHILST DISQUALIFIED

That you did on 19 April 1997 drive a motor car on a road called North Road, Oldcastle whilst disqualified from holding or obtaining a driving licence contrary to section 103, Road Traffic Act 1988.

SPECIMEN

- O.I.C.: DCP Stubbs 2345 Central
- Officer Charging: P Stubbs
- Receipt for copy of charge(s) (Pros. 56): YES/NO
- Receipt for Disclosure Notice (Pros. 56): YES/NO
- Time and Date of Charging: 10.18 a.m. 19/4/97
- Officer Accepting Charge: Williams Sgt 4567

NOTICE OF BAIL

The above named has this day been released on bail in accordance with Section 38(1) of the Police and Criminal Evidence Act 1984 and the Bail Act 1976 in connection with the alleged offence(s) as outlined above, and is required to surrender to custody at the Magistrates' Court sitting at the place and time shown above to answer the charge(s).

I have been informed that unless I surrender to Custody as shown above I may be liable to a fine, or imprisonment or both.

Signature of person bailed: S. Rushkin

- Signed (Officer granting bail): D. Williams
- Rank: Sgt   No. 4567
- Date: 19/4/1997   Time: 10.18 am

SURETIES
I/we acknowledge my/our obligation to pay the Court the sum specified by my/our signature if the accused fails to surrender to custody as shown.

(1) Signature / Name (Block Capitals) / Address — £
(2) Signature / Name (Block Capitals) / Address — £

MG4 (4.94)

1. Blue-Custody Record Copy
2. Yellow-Copy for Magistrates' Clerk
3. White-Copy for Accused
4. Green-Copy for Court Office
5. Pink-Copy for O.I.C

R v RUSHKIN

Document 5B

NORTHUMBRIA POLICE   Form MG 4A

CONDITIONAL BAIL AFTER CHARGE   ASU URN

Police Station: OLDCASTLE CENTRAL   Code: Other refs: Custody No.

Name: Steven Rushkin   Date of birth: 12 / 1 / 53
(Full name of accused)

The above named, has been granted bail *WITH CONDITIONS AS BELOW in accordance with the Bail Act 1976 and is under a duty to surrender to the custody of Oldcastle Central Police Station [*Youth] [*Magistrates] Court
situated at (full address) Beech Street, Oldcastle
at (time) 2.00 *a.m./p.m. on Fri DAY 2 / 5 / 97

*Conditions *(complete sections which apply).*

(a) Surety:
I have been informed of the conditions set out below and; I acknowledge my obligation to pay the Court the sum specified by my signature if the above named person fails to surrender to custody as shown above.

Signed .... £ ....

Name: ....
(Block capitals)
Address: ....

(b) Security:
The sum of £ .... (cash only)
has been accepted from:

Name: ....

Address: ....

for the surrender to custody as shown above of the above named person.

Signed: ....
Inspector

(c) Other: The grant of bail is subject to the following conditions *(number each separately, e.g. "1- To be indoors at (address) between 10 pm and 8 am"):–*

....
....
....

The above conditions are imposed because they appear necessary to prevent the above named person from [*failing to surrender to custody] [*committing an offence whilst on bail] [*interfering with any witnesses or otherwise obstructing the course of justice], for the following reasons:

SPECIMEN

If this record is not part of the custody record, a note of the reason(s) must be made on the custody record s.5A(3) and (4) Bail Act 1976)   (Continue on separate sheet if necessary)

Acknowledgement of obligations
I have been informed that:
(i) If I fail to surrender to custody at the time and place shown above, I may be liable to a fine or imprisonment or both.
*(ii) If I fail to comply with any of the conditions set out above, I may be liable to arrest and that if I wish to vary any of the conditions, I may apply to either the police station or court specified above, stating my reasons.

Signed (person bailed) S. Rushkin   Date 19 / 4 / 97   Time: 10.22 *a.m./p.m.

Appropriate Adult (Name & Address) ....
Signed: .... Date: / /   Time: *a.m./p.m.

Custody Officer granting bail:
I have granted bail as above under the provisions of s.38(1) of the Police and Criminal Evidence Act 1984 **and given a copy this record and continuations thereof to the person bailed [*and to the surety].**

Signed: A. Williams   Date: 19 / 4 / 97   Time: *a.m./p.m.
Name: A. WILLIAMS   Rank: Sgt   No: 4567

* delete the words or sections as appropriate.

Summary of Variations	MG 4B/......serial no.	MG 4B/1	MG 4B/2	MG 4B/3	Court Applicat'n	Date notified	
(Update after each request dealt with)	Date of request				(precludes further variation by police)	Date heard	
	Bail changed? 'Y' 'N'					Bail changed? 'Y' 'N'	

1. Custody Record *(Blue)*   2. Accused *(White)*   3. Court *(Yellow)*   4. Case Papers *(Pink)*

Did the police have to grant Steven bail?

In respect of the burglary matter they had no choice. They do not have sufficient evidence to charge him. It is going to take time to arrange an identification parade and to obtain the results of the forensic tests. The police do not want to bail him. They know he has a previous history of absconding. Indeed, you will see that later in the case, once he has been charged with the attempted burglary, the police refuse bail. However, at this stage, unless they wish to try and keep him in custody until they use up the limited time on the detention clock, they must let him go. (They would have to charge or release him at the end of that period in any event, long before the forensic evidence is ready.)

Do the police have to grant bail now that he has been charged with driving whilst disqualified? They do not. Section 38, PACE 1984 gives the power for the custody officer to refuse bail on a number of grounds, including situations where he believes the accused will fail to attend at court. But driving whilst disqualified, although imprisonable, is nowhere near as serious an offence as the burglary and he would almost certainly be granted bail when he was produced at court on Monday (i.e., the next available sitting of the court).

Before leaving the police station at 10.20 a.m., Jane confirms the court date and the return date for the identification parade with Steven. She arranges for Steven to come and see her at the office at 4.00 p.m. on the following Monday to discuss the cases.

Back in her car, Jane immediately dictates an attendance note while everything is still fresh in her memory.

Document 6

Attendance Note

Your name   JW

Client's name   S. Rushkin

Time start   7.14

Date 19 April 1997

Person attended   Client

Time finish 10.40.

Call from Central Police at 7.14 a.m. Sergeant Williams, custody officer, informed me that Steven Rushkin is detained on suspicion of burglary, together with a Robert Chapman. Rushkin arrived at station at 12.30, detained for questioning and possibly identification and forensic, 'insufficient evidence yet for charging'. Asked when they plan to interview, told no need to come before 8.30. Spoke to Rushkin on phone, said I would be coming and advised him to answer no questions until I had spoken to him.

Apparently Rushkin also caught driving while disqualified and will be charged. Asked Sgt Williams why the seven hour delay in interviewing, told needed to 'make further enquiries, and allow Mr Rushkin a rest period'. Asked what further enquiries, told 'interview witnesses, obtain statements'.

Travel to Central Police Station: 15 minutes

Attendance on Sergeant Williams 9.05–9.10 a.m.: Asked to see custody record, asked what matters they wished to question Rushkin about. Apparently seen in Burn Street trying to break in and then running away from back of MegaWin Amusement Arcade at 11.55 p.m.

Witness apparently obtained clear description fitting Rushkin and Chapman. Evidence of attempt at window break in and screw driver found on ground. Asked for actual words used by witness identifying person alleged to be Rushkin: 'about 6 feet tall, dark hair, bald, slim build, wearing blue

R v RUSHKIN

jeans, trainers, anorak and glasses; has some kind of scar on his cheek.' I asked whether the witness said whether she would recognise this person again: apparently 'fairly sure'.

Rushkin and Chapman stopped by police travelling north out of Oldcastle on North Road at 12.15, arrested on suspicion of attempted burglary; searched and screwdriver set with one screwdriver missing found in Mr Rushkin's car, similar to one found at scene; brought in at 12.27.

Purpose of police interview to seek Rushkin's account of movements at relevant time. According to custody officer Chapman has admitted offence in conversations with police.

Williams then asked me to advise Chapman. In view of Chapman's admissions, declined until I saw Rushkin. Asked for private interview before questioning.

Attending Mr Rushkin: 9.10 – 9.20 a.m.

Took preliminary instructions as follows:

Mr Rushkin wishes his wife to be informed of his arrest. He was not aware of right to have her informed and was very worried. Arranged with custody officer at 9.15 for call to be made, telling her where car can be collected.

Rushkin has pre-existing back injury, has received painkillers, no complaints.

Mr Rushkin agrees that he was driving whilst disqualified. Advised it would help for sentencing to admit offence after charge.

Told Rushkin what police allege. Mr Rushkin denies any involvement in any attempt at burglary, admits being in the area in his car at time, coming home from evening work as barman at King's Arms, North View. Saw Chapman and offered a lift, as they are neighbours. Left work after midnight. Screwdriver missing for months.

Advised him of his right not to reply, but advised that as he can explain his movements, should do so at an early opportunity. Advised him that if charged court might take into account any failure to explain his movements. Mr Rushkin wished to give full account as he has nothing to hide. Advised that police likely to check out anything he says before releasing him, e.g. alibi. Still clear he wished to answer questions.

Checked if he had any further convictions since we last acted. Yes:

excess alcohol Feb 97 for driving over limit at New Year. Fined and 12 months' disqualification.

Advised client and police that possible conflict of interest in seeing Chapman. Advised client that unlikely that Chapman's evidence going to be used against him at trial, whatever he's saying to the police. Not a reason for confessing if he hasn't committed crime, but given what Chapman apparently said to police, Mr Rushkin can expect intense questioning.

Rushkin interviewed in my presence by DC Stubbs 9.20 – 9.35, no admissions made. (See handwritten notes of interview on file – note in particular clear statement of alibi, meeting Chapman outside King's Arms, explanation of screwdriver set.)

> After interview Sgt Williams 'not yet ready to charge' and will hold parade as soon as possible. Would like to obtain forensic evidence and release until parade. Asked what forensic and why: fingerprints on screwdriver found at scene of crime; hat nearby – want hair sample from Rushkin.
>
> Advised client that co-operation with parade advisable, alternatives more likely to lead to positive i.d. Client agreed.
>
> Advised client to co-operate with hair sample and fingerprint. Procedures completed 10.17.
>
> Rushkin charged with the driving whilst disqualified 10.18. Client admitted offence when cautioned after charge. To appear in court (Central Magistrates) 8 May and bailed unconditionally on that matter.
>
> Released on bail till 2 May at 2.00 p.m for parade. Advised Rushkin that could well be charged then for attempt burglary.
>
> Arranged to see Rushkin in office 4.00 p.m. Monday.
>
> Return travel: 10.20 – 10.35 a.m.
>
> Mileage – 10

This attendance note is longer than many solicitors would write. An experienced solicitor might well summarise many of the points made. However, attendance notes are not just for the person who makes them, but also for Jane's colleagues who may deal with the case if they are covering the magistrates' court on the day it is listed for hearing. As I have only included attendance notes in this case study where they are of importance (otherwise the book would be cluttered with relatively unimportant notes), I have made sure that the first attendance note is relatively comprehensive.

In any attendance note, the bottom line is:

(a) a solicitor must be absolutely clear about the client's instructions;

(b) a solicitor will only be paid for work actually done, and the attendance note therefore records the times and the form of the work undertaken.

What about payment?

Payment for work at the police station is made under the Legal Advice and Assistance at Police Stations (Remuneration) Regulations 1989 (as amended). This permits a solicitor to be paid for travel, waiting, telephone advice, other phone calls and giving advice and assistance to the person being questioned, whether under arrest or attending as a volunteer. Jane's attendance note has therefore identified the timings for all the different elements of her attendance on Steven.

Unlike 'green form' advice, the police station legal advice scheme does not involve any means test. It is free and available to any person being questioned by the police. The amount that can be claimed is, however, limited to £90, but claims which exceed this limit will be paid if the Legal Aid Board accepts that the work was necessary in the interests of justice and as a matter of urgency (see regs 5 and 6 of the Police Station (Remuneration) Regulations 1989). Frequently claims will exceed this limit.

Here, since Jane knows that Steven will be returning to the police station on 2 May for the identification parade, she does not submit her claim at this stage. She will wait until the police station work is completed and will then submit the claim for all the work on a single form.

The First Interview with Steven: 21 April 1997: 4.00 p.m.

Steven has been charged with driving while disqualified, and his first appearance at court will be on 8 May 1997. He is clearly going to be entering a guilty plea and if this was the only outstanding matter Jane would complete the legal aid forms at this point and would prepare to attend court in two weeks' time to enter a guilty plea. Steven might be sentenced there and then, or, given that driving while disqualified carries a custodial penalty (discussed below at page 56), the court might adjourn for pre-sentence reports to be prepared.

However, there is still the burglary investigation in progress. The evidence against Steven so far is not strong. However, if there is a successful identification on 2 May, when Steven is bailed to return to the police station, he will almost certainly be charged and the court will then want to look at both offences together. So, with this in mind, Jane does not complete the application for legal aid at this stage, but instead uses the 'green form' scheme. This will permit her to do two hours work on most issues of English law (a few matters such as conveyancing and most wills are excluded).

What work needs doing at this stage?

Jane will not want to take a full statement from Steven until she sees whether he is going to be charged, but she can use this opportunity to make sure that the background information that she has is up-to-date. However, the key matter that needs to be dealt with is Steven's alibi. The alibi concerns a matter of minutes — the offence is alleged to have occurred at 11.55 p.m. and Steven says he left the pub at midnight. If Jane waits until after the identification parade, the witness(es) may well have forgotten the exact times involved. Jane therefore needs to take a statement from Steven's employer the publican, Mr Gramsci, and to find out if there are any other witnesses.

Is Steven eligible for Legal Advice and Assistance?

Legal Advice and Assistance is the formal name for the 'green form'.

If you look at the GF1 (Document 7) and the 'keycard' (Document 8) you will see that Steven is automatically eligible because he receives income support. (Note that income-related job seekers' allowance has now replaced income support for most unemployed claimants, and this also will ensure eligibility for green form advice. However, Steven is submitting sick notes and is therefore treated as 'incapable of work' rather than unemployed; he therefore continues to receive income support.)

How should Jane deal with the awkward fact that Steven is actually working in a pub while claiming income support? Does she have to declare these earnings on the form? Here the Legal Advice and Assistance Regulations 1989 (reg. 13(2)) provide that the solicitor can assume that the person is within the income limits if he or she receives income support, family credit, disability working allowance and income-related job seekers' allowance. So, under the regulations, Steven's other 'earnings' are irrelevant. Jane would be in breach of her duty of confidentiality to Steven if she declared the money. (In contrast, on the application for legal aid, Jane must ensure the income is declared accurately!)

Jane therefore uses the interview to complete the green form, to update her instructions from Steven and to find out how and where to contact Mr Gramsci. The green form is never in fact sent off for payment in this case since where a criminal legal aid order is subsequently granted, the costs of earlier green form advice and assistance are recovered under the legal aid order. However, it is wise to have the form completed if possible in case legal aid is not granted. Here, of course, Jane is hoping that the burglary case will not proceed and Steven will not be charged. In that case there would then be no later legal aid application.

R v RUSHKIN

Document 7

Green Form

To be used by solicitors with **NO** franchise contract which covers the category of work into which this green form falls

LEGAL AID BOARD LEGAL AID ACT 1988

Legal aid account no: **A 123 B**

Ref: **JW/RUSH**

(Copy from extension authority before sending claim)

➤ If you have a franchise contract covering the category of work into which this claim falls, complete form GF7.
➤ If you give advice and assistance about making a will you must submit form GF4 with your claim.
➤ You should keep a copy of the entire green form.

Client's details
*Please use block capitals *Delete the one which does not apply*   Male/~~Female~~*

Surname: **RUSHKIN**   First names: **STEVEN**
Address: **12 PARK VIEW, LONGFIELD, OLDCASTLE**
                                   Postcode: **OL10 2AB**
National Insurance No: **YP 90 84 25 A**   Date of Birth: **12·1·53**

Capital details
(give these details even if the client gets income support, income-based Jobseeker's Allowance, family credit or disability working allowance)

How many dependants (partner, children or other relatives of his/her household) does the client have? _____

Give the total savings and other capital which the client has (and if relevant his or her partner)

Client: £ **NIL**
Spouse (or person living as if a spouse of the client): £ **NIL**
Total: £ **NIL**

Income details

Does the client get Income Support, any income-based Jobseeker's Allowance, Family Credit or Disability Working Allowance?

☐ Yes: ignore the rest of this section   ☐ No: give the total gross weekly income of

The client: £ _____
The client's spouse (or person living as if a spouse of the client): £ _____
Total: £ _____

Calculate the total allowable deductions: Income tax: £ _____
National Insurance contributions: £ _____
Spouse (or person living as if a spouse of the client): £ _____
Attendance allowance, disability living allowance, constant attendance allowance and any payment made out of the Social Fund: £ _____
Dependent children and other dependants: Age   Number
Under 11 _____ £ _____
11 to 15 _____ £ _____
16 to 17 _____ £ _____
18 and over _____ £ _____

Less total deductions: £ _____
Total weekly disposable income: £ _____

SPECIMEN

Client's declaration

I confirm that:
➤ I am over the compulsory school-leaving age (or, if not, the solicitor is advising me under Regulation 14(2A) Legal Advice & Assistance Regulations 1989);
➤ I ~~have~~/have not *(delete whichever one is not correct)* previously received help from a solicitor on this matter under the green form; and
➤ I understand that I might have to pay my solicitor's costs out of any property or money which is recovered or preserved for me.

As far as I am aware, the information on this page is correct. I understand that if I give false information I could be prosecuted.
Signed: **S. Rushkin**   Date: **21 / 4 / 97**

33

R v RUSHKIN

Document 8

GREEN FORM AND ABWOR KEY CARD
(No. 29)

Effective from 7th April 1997

Please see over for further explanatory notes.

CAPITAL means the amount or value of every resource of a capital nature.
In computing Disposable Capital disregard
(i) the first £100,000 equity in the main or only dwelling in which the client resides, (see note 3(c)(i) overleaf) and
(ii) the value of the household furniture and effects, personal clothing and tools or implements of the client's trade and
(iii) the subject matter of the advice and assistance.

If you advise a client who returns to you for further advice on the same matter under a Green Form within 6 months of you submitting your claim for payment, fill in the client's details and the date of your claim only then strike through the rest of the front page. Set out your further claim on the back of the Green Form.

Maximum Disposable Capital for Financial Eligibility (dependant=partner, child or dependant relative)

Advice and Assistance*	ABWOR**
£1000-client with no dependants	£3000-client with no dependants
£1335-client with 1 dependant	£3335-client with 1 dependant
£1535-client with 2 dependants	£3535-client with 2 dependants

Add £100 for each additional dependant

* Capital must be assessed for advice and assistance even if client is on income support, income-based jobseekers allowance, family credit or disability working allowance. See note 3.
** All capital is disregarded if client is on income support or income-based jobseekers allowance. See note 3.

INCOME means the total income from all sources which the client received or became entitled to during or in respect of the seven days up to and including the date of the application for advice and assistance.

The capital and weekly income of both partners must be taken into account unless:
(a) they have a contrary interest
(b) they live apart
(c) it is inequitable or impractical to aggregate their means

Some types of income are ignored. See note 3.

In computing Disposable Income deduct:-
(i) Income Tax
(ii) Contributions paid under the Social Security Acts 1975-88
(iii) £28 in respect of the client's partner (if living together) whether or not their means are aggregated. Where they are separated or divorced, the allowance will be the actual maintenance paid by the client in respect of the previous 7 days.
(iv) The following payments made under the Social Security Contributions and Benefits Act 1992:
   i) disability living allowance;
   ii) attendance allowance paid under section 64 or Schedule 8 paragraphs 4 or 7(2);
   iii) constant attendance allowance paid under section 104 and 105 as an increase to a disablement pension; or
   iv) any payment made out of the social fund.

These deductions also apply to the partner's income if there is aggregation.

v) £16.90 for each child under 11
For 11 year olds £24.75 if the child became 11 before 7th April 1997, otherwise £16.90. See opposite if applying after 1st September 1997.
£24.75 for each child aged 12-15
For 16 year olds £29.60 if the child became 16 before 7th April 1997, otherwise £24.75. See opposite if applying after 1st September 1997.
£29.60 for each child aged 17
For 18 year olds £38.90 only if the child became 18 before 7th April 1997, otherwise £29.60.
£38.90 for each dependant aged over 18 (but see opposite).
vi) Back to work bonus under section 26 of the Jobseekers Act 1995.
vii) Payments under the Earnings Top up Scheme 1996.
viii) Payment under the Community Care Direct Payment Scheme.

Where the child or dependant relative is not a member of the household the allowance will be the actual maintenance paid by the client in respect of the previous 7 days.

The rules for 11 and 16 year olds will change if applying on or after 1st September 1997. From that date for 11 year olds the allowance will be £24.75 only if child became 11 before 1st September 1997, otherwise it will be £16.90. Similarly for 16 year olds the allowance will be £29.60 only if child became 16 before 1st September 1997, otherwise it will be £24.75. These allowances apply to dependant children and relatives of the household of the ages specified. There is no allowance in relation to a foster child.
At the time of printing the regulations providing for an allowance for dependants over 18 have not yet been finalised. Solicitors should check the Handbook or with the area office to confirm when the allowance will be payable.

Maximum Weekly Disposable Income for Financial Eligibility.
Advice and Assistance
Green Form advice and assistance is only available to people who get income support, income-based jobseekers allowance, family credit, disability working allowance or have not more than £77 a week disposable income (and who come within the maximum capital limit). They will pay no contribution.

ABWOR
Lower limit £69 a week (no contribution to pay)
Upper limit £166 a week (people with disposable income between the lower and upper limits will be liable to pay a **weekly** contribution (collected by the solicitor) from the date of the ABWOR approval to its withdrawal or the end of the proceedings.
The amount of weekly contribution is calculated as 1/3 of the weekly disposable income over £69.

The Green Form must be signed by or on behalf of the client at the initial interview as soon as his/her eligibility has been determined except in the case of an authorised postal application or where a franchisee is exercising his or her powers.

Interviewing the Alibi Witness: 22 April 1997: 3.30 p.m.

Jane manages to contact Philip Gramsci, the landlord of the King's Arms, the following day. He comes into the office after the lunchtime shift and Jane is able to take a short statement confirming the events of the evening of 18 April 1997. By this stage he has, however, already been contacted by the police, although he has told them the same thing: namely that Steven left at midnight.

Jane prepares the statement and sends two copies to Mr Gramsci; one to sign and return to her, the other to keep for his own reference.

Mr Gramsci has confirmed that there are no other witnesses since all the other staff had left some time earlier. There is therefore no more work to do on the case until the identification parade.

Document 9

Statement of Philip Gramsci, of the King's Arms, North View, Oldcastle, who will say as follows:

I am the landlord of the King's Arms and have been employed in this capacity by Northern Breweries for five years.

I am aged 32 and have no criminal convictions.

I can remember the evening of 18 April 1997. We were open as usual, and I was serving all evening in the bar, which serves the lounge and the public bar. We also had a private function in the upstairs room, where we served a buffet and drinks to about 50 people.

One of my casual staff is Steven Rushkin, who works in the pub on an ad hoc basis when I need extra staff. I would estimate he works for me about two or three evenings a week, and I pay him cash in hand. During the week of 18–25 April I had asked Steven to come in every evening from 7.00 p.m. until whenever we finished clearing up, as one of the regular staff was sick.

On Friday 18th Steven had come in early at 5.30 at my request and was on duty in the bar to my knowledge until midnight. He was the last of the staff to leave. I know he did not leave until midnight because when we had finally finished clearing up, a good deal later than usual because of the buffet, I remarked to him: 'look, it's midnight, hope your coach doesn't turn into a pumpkin on the way home', or words to that effect. He remarked that he was pleased he had the car as he did not want to have to wait for a taxi. I remember looking at the clock. I also remember the time because I pay Steven at the end of every night according to the hours worked, so I have to check the time when he is finished.

I keep an accurate clock, because of the need to comply with licensing hours.

I have already been approached by the police. I have told them exactly the same.

I am willing to attend court if necessary.

Signed P. Gramsci   Dated 25.4.97

Attending the Identification Parade: Friday Afternoon: 2 May 1997: 2.00 p.m.

Jane meets Steven at the Central Police Station just before 2.00 p.m. on Friday 2 May. They go into the police station and Steven surrenders to his bail. The custody record is revived and the detention clock (under s. 41, PACE 1984) starts to run again.

As has been discussed above Steven is not obliged to take part in a parade. Some clients dislike parades and feel that group identifications (where the suspect is released in a controlled but crowded environment such as a railway or underground station) are a better bet. Here, however, Steven continues to deny involvement and Jane advises that the controlled process of a formal identification parade is the most satisfactory procedure.

Jane herself attends the parade to ensure that it is properly organised, that the other participants are appropriate, and to advise Steven if necessary on any objections that should be raised. She has asked for confirmation as to the witness' original description, and she also checks what it was that the witness says she saw the suspect doing. She keeps an eye on the arrangements for ensuring that the investigating officers are kept separate from the witness, and if there were several witnesses she would also make sure that they were kept separate from one another.

The precise arrangements for the holding of a parade are laid down in PACE Code D, paras 2.3 to 2.6:

> 2.3 *Whenever a suspect disputes an identification, an identification parade shall be held if the suspect consents unless paragraphs 2.4 or 2.7 (group identification) or 2.10 (video film identification) apply. A parade may also be held if the officer in charge of the investigation considers that it would be useful, and the suspect consents.*
>
> 2.4 *A parade need not be held if the identification officer considers that, whether by reason of the unusual appearance of the suspect or some other reason, it would not be practicable to assemble sufficient people who resembled him to make a parade fair.*
>
> 2.5 *Any parade must be carried out in accordance with Annex A. A video recording or colour photograph shall be taken of the parade.*
>
> 2.6 *If the suspect refuses or, having agreed, fails to attend an identification parade or the holding of a parade is impracticable, arrangements must be made to allow the witness an opportunity of seeing him in a group identification, a video identification or a confrontation.*

Annex A to Code D then lays down a number of detailed provisions regarding the conduct of the parade:

(a) A suspect has a right to have a solicitor or friend present: paragraph 1.

(b) The parade can take place in a normal room or with the witnesses hidden behind a screen. In either case the suspect must be given details of the first description by any witnesses and must (if practicable) be shown any material released to the media by the police for the purpose of tracing the suspect: paras 2 and 2A.

(c) The suspect must be cautioned.

(d) Once the parade is formed everything must take place in the suspect's presence and hearing, unless there is a screen (in which case the solicitor must still be present or it must be videoed): para. 7.

(e) The parade 'shall consist of at least eight persons (in addition to the suspect) who so far as possible resemble the suspect in age, height, general appearance and position in life': para. 8.

(f) The suspect must be asked if he has any objections before the parade. He may select his own position in the line, and can change position in between witnesses: paras 10 and 11.

(g) Witnesses are brought in one at a time. They are told that the person they saw may or may not be on the parade and that if they cannot make a positive identification they should say so, but not until they have looked at each person on the parade at least twice: para. 14.

(h) If they ask to hear any parade member speak, adopt a posture or move, they must first be asked if they can identify anyone on the basis of **appearance only**. If the request is to hear a person speak, they must be reminded that the participants have been chosen on the basis of their physical appearance only, but the members of the parade may then be asked to move, speak or adopt a posture: para. 17.

(i) At the end of the parade the suspect must be asked for any comments on its conduct. A photograph or video of the parade must be taken and a record kept of all those present at the parade.

Typical identification parade documents are shown below (Documents 10A to 10C below). Jane does not receive copies of these documents at this stage. They are supplied to her later in the proceedings with the committal papers.

R v RUSHKIN

Document 10A

NORTHUMBRIA POLICE   FORM A

IDENTIFICATION PARADES, GROUP AND VIDEO IDENTIFICATIONS

PART I — NOTICE TO SUSPECT

1. **PURPOSE**

    The purpose of an identification procedure is to test the ability of a witness to pick out from a group, if he is present, a person whom the witness has said that he has seen before on a specified occasion.

    The arrangement for and conduct of an identification procedure are the responsibility of a police officer in uniform of the rank of inspector or above who is not involved in the investigation. This officer is called the 'identification officer'.

2. **FREE LEGAL ADVICE**

    You are entitled to free legal advice before making any decisions regarding the identification procedures proposed. This includes the right to speak to a solicitor on the telephone.

3. **METHOD**

    a) An identification parade or group identification may take place either in a normal room or in one equipped with a screen permitting witnesses to see its members without being seen. The procedures for the composition and conduct of an identification parade are the same whether or not a screen is used and in either event a colour photograph or a video film of the parade shall be taken.

    b) If you refuse or, having agreed, fail to attend an identification parade or the holding of a parade is impracticable, arrangements will if practicable, be made to allow a witness an opportunity of seeing you in a group of people. Such a group identification may also be arranged if it is considered that, whether because of fear on behalf of the witness or for some other reason, it is in the circumstances more satisfactory than a parade.

    c) If you significantly alter your appearance between the taking of any photograph at the time of your arrest or after charge and any attempt to hold an identification procedure, this may be given in evidence if the case comes to trial. The Officer in charge may then consider other forms of identification. If in any event you change your appearance before a parade it may not be practicable to arrange one on the day in question and alternative methods of identification may be considered.

4. **PROCEDURES**

    Identification Parade

    a) You will be asked to stand in a line with a number of persons who are as far as practicable, of similar age, height and general appearance to yourself. You may stand in any position in the line you choose.

    b) You may object to anyone else on the parade or to the arrangements made. Such objection should be directed to the Identification Officer.

    c) The parade will be inspected by the witness. If there is more than one witness, each witness will be brought in separately.

    d) You will be allowed to change your position in the line after each witness has left. The witness will not be told who is the suspect.

    e) At the conclusion of the parade, you can make any comments you wish and these will be recorded.

    Group Identification

    f) A group identification should be held in a place other than a police station, but may be held in a police station when the identification officer considers it not practicable to hold it elsewhere.

    g) The arrangements for a group identification are the responsibility of the identification officer and must follow as far as possible the arrangements for holding an identification parade.

    Video Identification

    h) The video film must include you and at least eight other people who as far as practicable resemble you in age, height, general appearance and position in life.

    i) Both you and the other persons shall as far as possible be filmed in the same positions or carrying out the same activities and under identical conditions.

    j) You and your solicitor will be given a reasonable opportunity to view the complete film before it is shown to witnessess. Any reasonable objection to the film will be taken into consideration and if practical, steps will be taken to remove the grounds for objection.

    k) You and your solicitor will, if practicable, be given reasonable notification of the time and place that the film will be shown to witnessess. Whilst you yourself may not be present your solicitor or other representative may, and in the absence of your representative the showing of the video to witnessess will itself be recorded on video.

    l) Only one witness will see the film at a time, and the witness will not be told who is the suspect.

    m) All copies of the video film made under these provisions must be destroyed if you are prosecuted for the offence and cleared or if not prosecuted (unless you admit the offence and are cautioned for it). You may witness this destruction if you so request within five days of being cleared or informed that you will not be prosecuted.

5. **SOLICITORS, APPROPRIATE ADULTS OR OTHER REPRESENTATIVES**

    a) You will be given a reasonable opportunity to have a solicitor and an appropriate adult or friend present, and the identification officer will ask you to indicate on Form B(1) whether or not you so wish.

    b) Any procedure involving the participation of a person (whether as a suspect or witness) who is mentally disordered, mentally handicapped or a juvenile must take place in the presence of the appropriate adult, but the adult must not be allowed to prompt any identification of a suspect by a witness.

6. **CONSENT**

    a) You do not have to take part in a parade, or co-operate in a group identification, or with the making of a video film and, if it is proposed to hold a group identification or video identification, you are entitled to a parade if this can practicably be arranged.

    b) If you do not consent to take part in a parade or co-operate in a group identification or with the making of a video film, your refusal may be given in evidence in any subsequent trial and police may proceed covertly without your consent or make other arrangements to test whether a witness identifies you.

    c) You are asked to sign Form B(1) to indicate whether you are willing to take part in a parade or group identification or co-operate with the making of a video film. If you do not consent or co-operate you are not obliged to give your reasons, but any reasons you give will be recorded and may be given in evidence in any subsequent court proceedings.

7. **GENERAL**

    a) Where a witness has been shown photographs, photofit, identikit or similar pictures by the police during the investigation you and your solicitor will be informed.

    b) Before the parade takes place you will be provided with details of the first description provided to the Police by any witnesses who are to attend the parade. In addition, you will be allowed to view any material released to the media by the Police for the purpose of recognising or tracing a suspect, provided it is practicable to do so and would not unreasonably delay the investigation.

    c) These procedures are provided by the "Code of Practice for the Identification of Persons by Police Officers", which you may consult.

PART II

Station: Oldcastle Central Crime No.: C.R. No.:

Name: Steven Rushkin

Address: 12 Park View

Longfield Oldcastle OL10 2AB

I am aged 17 years or over ☑ I am under 17 years of age ☐

I have read this notice.

I am willing ☑ not willing ☐ to take part in an identification parade

I am willing ☐ not willing ☐ to take part in a group identification.

I am willing ☐ not willing ☐ to take part in a video identification.

My reasons for not wishing to take part are:- (Note: You do not have to give any reasons for your decisions but if you do these reasons may be given in evidence in any subsequent court proceedings).

....

....

SPECIMEN

....

....

I would ☑ would not ☐ like my solicitor or other representative to attend the identification procedures.

Signed: S. Rushkin Date: 2.5.97

Name of Solicitor: J. Watkins

Address: Watkins & O'Dwyer

17 Sycamore Avenue Oldcastle OL10 2AB

Signed: S. Rushkin Date: 2.5.97

Parent or Guardian (for juveniles)/appropriate adult (for mentally disordered or handicapped).

Name: Age:

Address:

....

Status to suspect:

Signed: Date:

I certify that I have explained the content and served a copy of this notice.

Officer's Signature: D. Edmonds

Date/Time: 14:30 2.5.97

R v RUSHKIN

Document 10B

NORTHUMBRIA POLICE

FORM B(1)

IDENTIFICATION PROCEDURE REPORT

Area Command...... Oldcastle

Place of parade ...... Oldcastle Central
Date of parade ...... 2 May 1997
Rank/Name of Identification Officer ...... Insp. D. Edmonds
Name: SUSPECT 'X' ...... Steven Rushkin
SUSPECT 'Y' ......

SPECIMEN

TICK APPROPRIATE BOXES

Screen Used   YES [ ]   NO [✓]

If YES video recorded [ ]

Solicitor [✓] , friend [ ] , or appropriate adult [ ] present.

Name ...... J. Watkins

Identification Parades are carried out in compliance with the Police and Criminal Evidence Act, 1984, Codes of Practice and Home Office Circular No. 88/85.

Notes:

(a) The arrangements for the identification procedure and its conduct will be made by an officer in uniform, not below the rank of inspector, and not being an officer involved in the investigation of the case.

(b) If a one-way screen is used a solicitor, friend or "appropriate adult" should be present or the parade must be recorded on video (PACE Act 1984, Codes of Practice, Code D).

(c) In the case of a group identification a solicitor, friend or "appropriate adult" should be present where practicable.

(d) A coloured photograph or a video film of the parade shall be taken. A copy of the photograph or video film shall be supplied on request to the suspect or his solicitor within a reasonable time. Where a screen is used and the suspect is not accompanied by a solicitor, friend or "appropriate adult" the parade must be video recorded.

(e) Witnesses will be kept in a place where they cannot see the parade or the suspect, or hear any of the proceedings, and will be introduced one at a time. Witnesses who have previously seen a photograph or description of the suspect should not be shown the photograph or description again before inspecting the parade.

While waiting to enter the parade room they should be prevented from talking with each other about the case.

On leaving they will not be allowed to communicate with witnesses still waiting to see the persons paraded.

(f) Form C is NOT to be given to the suspect, the "appropriate adult" or the suspect's solicitor except on the authority of the court. (Paras. 2.5 and 2.6 of Identification Parades Administrative Guidance. H.O. Circular No. 88/85).

(g) A video film identification may be made if the investigating officer considers, whether because of the suspect's refusal to take part in an identification parade or group identification or other reasons it is in the circumstances the most satisfactory course of action. This procedure is only adopted if the officer in charge of the investigation considers it necessary. It is NOT at the discretion of, or an option which is open to, the suspect.

Misc 61(a) (3.95)

R v RUSHKIN

SUSPECT(S)

1. **Suspect 'X'**
   Name: Steven Rushkin DOB: 12.1.53
   Address: 12 Park View, Longfield, Oldcastle OL10 2AB
   Alleged Offence: Attempted Burglary
   Form 'A' Notice to Suspect served at: 14.05 (time) 2.5.97 (date)
   By: Insp. D. Edmonds

   Suspect 'Y'
   Name: .... DOB: ....
   Address: ....
   Alleged Offence: ....
   Form 'A' Notice to Suspect served at: .... (time) .... (date)
   By: ....

2. Officer in case: D.C. P. Stubbs 2345
   Not present and took no part in the arrangements, or the conduct of, the parade (PACE Act 1984, Codes of Practice, Code D. Para. 2.2).

3. Provision for a suspect who is mentally ill, mentally handicapped, seriously visually handicapped or a juvenile.

   Suspect 'X'
   Name of appropriate adult: ....
   Age: .... Relationship: ....
   Address: ....
   Tel. No. ....

   SPECIMEN

   Suspect 'Y'
   Name of appropriate adult: ....
   Age: .... Relationship: ....
   Address: ....
   Tel. No. ....

4. Immediately before the parade I confirmed that the suspect had received a 'Notice to Suspect on Identification Parades' (Form A)
   at 'X' 14.05 (time) on 2 May 1997 (date)
   'Y' .... (time) on .... (date)
   I explained the procedures which would be followed during the parade and I advised Steven Rushkin that he/~~she~~ did not have to say anything but it may harm his/~~her~~ defence if he/~~she~~ did not mention when questioned something which he/~~she~~ would later rely on at court and that anything he/she did say in the course of the parade would be recorded and might be given in evidence in subsequent court proceedings.

   Identification Officer: D. Edmonds Time: 15.05

   * *delete as applicable*

R v RUSHKIN

NOTICE TO SUSPECT

SUSPECT 'X'

THIS IS THE PART OF THE IDENTIFICATION PROCEDURE REPORT WHICH YOU WILL BE ASKED TO SIGN WHEN YOU HAVE READ FORM 'A' — NOTICE TO SUSPECT.

1. Name: *Steven Rushkin*
   Address: *12 Park View, Greyfield, Oldcastle OL10 2AB*

   TICK APPROPRIATE BOX

   I am aged 17 years or over [✓]   I am under 17 years of age [ ]

   I have read Form 'A' — Notice to Suspect [✓]

   I am willing [✓]   not willing [ ]   to take part in an identification parade.
   I am willing [ ]   not willing [ ]   to take part in a group identification.
   I am willing [ ]   not willing [ ]   to take part in a video identification.

   I have been informed that before this parade was arranged *no* witness(es) who are taking part have been shown photographs, photofit, identikit, compusketch or similar pictures by the police during the investigation.

   Signed: *S. Rushkin*   14.30   Time/Date: *2.5.97*

   My reasons for not wishing to take part are:— (Note: You do not have to give any reasons for your decision but if you do these reasons may be given in evidence in any subsequent court proceedings).

   SPECIMEN

   Signed: .... Time/Date ....

2. **Opportunity given to suspect/solicitor to view films/photographs released to media for broadcast.**

   Material released by police to media for the purpose of recognising or tracing suspect   Yes [ ]   No [✓]   (tick one box).

   If 'Yes' complete (i) or (ii) as appropriate:

   *(i) Material shown to *suspect/solicitor on (date) .... by ....

   *(ii) Material NOT viewed by suspect/solicitor because (tick all reasons which apply and/or complete other):—

   suitable facilities/equipment were not available [ ]

   unreasonable delay would be caused to the investigation [ ]

   suspect/solicitor declined the opportunity to view material [ ]

   other (describe) ....

   Providing details of first description to suspect/solicitor

   Details of first description of the suspect given by first witness provided to (suspect) (solicitor) on (date) ....
   by .... Name and station/branch ....

3. I would [✓]   would not [ ]   like my solicitor or other representative to attend the identification procedures.

   Signed: *S. Rushkin*
   Time/Date: *14.30 2.5.97*
   Name of *Solicitor/~~Representative~~ *J. Watkins*
   Address: *Watkins & O'Dwyer*
            17 Sycamore Avenue, Oldcastle OL10 2AB

   * delete as applicable

R v RUSHKIN

4. Parent or guardian (for juveniles)/appropriate adult (for mentally handicapped).

   Name .... Age................

   Address ....

   .... Tel. No.....................

   Status/Relationship to suspect ....

5. I certify that I have explained the content and served a copy of Form 'A' — Notice to Suspect. I have caused the *solicitor/friend/appropriate adult to be informed.

   Officer's signature ...... *D. Edmonds*

   Time/Date *14.30   2.5.97*

If the **suspect** consents to an identification parade go to No. 10 otherwise continue below.

GROUP IDENTIFICATION

6. QUESTION TO SUSPECT

   "Since *you have refused to attend an identification parade   I propose to take
           *it has not been possible to arrange an identification parade

   you to .... where you will be asked to mingle informally with members of the public before the witness(es) are asked to attempt an identification. Are you willing to take part in this procedure

   Reply ....
   ....

   The **suspect** must be asked to sign his/her consent on page 3 (PACE Act 1984, Codes of Practice, Code D, Para. 2.8).
   If the **suspect** consents to a group identification parade go to Form B(2) or B(3). Otherwise continue below.

VIDEO IDENTIFICATION (See Note G on Page 1).

SPECIMEN

7. QUESTION TO SUSPECT

   "Since you have also refused to take part in a group identification I propose to make a video film from which the witness(s) will be asked to attempt an identification. Are you willing to take part in the making of such a film?"

   Reply ....
   ....

   The suspect must be asked to sign his/her consent on Page 3 (PACE Act 1984 Codes of Practice, Code D, Para 2.11).
   If the suspect consents to a video identification go to No. 9, otherwise continue below.

CONFRONTATION

8. QUESTION TO SUSPECT

   "Since you have refused to take part in either an identification parade, a group identification or video identification I shall be confronting you with the witness(es). This is your final opportunity to take part in either a parade, a group identification or video identification. I must warn you again that your refusal to take part in a parade may be given in evidence in any subsequent criminal proceedings".

   Reply ....
   ....

9. If the suspect refuses to take part in an identification parade or a group identification but agrees to video identification the procedure should be suspended to enable arrangements to be made. Otherwise continue on Page 7.

Note to Reader: pages 5 and 6 are identical and relate to suspect Y only.

*delete as applicable

R v RUSHKIN

10. **Where parade held**
    *Identification Parade Centre/Other (specify) ....
    Type of lighting: *Fluorescent/Other (specify) ....
    If a group identification see Form B(2) or B(3).

11. **Location of suspect/witnesses before parade**
    Where was **suspect** placed before the parade and how was *he/~~she~~ introduced to parade?
    .... *Interview room B; brought by P.C. Johnston* ....
    Where were **witnesses** placed before the parade and who was posted with them?
    .... *CID Rest room. P.C. Andrws* ....

12. One way screen used *~~Yes~~/No.

13. Time parade began .... *14:35* ....
    If a group identification go to Form B(2) or B(3). If a confrontation go to No. 36.

14. QUESTION TO SUSPECT(S)
    "Do you object to any of the persons paraded"?   **SPECIMEN**
    Answer 'X' .... *No* ....
    Answer 'Y' ....

15. State any arrangements made in conseuqence of any objection and if any person is replaced, cross through his/her name on Form C. all copies of Form C are to be attached to the final report and not destroyed.
    ....

16. QUESTION TO SUSPECT(S)
    "Do you object to any other persons being present who are not on the parade or to any of the arrangements for the parade"?
    Answer 'X' .... *No* ....
    Answer 'Y' ....

17. State any steps taken to comply with suspect's objection.
    ....

18. State names of all persons present during the parade, showing in the case of police officers whether under training instruction or connected with the investigation of the above offence.
    .... *Insp D. Edmonds; P.C. J. Fernandez (not connected with the investigation) P.C. P. Vines (video camera); P.C. Johnson (escorting officer) J. Watkins (solicitor)* ....

    If a group identification go to Form B(2) or B(3).

    Note: Explain to suspect(s) before the witness appears. "You may select any place you like among the persons paraded".

19. **INTRODUCTION OF WITNESS(ES)**
    After the suspect has taken his/her position in the line it is important that no-one leaves the room. The officer collecting the witness(es) should not be permitted to know the position of the accused. Witnesses will be kept in a place where they cannot see the parade or the suspect, or hear any of the proceedings, and will be introduced one at a time. Witnesses who have previously seen a photograph etc., or description of the suspect should not be shown the photograph etc., or description again before inspecting the parade. While waiting to attend the parade they should be prevented from talking with each other. On leaving they will not be allowed to communicate with witnesses still waiting to view the parade.

R v RUSHKIN

Conduct of witness's inspection on the parade.

		WITNESS 1
20.	Witness(es) (if more than 5 use Form B(1)(b)) Name	~~Mr/Mrs/Miss~~/Ms Rachel Paling

21. (a) The numbers in the top row refer to the position of the volunteers/suspects in the parade.
    (b) The position of the volunteers should be marked with the letter of the alphabet shown opposite their names on Form C.
    (c) The position of the suspects should be marked as X and Y.
    (d) The person identified should be ticked in 'Person Ident.' row.

Statement to suspect (before witness appears)
"You may select any place you like among the persons paraded".

Number	1	2	3	4	5	6	7	8	9	10	11	12	13	14		
Letter	E	G	B	C	A	F	X	D	H	/	/	/	/	/		
Person Ident.							✓									

22. Who ushered witness in and when?   P.C. Johnson   Time: 14.36

23. "You have been asked here today to see if you can identify the person you saw on (date(s)) ..... 18 April just
    (Describe incident(s)) before midnight attempting to break in at Megawin Amusement Arcade

"I am going to ask you in a moment to look at each person on the parade at least twice, taking as much care and time as you wish. I want to make it clear to you that the person you saw may not be here. If you cannot make a positive identification you should say so but should not make a decision until you have looked at each member of the parade at least twice. Please indicate the person by calling out his/her number".

24. Describe what witness does and says (eg walked L to R along front three times and said: "I think it's number three").

    Looked at line up, walked along L to R, looked from static position, identified no 7 by saying: "It's number 7."

    Witness reply ....

25. Describe what parade was asked to do at request of witness, if applicable (eg walk, speak, remove hat, etc.). See footnote.

    SPECIMEN

26. Was 'X' identified?   *Yes/~~No~~
    Record any comments by 'X' (if identified did *he/she say anything in the presence of the witness?).   No comment made

27. Was 'Y' identified?   *Yes/No
    Record any comments by 'Y' (if identified did *he/she say anything in the presence of the witness?).

28. Time witness left parade.   14.38

29. Where was witness taken after the parade and who escorted *him/~~her~~ there? Who was posted with *him/~~her~~?
    To CID Rest Room
    P.C. Johnson

* delete as applicable

R v RUSHKIN

After the witness has viewed the parade he/she shall be asked if he/she has seen any broadcast or published films or photographs relating to the offence.

Reply .... No

30. Any comments made by suspect after witness left.
.... No

Footnote: It may happen sometimes that a witness desires to see the suspect with a hat on or off and there is no objection to the person paraded thereupon being asked to wear or remove hats. If a witness asks to hear members of the parade speak or see them move, he/she **should be asked whether he/she can first identify any persons on the parade on the basis of appearance only, and his/her reply should be noted.** When the request is to hear members of the parade speak, he/she should be reminded that the participants in the parade have been chosen on the basis of physical appearance only. Members of the parade may then be asked to comply with the witness's request to hear them speak or see them move. Full details of the incident including the stages at which any identification was made, should be recorded.

[Note to Reader: the remaining pages are used when there is more than one identification witness.]

SPECIMEN

delete as applicable

9

R v RUSHKIN

Document 10C

FORM C

NORTHUMBRIA POLICE

Record of Persons forming Identification Parade or Group Identification
(Both hereinafter referred to as "Parade")

Date held: 2.5.97

Name(s) of suspect(s): X: S. Rushkin

Y:

Ref. No.: OL/GE/3099

	Names and addresses of persons forming the parade	Signature for expenses
A	Name: John Stevens Address: 15 Forest Avenue, Oldcastle OL21 2OR	J. Stevens
B	Name: Paul Healy Address: Flat 2, The Copse, Oldcastle Street, Oldcastle	P. Hardy
C	Name: Arthur Bailey Address: 107 Tus Street, Oldcastle OL5 9BX	A. Bailey
D	Name: Maurice Montgomery Address: Beach Hotel, Beech St, Oldcastle OL5 2AB	M. Montgomery
E	Name: Percy Hedley Address: 1 College Street, Oldcastle OL1 9HJ	P. Hedley
F	Name: Kenneth O'Brien Address: 19 Wilton Avenue, Oldcastle OL14 1AJ	K O'Brien
G	Name: Anthony McVeigh Address: 95 Anchor Street, Oldcastle OL2 10KL	Anthony McVeigh
H	Name: Mark Gibson-Smythe Address: Headmaster's Cottage, Gibson School, Gibson Street, Oldcastle OL5 2AB	M. Gibson-Smythe
I	Name Address	
J	Name Address	
K	Name Address	**SPECIMEN**
L	Name Address	
M	Name Address	
N	Name Address	
O	Name Address	
P	Name Address	

Note:

1. *If the suspect objects to any of the persons forming the parade, that person should not be used, and his name and address should be crossed through.*

2. *In all cases a colour photograph or a video film of the parade shall be taken. A copy of the photograph or film shall be supplied on request to the suspect or his Solicitor within a reasonable time.*

3. *When a group identification is held in a public place and the witness identifies a person other than the suspect, an Officer should inform that person what has happened and ask if they are prepared to give their name and address. There is no obligation upon any member of the public to give these details.*

Misc. 63 *(Amended 3.95).*

As you can see from section 24 of Document 10B, Steven was identified by the witness, Rachel Pa'ing, during the parade. At the conclusion of the parade, Steven is therefore taken to the interview room to consult with Jane.

After The Parade — The Second Police Interview: Friday 2 May: 14.45 p.m.

Arguably the police now have sufficient evidence to charge, but they will normally wish to put the identification to the suspect 'in order to give him an opportunity to comment on it'. Jane therefore now takes further instructions from Steven. She explains that he will certainly now be charged with the attempted burglary and she completes the legal aid forms for him to sign (these forms are set out later).

Jane also takes the opportunity to take Steven's instructions about bail. She warns Steven that the police are unlikely to grant bail once he has been charged, and that he will therefore be kept in custody until he is produced at the magistrates' court the following day. She advises Steven that he should continue to answer the police questions in interview, putting forward his version of events (i.e., the 'defence facts' for s. 34, Criminal Justice and Public Order Act 1994 purposes).

There is then a further interview in which Steven re-iterates that it was not him at MegaWin and that Phil Gramsci can confirm his alibi. (A transcript of this interview is obtained just before trial and is set out at Document 68 on page 163.)

After the interview Jane talks to the custody officer who confirms that there is now sufficient evidence and he intends to charge. Jane asks about progress on the forensic analyses, but is told these are still outstanding. Jane asks about bail but, as she expects, the custody officer indicates that he intends to refuse bail.

Under s. 38, PACE 1984 the custody officer must grant bail unless:

(a) the suspect's name or address either cannot be ascertained, or there are reasonable grounds for doubting the accuracy of the details given by the suspect;

(b) there are reasonable grounds for believing the suspect will fail to appear in court to answer his bail, bearing in mind the nature and seriousness of the offence, the defendant's character, antecedents, associations and community ties, the defendant's previous bail record and the strength of the evidence against him;

(c) there are reasonable grounds for believing detention is necessary to prevent the defendant from committing an offence (imprisonable offences only);

(d) there are reasonable grounds for believing detention is necessary to prevent the defendant injuring someone else or causing loss or damage to property (non-imprisonable offences only);

(e) there are reasonable grounds for believing the detention is necessary to prevent the defendant interfering with the administration of justice or the investigation of an offence;

(f) there are reasonable grounds for believing that the detention is necessary for the person's own protection.

Here the custody officer refuses bail on the basis that he believes Steven will not answer his bail, taking into account the strong evidence, the seriousness of the charge and his previous very poor bail record.

The custody officer has a power to grant bail but to impose conditions (such as a surety, or a condition of residence at a specified address, or a condition of reporting at specified times to a given police station). Jane has instructions from Steven that his wife and Philip Gramsci are both possible sureties. She argues strongly that this condition would meet the custody officer's concerns. She is very conscious that the court will often be very influenced in deciding whether it will grant bail by whether the police have granted bail. She also points out that Steven has answered the police bail by attending today.

However, the custody officer is not persuaded and Steven is now produced for charging.

The Attempted Burglary Charge: Friday 2 May 1997: 15.45 p.m.

Steven is charged with attempted burglary and, as you will see from the custody record (at 15.45 p.m.) Jane indicates that he has no further comment to make, having given a full account in interview. (Bear in mind that a s. 34 inference from a failure to mention defence facts can also arise at charge.)

R v RUSHKIN

Document 11

NORTHUMBRIA POLICE
NOTICE OF OFFENCE(S) CHARGED

ORIGINAL / AMENDED / ADDITIONAL

Sheet No. 1 of 1
Custody Record No. OLC/97/293

CRO No. R1234　　OIC No. 2345　　URN COMPLETED AT ASU

Area Command: OLDCASTLE
Section: CENTRAL
Court: CENTRAL MAGISTRATES' at 10 a.m., on SATUR DAY 03/05/1997

PERSON CHARGED: Steven Rushkin
ADDRESS: 12 Park View, Longfield, Oldcastle
Date of Birth: 12.7.53
Occupation/Place of Education: Unemployed
Male/~~Female~~

YOU ARE CHARGED WITH THE OFFENCE(S) SHOWN BELOW
You do not have to say anything unless you wish to do so, but what you say may be given in evidence.

ATTEMPT BURGLARY

That you did on 18th April 1997 attempt to enter a building namely Megalon Amusement Arcade, Castle Street, Oldcastle as a trespasser with intent to steal therein CONTRARY to Section 1 Criminal Attempts Act 1981

SPECIMEN

O.I.C.: DC Stubbs 2345 Oldcastle, Central
Officer Charging: DC 2345 Stubbs
Receipt for copy of charge(s): YES/~~NO~~
Receipt for Disclosure Notice (Pros. 56): YES/~~NO~~
Time and Date of Charging: 15.45 pm 02/05/97
Officer Accepting Charge: Sgt. Smith 6789
Signature: S. Rushkin

NOTICE OF BAIL

The above named has this day been released on bail in accordance with Section 38(1) of the Police and Criminal Evidence Act 1984 and the Bail Act 1976 in connection with the alleged offence(s) as outlined above, and is required to surrender to custody at the Magistrates' Court sitting at the place and time shown above to answer the charge(s).

I have been informed that unless I surrender to Custody as shown above I may be liable to a fine, or imprisonment or both.

REFUSED

Signature of person bailed: —
Signed (Officer granting bail): —
Rank: — No: —
Date: —/—/19— Time: —

SURETIES
I/we acknowledge my/our obligation to pay the Court the sum specified by my/our signature if the accused fails to surrender to custody as shown.

(1) Signature / Name (Block Capitals) / Address £
(2) Signature / Name (Block Capitals) / Address £

MG4 (4.94)

1. Blue—Custody Record Copy.　2. Yellow—Copy for Magistrates' Clerk.　3. White—Copy for Accused
4. Green—Copy for Court Office.　5. Pink—Copy for O.I.C.

As expected the custody officer refuses bail. Steven will therefore be produced at the first available court hearing, which will be on Saturday morning. Jane therefore confirms with Steven that she will be attending court to represent him tomorrow and to apply for bail from the court. Steven is taken back to the cells and Jane goes back to the office to dictate her attendance note.

Document 12

Attendance Note

Your name JW   Date 2 May 1997

Client's name   S. Rushkin   Person attended   client at police station

Time start   2.00   Time finish   3.05

Arrived police station 2.00. waiting 2.00 – 2.15, attending Insp. Edmonds on parade arrangements 2.15 – 2.30.

Attended parade at 2.30 p.m. conducted by Inspector Edmonds. Witness a Mrs R. Paling, wore glasses, appeared elderly and hesitant. Stated 'I think it's him (pointing at Rushkin's position); yes, I'm almost sure it was him.' Parade conducted in accordance with codes and videoed at my request.

Paling had apparently seen two people from her first floor flat in Castle Street opposite MegaWin. A person she now identifies as Rushkin and another person were seen beside the broken window of the downstairs toilet in the enclosed rear yard of MegaWin. They both ran off over the rear wall behind MegaWin and ran away down Burn Street.

Waiting with client 2.45 – 3.35, took instructions for bail if necessary.

Further interview after parade 3.30 – 3.35 with DC Stubbs: no new replies, denial as before. Rushkin stated to me beforehand and on my advice repeated in interview that there is no way he could climb over a tall wall because of his injury.

Attending Sgt Smith 3.40; he has decided he now has enough evidence for a charge. Asked for bail, but Smith says will not grant bail in view of the seriousness of the offence and Rushkin's repeated absconding in 1996. I made representations that unlikely to abscond now – has been on bail for two weeks and reported without a problem today, and explanation of the absconding. Suggested a surety could be contacted shortly. No success.

Asked if fingerprint and hair analyses yet ready. 'Nothing to report'.

Saw Rushkin 3.40, advised to make no further statement after caution. Client charged. Advised him he would be in court tomorrow. I or a member of firm will see him in cell before court starts.

Instructions for a bail application at court tomorrow. The 'repeated absconding' in 1996 was at a time when he was suffering considerable trauma from a road accident two months previously, and was incapable of organising his life. That had been the reason he took part in the burglary as well. Mr Rushkin thinks he failed to turn up some three times, and on the third occasion was both refused bail and convicted of absconding. (Obtain file and check.)

Instructed to contact wife Jocelyn and employer, Philip Gramsci, as possible sureties. He will agree to any other conditions in order to get out.

Left at 3.45 after charge.

travel – 20 min, 10 miles

Getting paid for the police station work

As previously discussed (see page 31) Jane will claim for the work at the two police station attendances under the police station advice and assistance scheme. The work is claimed on a form DSPS 1, which divides up the different types of work (advising, travelling, waiting, telephoning etc.) and also makes a distinction between own solicitor and duty solicitor work. Just to make things even more complicated, there are different rates for firms with a legal aid franchise (you do not currently have to have a 'franchise' to do legal aid work, but there are carrots such as better payments to encourage firms to apply).

Document 13 below shows the completed DSPS 1 in this case.

R v RUSHKIN

Document 13

DSPS.1
Area Reference

LEGAL AID BOARD - LEGAL AID ACT 1988
ADVICE AT POLICE STATIONS REPORT

SPECIMEN

Date of receipt of claim   Total claim £

Legal Aid

This form should be completed whether you acted as own solicitor or 24-hour duty solicitor.

Please complete Sections 1,2,3,4 and 5

Section 6 should be completed where a client has been represented on an application for a warrant of further detention or extension of such a warrant

You should retain the copy of this form marked "Solicitor's Copy".

The remaining two copies should be sent to your Legal Aid Area Office.

Claims for standby and hotel expenses should be made on form DSPS 2.

SECTION 1

Client's Surname: RUSHKIN

Client's address: 12 PARK VIEW, LONGFIELD, OLDCASTLE OL10

Acted as: ✓ own solicitor

Police Station where client was located:

Date of first attendance (day, month, year): 19 4 97

Was your client: ✓ adult (civilian)

State offence for which client is being investigated (if more than one, state the most serious): ATTEMPT BURGLARY

Is this offence: ✓ an arrestable offence (11)

Did you advise and assist the client when he/she was attending the police station: ✓ under arrest (14)

Did you advise the client: ✓ in office hours (16)

Legal Aid Account No.: A123B
Solicitor's Reference: JW/RUSHKIN
VAT Registration No. (if required): 123456

SECTION 2 WORK DONE

Visits to Police Station	1st visit	2nd visit	3rd visit	4th visit
From	9 05	14 00		
To	10 20	15 40		

Own solicitor	Time (in mins)	Cost claimed	Office Use £ p
Travelling	40	16 83	
Waiting	20	8 41	
Advice and assistance/detention	150	121 25	
Sub Total		146 49	

Duty Solicitor			
Travelling			
Waiting and advising			
Sub total			

Telephone calls			
Total time on duty and assistance calls			
No. of advice and assistance calls			
No. of routine calls	1	3 60	
Sub Total		3 60	

ABWOR

Sub total profit costs: 150 09
VAT on profit costs: 26 27
Total profit costs inc VAT: 176 36

Disbursements and travel
Total disbursements:
Mileage (if appropriate): 20 — 7 20
VAT on travel and disbursements: 1 80
Total disbursements and travel inc VAT: 9 00

Has your client previously received advice and assistance in respect of this matter: NO ✓

Date: 7 5 97   Signed (for solicitor)

DECLARATION AS TO CERTIFICATION: I hereby declare that I have at all times during the conduct by me of the matter to which the claim relates held a valid practising certificate.

J. Watkins   Signed by Conducting Solicitor

Duty Solicitor Region   Scheme identifier

Provisional Assessment   Y   N

Signed Authorised Signatory

Legal Aid Area No.   Date

ACCOUNTS DEPARTMENT'S COPY

R v RUSHKIN

SECTION 3

Details of disbursements *Please include the amount of VAT (if any) on disbursements where indicated below*

Disbursements	
VAT on disbursements	

(include these amounts in 'Disbursements' and 'VAT on travel and disbursement' boxes in Section 2)

If the client has previously received advice and assistance in respect of this matter, please state the date of the advice, the amount of the claim and the name and the address of the solicitor.

Does the office have a crime franchise?
Tick one box

If the office does not have a crime franchise and you have exceeded the costs limit, please explain why it was necessary in the interests of justice that advice and assistance was given as a matter of urgency.

Mr Rushkin was advised on 15.4.97 charged on one matter and bailed to attend an identification parade. I had to advise and assist with interviews on both occasions, assist at the parade and taking non-intimate samples and fingerprints

For office use
Authority to exceed costs limit
- Granted
- Refused

Date
Signed

SECTION 4

Details and category of the person advising
- Duty Solicitor = 1
- Duty Solicitor Representative = 2
- Own Solicitor = 3
- Trainee Solicitor representative = 4
- Accredited representative = 5
- Probationary representative = 6
- Immigration representative = 7

For initial telephone advice
Name			
Date		Category (1 - 7)	PIN no.

For first attendance at police station
Name	J. Watkins		
Date	19.4.97	Category (1-7)	PIN no.

For any subsequent attendance at police station
Name	J. Watkins		
Date	2.5.97	Category (1-7)	PIN no.
Name			
Date		Category (1-7)	PIN no.
Name			
Date		Category (1-7)	PIN no.

Type of case: *Tick one box only*
| Immigration | Indictable only | either way | summary |

SECTION 5

Solicitor's name
J. Watkins

Firm's name, address and telephone number
17 Sycamore Avenue
OLD CASTLE CLIO 2BR

Document exchange number
DX 1234 2BR

SECTION 6

To be completed only if you represented a client on an application for a warrant of further detention or an extension of such a warrant (ABWOR)

Total time spent *(Use 24-hour clock for times)*
From	
To	

Travelling
	Time (in mins)	Claimed £ P	Assessed £ P

Personal attendance

Preparation

Waiting for advocacy
- Waiting
- Advocacy

Letters and telephone calls
- No. of letters written
- No. of telephone calls

Total for Section 6 so far
(enter this amount in 'ABWOR' box in Section 2)

Travel expenses
Mileage *(if appropriate)*
(include this amount in 'Travel expenses' box in Section 2)

Details of disbursements *Please include the amount of VAT (if any) on disbursements where indicated below*

SPECIMEN

Disbursements	£
VAT on disbursements	£

(include these amounts in 'Disbursements' and 'VAT on travel and disbursement' boxes in section 2)

PART B — THE MAGISTRATES' COURT

Steven is now due to be appear before the magistrates' court on two different dates for two different matters. He is in custody for the attempted burglary and will be brought to court on Saturday morning. He is on bail (although only technical bail, since he is in fact in custody on the burglary) for the driving offence, and must attend court on the following Thursday.

Jane therefore now needs to consider:

(a) the legal elements of the offences;

(b) obtaining legal aid;

(c) preparing to apply for bail.

Bail is obviously critical and if you have ever been in a prison (whether long-term or just visiting) you will know why clients are desperate to get bail. Indeed, at this stage, getting bail is often the client's number one consideration, and it can sometimes be hard to persuade clients to think about the case against them until bail has been sorted out. But equally, from Jane's perspective, legal aid is critical. If Steven is not granted legal aid, he will not be represented at court unless Jane (or her firm) consider that they are prepared to do the work pro bono on this occasion. Even if they are, pro bono work will not help Jane meet her monthly billing targets!

First, however, Jane must look briefly at the legal elements of the charges, to make sure that she is not overlooking anything relevant in her preparation for the burglary trial and the driving disqualified mitigation.

The Legal Elements of the Charges

The solicitor now has two charge sheets and each should be read very carefully. The case can be prepared only in the knowledge of the exact allegations which the defence have to meet.

The solicitor, if not familiar with the exact components of the offences, checks them later, for example in *Stone's Justices' Manual*.

The attempted burglary

Section 1 of the Criminal Attempts Act 1981 states:

If, with an intent to commit an offence to which this section applies, a person does an act which is more than merely preparatory to the commision of the offence, he is guilty of attempting to commit the offence.

Section 2 states that the offence is tried in the same manner in the same court as if it were the substantive offence.

Section 4 states that the penalty for an attempt is the same as for the substantive offence — in this case, burglary.

Burglary, in relation to Steven's circumstances, is defined in s. 9(1), Theft Act 1968:

A person is guilty of burglary if —
  (a) he enters any building or part of a building as a trespasser and with intent to commit any such offence as is mentioned in subsection (2) below)
  (b) ...
  (2) The offences referred to in subsection (1)(a) above are offences of stealing anything in the building or part of a building in question ...
  (4) A person guilty of burglary shall on conviction on indictment be liable to imprisonment for a term not exceeding fourteen years.

He is charged with attempting to enter in order to steal. Under s. 17 and sch. 1, para. 28, Magistrates' Courts Act 1980 such a burglary is triable either way. Under the Magistrates' Association Sentencing Guidelines, the entry point is a community penalty.

Driving while disqualified

The offence of driving while disqualified (charge sheet page 27) is defined by s. 103, Road Traffic Act 1988, as driving a motor vehicle on a road while disqualified for (sic) holding a licence. There are very few defences, and none of them are available to Steven according to his instructions (see, for example, McMahon, *A Practical Approach to Road Traffic Law* (London: Blackstone Press), 1994, ch. 14). It is a summary offence for which the penalties are six months' imprisonment, a level 5 fine, discretionary disqualification, and obligatory endorsement with six penalty points.

The entry point for sentencing is, according to Magistrates' Association Guidelines, custody (see e.g., Wasik, *Emmins on Sentencing*, 2nd edn (London: Blackstone Press), 1993, p. 361), although Steven's driving does not satisfy most of the seriousness indicators mentioned. However, if he is found to have driven in order to commit the burglary, the driving offence becomes more serious, because linked, under s. 29, Criminal Justice Act 1991.

Driving while disqualified is summary only, but under s. 41, Criminal Justice Act 1988, magistrates committing an either way matter to the Crown Court can also commit a summary only offence arising out of the circumstances of the either way offence. Such an offence must be punishable with imprisonment or disqualification. The Crown Court will not deal with the summary matter unless Steven is convicted of the either way offence (by pleading guilty or after a trial). At that point, if he pleads guilty to the summary offence, the Crown Court can sentence him without sending the case back to the magistrates.

(Certain summary offences, of which driving whilst disqualified is one, can actually be tried on indictment if factually connected to an either way offence which is tried on indictment — s. 40, Criminal Justice Act 1988. Here the prosecution use the s. 41 procedure, which only gives the Crown Court a power to deal with the summary offence if the plea to that offence is guilty. The driving offence does not therefore become part of the indictment.)

Applying for Legal Aid

Steven has instructed Jane to apply for legal aid. When she conferred with Steven at the police station after the identification parade, Jane quickly completed the legal aid forms (Form 1 and Form 5, which are often now printed as a single composite form).

Driving whilst disqualified attracts a custodial sentence and, as has been discussed, the link with an alleged burglary attempt may well mean that the court treats that offence as so serious that only a custodial sentence is appropriate. Equally, while burglary of commercial premises is less serious than domestic burglary, it too carries a potential custodial sentence. In a case of this seriousness and complexity there is little doubt that legal aid will be granted by the court.

Note, however, that in order to illustrate what happens if legal aid is refused, we will be taking a small 'detour' to look at the review process.

The legal aid application and statement of means are set out as Document 14. Steven is not required to complete most of the parts of Form 5 since he can show that he is in receipt of Income Support.

Document 14

Form 1 and Form 5 also known as Crown Courts 5131 and 5132

The Legal Aid in Criminal and Care Proceedings (General) (Amendment) No 3 Regulations 1996 ▮▮▮▮▮▮

Application & Statement of Means for Legal Aid in Criminal and Care Proceedings Magistrates'/Crown Court
(Including Youth Court)

General Notes on Use — see below for your age group and directions as to which forms you must complete

Aged 16 years and over
Complete Form 1 and Form 5

Aged 15 years or below
(i) If you make the application yourself complete Form 1 and Form 5 must be completed by your parent or guardian
(ii) If the application is made by your parent or guardian, he or she must complete Form 1 and Form 5.

WARNING
APPLICANTS MAY BE PROSECUTED IF THEY ARE FOUND KNOWINGLY TO HAVE MADE A FALSE STATEMENT AS TO THEIR FINANCIAL CIRCUMSTANCES. ANY CHANGE OF FINANCIAL CIRCUMSTANCES MUST BE NOTIFIED TO THE LEGAL AID CLERK IMMEDIATELY.

NOTE: To avoid delay in your application being considered, please ensure that you answer all relevant questions fully and send all the documents to be sent. Write "NONE" where this is appropriate and where a question is not applicable in your case write "N/A" or cross the question out.

If the form is not completed properly it will be returned to you thus causing a delay; or may result in you being assessed to pay too high a contribution towards legal aid (if granted) or not being granted legal aid at all.

JUNE 1996

R v RUSHKIN

Application for Legal Aid in Criminal Proceedings
Magistrates' or Crown Court

Form 1
Reg 11 & 18
(also known as Crown Court Form 5131)

I apply for Legal Aid –
For the purpose of proceedings before the CENTRAL   Crown/~~Magistrates'~~/~~Youth Court~~*

1. Personal details: *(Please use BLOCK letters and BLACK ink)*

a) Surname: RUSHKIN   e) Date of birth: 12.1.53

b) Forenames: STEVEN

c) Permanent address: 12 PARK VIEW, LONGFIELD, OLDCASTLE OLIO 2AB

d) Present address *(if different from above)*:

2. Case Details:

a) Describe briefly what it is you are accused of doing, e.g. "stealing £50 from my employer," "kicking a door causing £50 damage."
1. Attempted burglary at an amusement arcade
2. Driving whilst disqualified

b) The following other person(s) is/are charged in this case.
Robert Chapman

c) Give reasons why you and the other persons charged in this case, if any, should not be represented by the same solicitor.
He admits the defence and I deny it

SPECIMEN

3. Court Proceedings: *(Complete section a or b whichever applies)*

a) I am due to appear before the Central on 3rd May 19 97 at 10 am/~~pm~~ Magistrates'/~~Youth Court~~*

or

b) I appeared before the _____ on _____ 19 __ at __ am/pm Magistrates'/Youth Court*

and *(tick whichever applies)*
☐ my case has been transferred to the Crown Court for trial
☐ I was convicted and committed for sentence to the Crown Court
☐ I was convicted and/or sentenced and I wish to appeal against the   conviction and/or sentence*

*Cross out whichever does not apply

A1

4. Outstanding Matters:

a) If there are any other outstanding criminal charges, or cases against you, give details including the court where you are due to appear (only those cases that are not concluded).

5. Your Financial Position: *(Tick the box which applies)*

a) [✓] I receive Income-based Jobseeker's Allowance, Income Support, Family Credit or Disability Working Allowance, and I attach documentary evidence that I am receiving such a benefit (e.g. order book).

(You may also tick this box if your spouse or partner receives any of these benefits, and you are living together)

Give:

i) The address of the Social Security or Jobcentre office dealing with the benefit

> BENEFITS AGENCY, WOULDHAVE HOUSE, HASSELL PLACE, OLDCASTLE OL33

ii) National Insurance number of person receiving benefit

> YP908425A

iii) Type of benefit

> INCOME SUPPORT

If you do not produce documentary evidence that you are receiving benefit, the court will assume that you are not receiving benefit and you will also have to complete a Form 5 (statement of means).

SPECIMEN

b) [ ] I have already given a statement of my means to the _____ Court and there has been no change in my financial position. *(A new statement is required if there has been any change)*

c) [ ] I attach a statement of my means in these proceedings *(details of your income and expenditure)*

d) [ ] I am under 16 and I attach a statement of my parents means. If you are unable to provide a statement of their means, give their name and address.

6. Legal Representation:

Note

a) If you do not give the name and address of a solicitor the court will select a solicitor for you.
b) You must tell the solicitor that you have named him, unless he has helped you complete this form.
c) If you have been charged together with another person or persons, the court may assign a solicitor other than the solicitor of your choice.

a) The solicitor I wish to act for me is

> JANE WATKINS

b) Give the firm's name and address (if known)

> WATKINS & O'DWYER, 17 SYCAMORE AVENUE OLDCASTLE OL10 2BR

A2

R v RUSHKIN

7. Reasons for wanting Legal Aid:

- To avoid the possibility of your application being delayed or legal aid being refused because the court does not have enough information about the case, you must complete the rest of the form.
- When deciding whether to grant legal aid, the court will need to know the reasons why it is in the interest of justice for you to be represented.
- If you need help in completing this form, and especially if you have previous convictions, you should see a solicitor. He may be able to advise you free of charge or at a reduced fee.

Note: If you plead **NOT GUILTY** neither the information in this form nor that in your statement of means will be made available to the members of the court trying your case unless you are convicted or you consent. If you are acquitted, only the financial information you have given in your statement of means will be given to the court

Tick any boxes which apply and give brief details or reasons in the space provided

		Details	Reasons for grant or refusal
a) It is likely that I will lose my liberty *(You should consider seeing a solicitor before answering this question)*	✓	1. The offence of driving whilst disqualified is normally considered a matter for custody. 2. I have a conviction for burglary in August 1996 which may make the present matter appear more serious. Court of Appeal guidelines suggest that burglary is serious enough to warrant custody	
b) I am subject to a: suspended or partly suspended prison sentence ☐ conditional discharge ☐ probation order ☐ supervision order ☐ deferment of sentence ☐ community service order ☐ care order ☐ combination order ☐ *Give details as far as you are able, including the nature of the offence and when the order was made.*		**SPECIMEN**	
c) It is likely that I will lose my livelihood ☐			
d) It is likely that I will suffer serious damage to my reputation ☐			
e) A substantial question of law is involved ☐ *(You will need the help of a solicitor to answer this question)*			

(Please give authorities to be quoted with law reports references)

A3

R v RUSHKIN

		Details	Reasons for grant or refusal *(for court use only)*
f) I shall be unable to understand the court proceedings or state my own case because: i) My understanding of English is inadequate ii) I suffer from a disability *(Give full details)*	☐ ☐	**SPECIMEN**	
g) Witnesses have to be traced and/or interviewed on my behalf *(State circumstances)*	☑	The case turns on what happened over a period of only five minutes. Alibi evidence and other possible witnesses to be interviewed.	
h) The case involves expert cross examination of a prosecution witness *(Give brief details)*	☑	Police have taken finger prints and hair sample — expert witnesses may be called. Identification evidence will be challenged.	
i) It is in someone's else's interest that I am represented	☐		
j) Any other reasons *(Give full particulars)*	☑	1. Need to obtain own expert evidence on my own capacity to climb six foot wall as alleged by identification witness. 2. Co-accused admits offence	

8. Declaration:

If you knowingly make a statement which is false, or knowingly withhold information, you may be prosecuted. If convicted, you may be sent to prison for up to three months or be fined or both *(Section 39 (1) Legal Aid Act 1988)*. After your application has been considered by the court, you may be asked to give further information or to clarify information or to provide further proof of the information you have given.
If you stop receiving Income-based Jobseeker's Allowance, Income Support, Family Credit, Disability Working Allowance or if your financial position changes in any way after you have submitted this form, you must tell the court. This is a requirement of the Legal Aid regulations. I understand that, if I do not produce all the information which the court needs, it may make such enquiries of the Benefits Agency as it considers necessary and I authorise it so to do. I consent to the disclosure of information to confirm that I am in receipt of benefit.

I understand that the court may order me to make a contribution to the costs of Legal Aid, or to pay the whole costs if it considers that I can afford to do so and, if I am under 16, make a similar order with respect to my parents.

Signed: S. Rushkin   **Dated:** 2nd May 1997

A4

R v RUSHKIN

For Court use only

Any additional factors considered when determining the application, including any information given orally.

Decision on the interest of justice test

I have considered all available details of all the charges and it is/is not* in the interests of justice that representation be granted because:

SPECIMEN

Signed: *Lee Gallade* Proper Officer
Dated: 23 . 5 . 97

* Cross out whichever does not apply

A5

R v RUSHKIN

Statement of Means by Applicant or Appropriate Contributor for Legal Aid purposes

Form 5
Regulation 23
(also known as
Crown Court Form 5132)

To apply for criminal legal aid you must complete this form unless you can prove that you are in receipt of Income-based Jobseeker's Allowance, Income Support, Family Credit or Disability Working Allowance and have provided documentary evidence that you receive one of those benefits when you completed Form 1. *(See Section 5 of Form 1 headed* **Your Financial Position**).

If you are not yet sixteen, then your mother or father may also be asked to complete one. If you have applied for legal aid for a child of yours who is aged sixteen or over **you** do not need to fill in this form. **Your child** should complete it, giving details of his or her **own income.**

To avoid delay in your application being considered please complete the form as fully and carefully as possible and provide the information and documentary evidence the form requires. If you cannot provide the documentary evidence you must explain why at Section 5.

1 Personal Details (please use BLOCK letters)

1. Surname   [ ]   Mr [ ]   Mrs [ ]   Miss [ ]   Ms [ ]

2. Forenames

3. Date of birth

4. Home address

5. Marital status (please tick one box)
   - Single [ ]
   - Single and living together [ ]
   - Widow(er) [ ]
   - Married [ ]
   - Married but separated [ ]
   - Divorced [ ]

6. Are you claiming legal aid for a dependent child who is not yet sixteen? YES [ ]   NO [ ] (go to section 2)

   If Yes, give the following details about the child

   Surname

   Forenames

   Date of birth

   Home address (if different from yours)

   Your relationship to the child (eg. father)

2 Financial Details – Part A : Income

In this section you are asked to give details of the money you receive. If you are living with your spouse or partner then you must provide details of the income of your spouse or partner as well. The details will be used to work out whether you have to pay a contribution towards legal aid and if so how much. The assessment is based on weekly income so your answers must show the amount you get *each week*. If any of the sections do not apply, write NONE in the space.

Work	Employer's name and address	Your Income	Income of Spouse or Partner	Official use
Enter gross earnings *per week* (before tax and insurance), including overtime, commission or bonuses. You must attach documentary evidence of the pay you have received over the past 13 weeks. Three monthly or 13 weekly pay slips would be the best evidence.		£	£	
If you are self-employed write SELF-EMPLOYED. Show your gross earnings and attach the most recent accounts, showing gross income.		£	£	
Part time work Enter gross earnings *per week* (before tax and insurance) from any part time job not included above and attach documentary evidence.		£	£	
State Benefits Enter *weekly amounts* eg. from unemployment benefit, child benefit, etc. Say which benefit(s) you get in the space provided. You should produce evidence of the benefit payment (eg. order book)	Types of benefit	£ £ £	£ £ £	
Money from property Enter *weekly amounts* (before any deductions) of money from sub-letting a house or rooms and attach documentary evidence		£	£	
Any other income Please give details *and weekly amounts* and attach documentary evidence		£	£	

Important - If the information you have given above is going to change soon please give details of the changes in Section 4 of this form.

2 Financial details – Part B : Capital and Savings

Please give details of all your capital and savings. If you are living with your spouse or partner you must also give details of their capital and savings.

Property. *Note: In the questions which follow the value of the equity means the sum which you would receive from the sale of the property after paying the mortgage or other loan on it.

1 – Main Dwelling

Do you or your spouse/partner own the house or property which you treat as your main dwelling? If so please provide the following information. *(Tick appropriate box)*

	You	Spouse or Partner
	Yes ☐ No ☐	Yes ☐ No ☐

i) What is the value of the equity* in your main dwelling? £ _____ £ _____   Official Use

ii) What is your main dwelling worth now, that is, what is its market value? £ _____ £ _____

iii) What is the mortgage on your main dwelling? £ _____ £ _____

2 – Other Houses or Property

Do you or your spouse/partner own a house or property other than the house or property which you treat as your main dwelling? If so, please provide the following information. *(Tick appropriate box)*

	You	Spouse or Partner
	Yes ☐ No ☐	Yes ☐ No ☐

i) What is the value of the equity* in the house(s)/other property? £ _____ £ _____

ii) What are the house(s)/other property worth now, that is, what are their market values? £ _____ £ _____

iii) What are the mortgages on the house(s)/other property? £ _____ £ _____

Savings

Give details of where your savings are, and the amounts. Include money in any bank, building society, National Savings Certificates, cash, stocks and shares or any other investments. You should produce pass books etc.

£ _____ £ _____

Articles of value

Give details of any articles of value that you own (eg. jewellery, furs, paintings) with their approximate value. You may be asked to produce valuation certificates.

£ _____ £ _____

3 Allowances and Deductions

1. Enter Tax and National Insurance Contributions deducted from your earnings *per week*.

   You
   Tax _____
   N.I. _____

   Spouse or Partner
   Tax _____
   N.I. _____

2. Enter the NUMBER of dependants who are living with you. If you are claiming legal aid for a child, please include that child. **N.B. Dependants are the people you and your spouse or partner look after financially.**

   Spouse or Partner ☐   Children 18 and over ☐   Children 16 and 17 ☐   Children 11 to 15 ☐   Children under 11 ☐

   Others (please say who)

   _____

   You should supply copies of agreements or court orders

3 Allowances and Deductions (continued)

3. If you pay **maintenance** to any dependant who does **NOT** live with you, please give details of the amounts **you**, or your spouse or partner, pay.

Age(s) of dependant(s)		Your relationship to the dependant		Amount per week	

4. Give the amounts of Council Tax which you and your spouse or partner pay.

(a) The amount of Council Tax paid. You must provide evidence of this (eg. the demand from the local authority).

£ [ ]
- ☐ a week
- ☐ a month
- ☐ a year

(b) Is Council Tax benefit received?

☐ YES   ☐ NO

(please say how much)

£ [ ]
- ☐ a week
- ☐ a month
- ☐ a year

5. Give the following details of housing expenses of you and your spouse/partner. If you own more than one house only give details for the house in which you live. If you are paying the expenses of a dependent who is not living with you, enter the details in the spaces on the right. You should produce rent books, evidence of mortgage instalments, and evidence of water and sewerage charges. It is in your interests to provide evidence of any other expenses claimed and you may be required to provide this.

Rent	£	/week	Amount for dependent(s)	£	/week
Mortgage Payment	£	/week		£	/week
Ground Rent	£	/week		£	/week
Service charge	£	/week		£	/week
Water and sewerage charges	£	/week		£	/week
Board and lodging	£	/week		£	/week
Bed and Breakfast	£	/week		£	/week

	You	Your spouse or partner
6. How much does it cost you and your spouse or partner **each week** to travel to and from work?	£	£
7. Give details of any other expenses which you think the court should know about. You may include any payments on court orders, and contributions to approved pension schemes, but not: money for food, clothing or heating. You should produce documentary evidence of the payments.	£	£

4

4 Further Information

1 Have you directly or indirectly transferred any resources (such as sums of money, stocks or shares, the equity value in your home or any other valuable items) to another person since you became aware that these proceedings would be brought? If so, please give details.

2 Has another person been paying your legal fees and expenses in respect of these or other proceedings before you applied for legal aid? If so, please give details.

3 Are the resources of another person available to you eg. is another person providing you with free accommodation or paying your bills? If so, please give details.

4 Please give any other financial information that you think that the court should have when deciding upon your application for legal aid. You should also include any future changes in circumstances that might alter your position.

5 If you have not produced documentary evidence of all income/benefits that you receive and each allowance you have claimed, you must explain why you cannot do so.

6 Declaration

If you knowingly make a statement which is false, or knowingly withhold information, you may be prosecuted. If convicted, you may be sent to prison for up to three months, or be fined, or both, *(section 39(1) Legal Aid Act 1988)*.

After your application has been considered by the court, you may be asked to give further information or to clarify information or to provide further proof of the information that you have given.

If your financial position changes in any way after you have submitted this form, you must tell the court. This is a requirement of the Legal Aid Regulations.

I declare that to the best of my knowledge and belief, I have given a complete and correct statement of my income, savings and capital (and that of my spouse or partner)*(and that of my child).**
I authorise the court to make such enquiries of the Benefits Agency as it considers necessary and I consent to the disclosure of information to confirm that I am in receipt of benefit.

Signed   Date

* Delete if you are single or if you are not living with your spouse or partner
** Delete if legal aid is not sought for your child

How to apply for legal aid

The most common error by solicitors is to fail to give sufficient information. It is not enough to tick the box that says Steven is likely to lose his liberty, Jane must also explain why this is likely. Similarly Jane is careful to specify why 'expert' cross-examination is needed. (Note that this does not mean cross-examination of experts, although this is in fact one of the reasons in this case; it requires the applicant to show why a standard of advocacy is required beyond that which an unrepresented defendant could be expected to produce by himself.)

Jane could send in the forms to the court. However, since she has told Steven that she will attend the Saturday court, she decides to hand in the forms at that stage and to make an oral application. The matter is sufficiently clear cut that she is confident the Bench will grant legal aid there and then, subject to confirmation that Steven is in receipt of income support. Here, Jane has asked Steven's wife to bring Steven's order book to court, and she is therefore able to hand up a copy of the order book. (Alternatively, most firms will have a pro forma letter for the client to sign authorising the local Benefits Agency to confirm that the client is in receipt of the relevant benefits.)

Note, however, that Jane is (at least in theory) risking not getting paid for attending court on Saturday. First, it is not guaranteed that legal aid will be granted in due course, and, even if it is granted, there is no guarantee that it will cover any work done before the grant. (Note that under Legal Aid in Criminal and Care Proceedings (General) Regulations 1989, reg. 44(7), a solicitor can claim for work done before the grant of criminal legal aid provided the court is satisfied that the work was urgent and that there was no undue delay in submitting the application. But even under this provision the onus is on the solicitor to satisfy the court that payment should be allowed.) However, if Jane does not attend court on Saturday, then Steven will have to see the Duty Solicitor. Not only may he feel aggrieved that he has been 'deserted' by Jane; he may decided to ask the Duty Solicitor to take on his case and Jane will lose her client.

Applying for Bail

In order to understand why bail is necessary, we need to consider what will happen at the first hearing.

Burglary (and therefore attempted burglary) is an either way offence. In due course the court will have to decide whether it can accept jurisdiction and can try the matter. If the court decides that it can try the matter, Steven will then have a choice about whether he wishes the matter to be heard by a jury at the Crown Court in any event. But before the defendant can make this decision, he will need to see the details of the case against him — in other words, he must be given 'advance information'. And indeed a requirement of disclosure is laid down by the Magistrates' Courts (Advance Information) Rules 1985 (discussed below at page 84). There is no way that the CPS will have this information ready at the first hearing, and the court will therefore need to adjourn the case for several weeks so that the papers can be prepared. This also gives time for legal aid decisions to be made, statements taken from witnesses and the like.

Because Steven is being produced from police custody, the court must make a remand decision: s. 18, Magistrates' Courts Act 1980. The court can either remand Steven on bail, or can remand him in custody.

Steven has a prima facie right to bail under s. 4, Bail Act 1976. The court, however, can refuse bail under the grounds in sch. 1, part I of that Act. Here, Jane knows that the court will again be primarily concerned with Steven's likely failure to surrender and so again she prepares arguments to show that this is unlikely to occur again.

The First Hearing: Central Magistrates' Court: Saturday 3 May 1997, 9.40 a.m.

Steven is to be produced at court at 10.00 a.m. Jane arrives early in order to have a quick chat to Steven in the cells before the hearing starts. She checks the legal aid forms, and the bail details. She also takes the opportunity to go over the statement she is drafting. She tells Steven that the court will almost certainly wish to 'consolidate' the cases — in other words, to have them heard together since they arise from the same set of facts. Steven confirms he is happy for this to happen.

Jane then has a quick word with the CPS representative, Mr Cairns. He confirms that he has only the charge sheet and antecedents forms. He has, however, discussed the case with the officer in the case. He and Jane agree that there will need to be an adjournment for the papers to be prepared. Mr Cairns indicates that he will object to bail because of the risk of absconding, especially given the client's previous bail history and the relative seriousness of this offence. Jane puts forward her arguments but he is not persuaded.

When court starts, the clerk checks with Steven his name, address and date of birth. The CPS explain that this is a first appearance and request an adjournment. Jane stands to confirm that she has no objection to an adjournment. She suggests that the matter be consolidated with the driving charge, which will be before the court on the following Thursday. She also hands up the legal aid forms and makes an oral application for legal aid, which is granted.

The court agrees to the suggested adjournment. Mr Cairns then explains that bail is opposed. He relies mainly on the ground that Steven is likely to abscond, but he also points out that Steven has previous convictions and is likely to reoffend. Jane explains the circumstances in which Steven's previous breaches of bail arose, and stresses that he is now settled with good community ties, that he vehemently denies the offence which rests almost entirely on potentially unreliable identification evidence and she suggests that sureties might meet the court's concerns. However, the court refuses bail on the basis of a likely failure to surrender to custody and the case is adjourned to Thursday 8 May.

A copy of the record of the court's refusal of bail is set out at Document 15. Note that the form states (at the bottom of the second section) that Steven can appeal to the High Court, but not to the Crown Court. This is because Steven will not have a right of appeal to the Crown Court until a 'certificate of full argument' is issued by the court; this will not happen until the next bail application after the first appearance (sch. 1, part IIA, para. 2, Bail Act 1976).

R v RUSHKIN

Document 15

Failure to surrender to bail or comply with bail conditions can result in your arrest. Failure to surrender to bail is an offence punishable by a maximum of 12 months imprisonment and/or unlimited fine.

CENTRAL MAGISTRATES' COURT (2853)
Bail Act 1976

Accused: Steven Rushkin Date of Birth: 12 / 1 / 53
Alleged Offences: Attempted burglary
Driving whilst disqualified

Stage of proceedings:
- [✓] Remand before trial
- [ ] Committal for trial
- [ ] Remand for reports after conviction
- [ ] Committal for sentence
- [ ] Variation of Time Place Conditions on application of Prosecution/Defence
- [ ] Appeal to Crown Court

DECISION THIS DAY

- [✓] Accused is remanded to appear before South Shields/Hebburn Magistrates'/Juvenile Court on Thurs day the 8th May 1997
- [ ] Accused is committed to appear before the Crown Court on such day, time and place as may be notified to the accused
AND
- [ ] Accused is granted bail
- [ ] Accused is granted bail with requirements
- [✓] Accused is refused bail and committed to custody and may apply to the High/~~Crown~~ Court to be granted bail

EXCEPTIONS TO RIGHT TO UNCONDITIONAL BAIL FOUND BY THE COURT: Sched. 1	GROUNDS FOR FINDING EXCEPTIONS TO RIGHT TO UNCONDITIONAL BAIL
[✓] Would fail to surrender Pt. 1, p 2(a)	[ ] Nature and gravity of offence and probable sentence
[ ] Would commit offence on bail Pt. 1, p 2(b)	[ ] Character, antecedents, associations, lack of community ties of accused
[ ] Would interfere with witnesses/obstruct course of justice Pt 1 p 2(c)	[✓] Record of fulfilment of previous grants of bail
[ ] Impracticable to obtain sufficient information for bail decision, want of time Pt. 1 p 5	[ ] Strength of evidence
[ ] Impracticable to obtain report or complete enquiries for sentencing purposes Pt. 1 p 7	[ ] Evidence of self injury, attempted suicide
	[ ] Serving sentence imposed on
[ ] Custody for own protection/welfare Pts 1 & 11 pp 3	[ ] Arrested a [ ] Identity and personal details not yet established
[ ] Serving custodial sentence Pts 1 & 11, pp 4	[ ] No likelihood of co-operation for purposes of obtaining reports
[ ] Arrested under S.7 Bail Act 1976 in these proceedings Pt 1 p 6 Pt 11 p 5	[ ] Behaviour towards/proximity to prosecution witnesses

REQUIREMENTS TO BE COMPLIED WITH BEFORE AND/OR AFTER RELEASE ON BAIL

- [ ] To give the following security
- [ ] To provide _____ suret _____ in £ _____ (each)
- [ ] To reside at _____ in the meantime to remain indoors at that address between _____ p.m. and _____ a.m. each day in the mea
- [ ] Not to communicate or interfere with prosecution witnesses
- [ ] To report to _____ Police Station each _____ a _____ a.m./p.m.
- [ ] To undergo medical examination at _____ by a/two m
practitioners and comply with the directions of _____
for the purposes of physical/mental report

SPECIMEN

Clerk of the Court present during these proceedings: A. Cleek   Dated 3 / 5 / 97

(Tick appropriate boxes; complete as necessary)

Document 16

Attendance Note

Your name   JW   Date   3 May 1997

Client's name   S. Rushkin   Person attended   Central Magistrates' Court

Time start   9.40   Time finish 10.35

Travel 30 min, 10 miles

Arrived 9.40, attended client in cell 9.40 – 10.00. Confirmed bail instructions. Checked he is receiving his medication. Took further details concerning attempted burglary. Obtained instructions to have both charges consolidated.

Completed legal aid application. Submitted application to court during hearing.

Asked CPS orally for advance information and agreed matter should be adjourned until 8 May to consolidate with driving while disqualified.

Mr Cairns prosecuting: said instructed to oppose bail on grounds of absconding; he mentioned seriousness of offence, and previous bail record. Countered with good community ties, explanation of previous absconding, offence not as serious as might be since, using mode of trial guidelines, nothing stolen, method amateurish, premises non-domestic; stressed client vigorously contests allegation and has alibi evidence, unlikely to want to abscond, answered police bail; willing to accept conditions and wife in court as surety.

Attending Mr Cairns: 10 min

Bail refused. Grounds stated as being substantial reasons to believe he may abscond, reasons: previous bail record and seriousness of offence. Adjourned to 8 May 1997.

Hearing 10.30 – 10.35

R v RUSHKIN

A diversion — what if legal aid had been refused?

If legal aid had been refused by the court, Steven could have reapplied to the court on subsequent occasions under regulation 14 (as often as he wishes — though Jane cannot be paid under legal aid for attending court to make the application, so would probably try to do so when at court on another matter.)

If legal aid is refused for an either way matter Jane can apply on Steven's behalf within 14 days for a review by the Legal Aid Board Area Committee. The following conditions must be satisfied:

(a) the reason for the refusal was that legal aid was not necessary in the interests of justice test;

(b) she has not applied again to the court;

(c) she applies at least 21 days before the committal proceedings or trial (if a date has been fixed, which is not likely).

(Regulation 15, Legal Aid in Criminal and Care Proceedings (General) Regulations 1989).

The Committee could not review a refusal of legal aid on the summary matter, although there is no reason not to re-apply to the court at the next hearing to add the driving while disqualified offence if an order for the attempted burglary is granted.

A note of refusal is set out below (Document 17, page 73), followed by Crim 9 (Document 18, page 74) for use in applying to the Area Committee for a review. The full grounds of appeal are best set out in a covering letter. I have filled it in, and shown a covering letter appealing the refusal, although in this case in fact the court grants legal aid for both matters.

Document 17

CENTRAL MAGISTRATES' COURT
NOTIFICATION OF REFUSAL TO GRANT LEGAL AID AND DETERMINATION
OF CONTRIBUTION (REGS 12, 13, 19 & 20)

TO: STEVEN RUSHKIN   APPLICATION NUMBER: 1011001

YOUR APPLICATION FOR LEGAL AID HAS BEEN REFUSED ON THE FOLLOWING GROUNDS:—

(a) IT DOES NOT APPEAR TO THE COURT OR PROPER OFFICER OF THE COURT DESIRABLE TO MAKE AN ORDER IN THE INTERESTS OF JUSTICE; and/or

~~(b) IT DOES NOT APPEAR THAT YOUR MEANS ARE SUCH THAT YOU REQUIRE ASSISTANCE IN MEETING THE COSTS YOU MAY INCUR.~~

DETERMINATION OF CONTRIBUTION:—

If legal aid had been granted you would have been ordered to pay a contribution of £ NIL per week from income and £ NIL from capital [payable on   ] towards the costs of your case/legal aid would have been conditional on immediate payment of £ NIL
You are entitled:

*(i) to apply for legal aid to an area committee (in some cases where your application has been refused under paragraph (a) above). If you wish to do this you should complete Form 3 overleaf. You must apply within 14 days of the date of this notification.

(ii) to renew your application to the court [to the Crown Court] at any time. If you wish to do so you should complete the bottom section of this form and return the whole form to the Court at the address stated.

(iii) in any event to apply for legal aid to the court of trial on the day of the trial.

*Delete as necessary

DATED THE 3RD DAY OF MAY 1997

SIGNED   A. CLERK

CLERK TO THE JUSTICES

COPY TO:
J. WATKINS
WATKINS & O'DWYER
17 SYCAMORE ST
OLDCASTLE

I wish to renew my application for legal aid to the court

I have/have not* made an application to an area committee

Signed:

Date:

Note: (i) You should enclose any additional or new information you think is relevant to your application.

(ii) If there has been any change in your financial circumstances you must complete and enclose a new statement of means form.

(iii) If you have made an application to an area committee you should enclose a copy of the notification of decision

*Delete as appropriate

Court Code _____

Offence Code _____

Solicitor's acc no _____

R v RUSHKIN

Document 18

Application in criminal proceedings

➤ Please read the notes overleaf before completing this form in block capitals.
➤ Do NOT use this form for an application for authority for prior expenditure. Complete form CRIM10 instead.

CRIM 9
LEGAL AID BOARD LEGAL AID ACT 1988

Legal Aid Order number (please copy this from the refusal or order) LA 0 981941

Has this application been granted over the telephone? ☐ YES ☑ NO

SPECIMEN

Defendant's details
Surname: Mr/Mrs/Miss/Ms RUSHKIN   First Names: STEVEN
Address: 12 PARK VIEW
LONGFIELD, OLDCASTLE OL10 2AB
Occupation: UNEMPLOYED

Solicitor's details
Name of Solicitor: WATKINS   Initials: J   Title: MS
Name & Address of firm: WATKINS & O'DWYER
17 SYCAMORE AVENUE
OLDCASTLE OL10 2BR
Legal Aid account no: A12313   Reference: JW/Rushkin   DX No: _____
Tel No: 011 111 1111   Fax No: 011 111 1111

Application type
Please refer to the notes overleaf, then tick the appropriate application type

Review of refusal of legal aid 01 ☑   Instruct Q.C. without junior 04   Withdrawal of Legal Aid Order 06
Assignment of counsel 03   Change solicitor 05

Court / charge details
Court Name: OLDCASTLE CENTRAL
Nature of Charges (including statute and section):
1. ATTEMPT BURGLARY, CRIMINAL ATTEMPTS ACT 1981, Section 1
2. DRIVING WHILST DISQUALIFIED, ROAD TRAFFIC ACT 1988, SECTION 103
Likely Plea: 1. NOT GUILTY 2. GUILTY   Date of next hearing: 8 5 97
Purpose of next hearing: CONSOLIDATION OF CHARGES, MODE OF TRIAL, BAIL

Give the full reasons for the application. In review cases please give full reasons why it is in the interests of justice for legal aid to be granted (refer to the criteria set out in Section 22 (2) Legal Aid Act 1988 [formerly known as the "Widgery criteria"]). If a solicitor has been assigned to act for co-defendants, please give details of any conflict of interest to justify separate representation.

PLEASE SEE ACCOMPANYING LETTER

Give a brief summary of the prosecution case. You may attach the advance disclosure or extracts

A PERSON MATCHING MR RUSHKIN'S DESCRIPTION WAS IDENTIFIED BY A WITNESS ATTEMPTING TO BREAK INTO AN AMUSEMENT ARCADE. ANOTHER PERSON WHO HAS ADMITTED THE OFFENCE WAS FOUND TRAVELLING WITH MR RUSHKIN IN HIS CAR SHORTLY AFTER THIS. MR RUSHKIN, WHO IS DISQUALIFIED FROM DRIVING, WAS SEEN DRIVING HIS CAR.

Give a summary of the defence or mitigation. Attach your client's statement and details of any previous convictions, if available in either case.

MR RUSHKIN WAS NOT PRESENT AT THE TIME THE ATTEMPT IS ALLEGED, BUT WAS CARRYING OUT CASUAL BAR WORK AT A PUB NEARBY.

Solicitor's signature: J. Watkins   Date: 7 5 97

Important notes

1. Review applications sent without a copy of the original legal aid application (which is available from the court which dealt with the application) may be refused. In such cases a further application for review to the Area Committee (as opposed to a renewed application to the court) is not possible. Review applications sent without a copy of the notification of refusal will be rejected.

2. Applications to assign counsel or change solicitor must first be made to the clerk at the court. When applying to the area office in such cases you must send a copy of the application made to the court and a copy of the court's notice of refusal. **Where these applications are sent without a copy of the notification of refusal they will be rejected.**

3. Check that the application has been sent to the appropriate area office and, except on review applications, that a legal aid order is held which covers the proceedings. The Board will deal with applications on the basis of the information sent by the solicitor and an Area Committee only has jurisdiction where it is the correct Area Committee and there is the appropriate legal aid cover.

4. Send applications to the Area Office in whose area the court is situated. A covering letter is not needed but you can continue on a separate sheet of paper if necessary.

For area office use only

COURT CODE:　　　　　　　　　　　　　DATE:

DECISION:

RF2	Request further information		CL4	Out of Time	
G10	Granted - Delegated		W10	Withdrawn	
G12	Granted - Committee		CL5	No Jurisdiction	
R21	Refused - Committee				

DOCUMENT CODES AND STANDARD WORDINGS CODES REQUIRED:

SUMMARY FOR COMMITTEE:

September 1993

Document 19

Watkins & O'Dwyer
Solicitors

17, Sycamore Avenue,
Oldcastle OL10 1BR.
Tel. 011-111-1111
Fax 011-111-1111
DX Oldcastle 1000

Partners: *J. Watkins*
A. O'Dwyer

The Secretary,
Area Committee 18,
Legal Aid Board,
Treasury Street,
Oldcastle OL2 2LA.

Your ref:
Our ref: JW/Rushkin

7 May 1997

Dear Sir/Madam,

R v Steven Rushkin

We enclose a refusal of legal aid from Central Magistrates' Court dated 3 May 1997, a copy of the original application for legal aid, and form Crim 9. Our client wishes to appeal the refusal in relation to the attempted burglary.

Our grounds for submitting that it will be in the interests of justice under s. 22, Legal Aid Act that Mr Rushkin be granted legal aid are as follows:

1. There is a risk of a custodial sentence. Mr Rushkin has a previous conviction for burglary in 1996, which will be taken into account in assessing the seriousness of this offence if he is convicted.

2. The principal evidence against Mr Rushkin consists of identification evidence, and will require expert cross examination of the witness in accordance with the Turnbull guidelines.

3. The prosecution have obtained fingerprint and hair samples from Mr Rushkin. He will need expert legal advice on the result of these analyses, and may need to instruct expert witnesses himself. Expert cross examination of prosecution witnesses will be required.

4. The prosecution allege Mr Rushkin climbed over a high wall. On our instructions Mr Rushkin is medically incapable of this feat, and it is necessary to obtain an expert opinion for the court. [Note to the reader – this is not one of the s. 22 criteria, but the Act does not make them the only criteria.]

5. The defence depends in part on alibi. Expertise is needed to trace the alibi evidence, and questions of law are involved in disclosing it according to the rules if Crown Court trial is to take place.

6. Mr Rushkin has been charged together with a co-defendant, who has apparently admitted the offence. If this co-defendant gives evidence, either for the prosecution or in his own defence, it will be necessary to cross examine him carefully, in the light of the need to treat his evidence with caution, and the risk that giving evidence against him or cross examining him on his character will lead to Mr Rushkin's convictions coming before the court.

In the light of these factors we trust that you will agree that it is in the interests of justice for Mr Rushkin to be represented.

Yours faithfully,

Watkins & O'Dwyer

Document 20

Notification of decision of the Area Committee on Review of Refusal to grant Legal Aid	**Form 4** **Reg. 17**

To: STEVEN RUSHKIN

Your application for legal aid has been granted/~~refused~~ because it appears/~~does not appear~~ desirable to make an order in the interests of justice on any of the following grounds:—

(1) You are in real danger of a custodial sentence.

~~(2) You are in real danger of losing your livelihood or suffering serious damage to your reputation.~~

(3) The determination of the case may involve consideration of a substantial question of law.

~~(4) You are unable to understand the proceedings or state your own case because:~~

   ~~(a) Your knowledge of English is inadequate~~

   ~~(b) You suffer from a disability, namely~~...

(5) Your case involves tracing and interviewing witnesses or expert cross-examination of a prosecution witness.

~~(6) It is in the interests of another that you be represented.~~

(7) Any other reasons.

*Delete as appropriate.

The Committee reached this decision because:—

Date: 16 May 1997

Lee Gallade
Secretary to the Area Committee

Area Committee 18
Treasury Street
Oldcastle OL2 2LA

If legal aid is granted by the Area Committee and not by the court, Jane has to return to the court to request legal aid for the summary matter. With luck the court will now see it as in the interests of justice for both matters to be dealt with together under legal aid.

After the First Hearing — Client Care and Case Preparation

At the first appearance the two charges have been consolidated. When Jane attends court on 8 May, she will have to deal with both the attempted burglary (where the defence are now waiting for advance information from the CPS so that a mode of trial decision can be made) and the driving disqualified matter (where Jane is ready to enter a guilty plea).

Jane has obtained fairly full instructions from Steven at this point. She therefore prepares a statement which is based on their original discussions at the police station and in interview at the office on Monday 21 April, with the additional details from the conversation before court on the 3 May.

It helps to have instructions put in writing and signed, to prevent any suggestion that the lawyer has acted without authority from the client. But on the other hand many solicitors would prefer to wait to take full instructions until their client has seen the advance information. This is either so that the client can give 'full' instructions that deal with all the prosecution evidence, or so that the client can adjust his evidence in the light of the case against him — depending on how cynical you are. Here, Jane has the benefit of legal aid, has clear instructions and is satisfied that she is already aware of most of the prosecution evidence.

Document 21

> Steven Rushkin of 12, Park View, Longfield, Oldcastle OL10 2AB
>
> I am 44, and was born on 12 January 1953
>
> I am unemployed and in receipt of income support of £104.05, and child benefit of £10.80.
>
> I live at the above property with my wife Jocelyn and our daughter Claire (age 16). Our two eldest children have left home.
>
> On 19 April I was arrested on suspicion of an attempted burglary alleged to have taken place the night before, together with Bob Chapman. I am not guilty of this offence. I am also charged with driving while disqualified arising out of the same incident, and will plead guilty.
>
> The burglary is supposed to have been attempted at MegaWin amusements on Castle Street. I have never even been in that street, and was not there that night. I was at work at the King's Arms, North View, all evening, from my arrival at 5.30 to when we finally cleared up at 12.00. Phil Gramsci, the manager, can attest to this. The other staff left once the main bars were cleaned up at about 11.30.
>
> When I left work I got the car from the car park and as I was coming out onto the street I saw Bob walking past, up towards the centre of town. I asked if he wanted a lift, as he lives in our street.
>
> When we got to the North Road we were pulled over by two officers in a car which had overtaken us. They said they wanted to search the car, and I agreed. I don't remember if they said why they wanted to. One of the officers went through everything, and removed a screwdriver set from the boot of the car. Then he said he was arresting us for attempted burglary and drove us to the Central Police Station.
>
> I understand Bob has admitted the burglary. Although he lives in our street I do not know him very well. I don't know what he does for a living. I did not see him once while I was on police bail. He did not mention anything about a burglary when I picked him up, and I did not notice anything unusual about his behaviour.
>
> I was told that part of the evidence against me is that I had a screwdriver set in my car from which a screwdriver was missing. The screwdriver found at the scene, which I was shown in the police station, was of the same size and type as the missing screwdriver. The set is one I bought at Woolfords about two years ago for use in the car; the biggest one has been missing for a considerable time, I cannot remember when I lost it. I doubt if anyone else would be able to confirm that it has been missing for a while.
>
> It has been alleged that I climbed over a tall wall to escape from MegaWin. This is impossible. My back injury after the accident in 1996 is such that I could not even climb a three foot wall, and cannot run at all. I am sure my doctor will confirm this, and I have stated this to the police in interview. My GP is Dr Khan of the Grove Medical Practice, Longfield, and my consultant at the Royal Northern after my accident was Dr Miller.

R v RUSHKIN

> I am also facing a charge of driving while disqualified, which is true. I was convicted of excess alcohol some time in February as a result of driving after a Christmas party. I was disqualified for a year. I drove to work that night (18 April) because I had missed the bus to work and decided to take the risk. It is the first and only time I have driven since the disqualification. I usually get a taxi home from work.
>
> I have four previous convictions :
>
> excess alcohol Feb 1997, disqualified 12 months, fined £100
>
> burglary of unoccupied house July 1996; this was shortly after a serious car accident in which I injured my back and am still in pain and likely to be permanently unable to work normally. I had to give up work as a self employed decorator, was very depressed for several months, and ended up getting involved in this spur of the moment burglary when a friend suggested we might find something worth having in a house that was being boarded up. We found nothing and were arrested as we were leaving. Fined £200 in Central Magistrates.
>
> absconding while on bail: I had unconditional bail while this offence was being dealt with. I was just so depressed that one time I simply could not motivate myself to get to court. I failed to turn up three times, and the last time I ended up being locked up for a week before the case was dealt with, as well as being fined £50 for the absconding.
>
> ABH summer 1995, following an argument with a neighbour who was always parking his car so as to block my driveway. After a bad argument he raised his fist, and I hit him on the face. I was fined £50.
>
> I have paid off all fines.
>
> Signed
>
> Dated

What happens if Steven later changes his instructions?

A solicitor must be familiar with the Professional Conduct rules and especially Chapter 21 of the *Law Society's Guide to Professional Conduct* (seventh edition), which deals with litigation and advocacy. Section 21.20 states:

> 6 *If either before or during the course of proceedings, the client makes statements to the solicitor which are inconsistent, this is not of itself a ground for the solicitor to refuse to act further on behalf of the client. Only where it is clear that the client is attempting to put forward false evidence to the court should the solicitor cease to act. In other circumstances, it would be for the court, and not the solicitor, to assess the truth or otherwise of the client's statement.*

Client care

Document 22

Watkins & O'Dwyer
Solicitors

17, Sycamore Avenue,
Oldcastle OL10 1BR.
Tel. 011-111-1111
Fax 011-111-1111
DX Oldcastle 1000

Partners: J. Watkins
A. O'Dwyer

Mr Steven Rushkin,
H.M.Prison Riversdale,
Irongate,
Riversdale RV1 1DT.

7 May 1997

Dear Mr Rushkin,

I am writing to set out how the case against you will now proceed, and to explain what I, as your solicitor, will be able to do in your case. What I will set out in this letter is what we discussed at court after your bail was refused. Having it in writing will, I hope, give you a chance to check that you understand everything clearly. Please let me know if there is anything at all that you do not understand – either by writing to me, or when we meet again at court next week.

You wish me to represent you on two charges: attempted burglary of MegaWin Amusement Arcade, together with Mr Chapman on 18 April, and driving whilst disqualified. You instruct me that you are not guilty of the attempted burglary, but you will admit the motoring offence.

The motoring offence will inevitably lead to a further period of disqualification from driving; and you will know from our discussion at court that driving while disqualified carries a real risk of a prison sentence. As you are pleading guilty, the sentencing for this will be dealt with after the trial of the attempted burglary – in the magistrates' court, unless you are tried and convicted in the Crown Court.

Attempted burglary can be dealt with either in the magistrates' court or at the Crown Court. If you are found guilty, you will know from our discussions that the court is likely to sentence you to several months in prison for this offence.

We do not yet know the details of the prosecution's case, and you will not have to make up your mind which court to choose until we have seen this. (You will not be given the choice if the magistrates think the case should be tried in the Crown Court.)

Your case comes before the magistrates again on Thursday. If I have had details of the prosecution case by then, the court will be able to deal with the question of where the trial should take place. I will have another attempt at getting you bail then, and I have been in touch with Mr Gramsci and your wife, as we discussed, and both of them are willing to come to court and be sureties if you are granted bail. I will discuss the bail application further with you before we go into court. You have told me you will be willing to agree to other conditions if necessary to get bail, in particular to stay at your own address, and to report to the police station.

You have been granted legal aid for me to represent you on both charges. At the time you were awarded legal aid you were receiving income support; there is therefore no contribution towards the cost of the legal aid. If you or your wife stop getting income support, or for any reason your financial position changes (including savings or items of value) you must let me know straight away, because the court will need to reassess whether you are entitled to legal aid, or whether a contribution is payable.

I will deal with this case personally, and if I ask anyone to assist me, they will do so under my supervision. If for any reason you are unhappy with the way I am dealing with your case, please let me know. If you are not satisfied with my response to any complaint, you should contact my partner, Ms Amanda O'Dywer. If there is still a problem, we will advise you how to contact the Solicitors' Complaints Bureau.

I am sending you a draft statement with this letter. This sets out what you have told me about the circumstances leading to your arrest, and your personal circumstances. Please will you check it through carefully, and make any alterations to it that are needed? If it is accurate will you please sign and date it? Will you please return the statement to me as soon as possible in the enclosed stamped addressed envelope or let me have it at court on Wednesday?

I do not need to visit you in prison at this stage, because until I have received the prosecution evidence, I have enough detail about the case from you. I will be able to have a brief chat with you when the case is before the magistrates this week, and as soon as I get the prosecution evidence, I will arrange to see you for a longer interview. I hope very much that by then you will be on bail.

I intend to visit Burn Street and MegaWin and get some photographs to help us understand what the case is about. The other thing I intend to do, as we discussed, is interview your wife to check her recollection about the missing screwdriver.

Yours sincerely,

Jane Watkins

Client care requirements

Chapter 13 of the *Guide to the Professional Conduct of Solicitors* makes clear what information a client should be provided with at the beginning of the retainer.

Solicitors' Practice Rule 15(1) requires the solicitor to inform the client whom to approach in the event of any problem with the service provided. There must be a complaints handling procedure in every firm. The rule does not require you to set this out in your letter to the client, but reference to it is good practice.

The client should also be told who is conducting the matter, and their status: in this case Jane is a partner. Although it is apparent from the notepaper, she explains this in the letter, as it is unreasonable to expect the client to understand what the notepaper means.

It is good practice to confirm advice on these matters, as well as confirming the advice on the case itself, in a letter to the client as soon as the retainer is established – which in this case was once legal aid was granted.

Further preparation

For the same reason – professional responsibility – statements of witnesses should be obtained sooner rather than later. We have already seen that Jane tried to get to see Mr Gramsci before the police, and while he was likely to remember exact times. She also wants to talk to Mrs Rushkin, and the sooner she does this the less the risk that under cross examination she is found to have discussed the matter of the missing screwdriver with Steven.

You should be familiar with Note for Guidance 17 in the Legal Aid Handbook. Paragraph 54 covers whether you will be paid for preparing the case for trial before the matter has been committed to the Crown Court. You will be paid if you can justify doing the work at this stage, in terms of loss of witness recollection, or preparing for committal. Paragraph 45 covers attendance on clients who are remanded in custody. (I presume this Note for Guidance will one day be altered to include preparation for the plea and directions hearing.)

Document 23

Statement of Jocelyn Rushkin, of 12, Park View, Longfield, Oldcastle OL10 2AB, who will say as follows.

I am the wife of Steven Rushkin, to whom I have been married for 23 years. I have lived with him at the above address for about 12 years. Our daughter Claire (16) lives there with us, and our oldest two children left home some two or three years ago.

I have no criminal convictions.

I am asked to recall a screwdriver set kept in the back of our car, a Ford Sierra. I can remember the set, as one Steve bought about two years ago. It is a Woolford's own brand set, and as far as I can remember, it has about six screwdrivers in it, ranging from very small (I presume for electrical use) to large (over 12 inches). The handles are all made of yellow plastic.

Steve has told me that the police are claiming the largest screwdriver from this set is the one used for the attempted burglary on 18 April. I can confirm that this is not the case. Although I cannot trace the screwdriver at present, I recall that I used it to lever off paint tin lids when I redecorated the hall and front room of our house last autumn. I remember Steve being angry with me for removing it from the car, and ridiculing me for getting it covered in paint, as I had used it to stir the paint. When I finished the painting I intended to put it back in the car, but I never got round to it, and now I cannot find it.

I am in no doubt of the above facts, and I am willing to attend court if necessary to give evidence.

Signed J. Rushkin   dated   10.5.97

Jane notes that Mrs Rushkin has come up with an explanation that Steven has not himself put forward (yet). Any evidence a solicitor has that is of benefit to her client must be put to him – so Jane informs Steven (who in fact has already been told by his wife). Of course there is a risk that the story will be seen as concoction, and Jane, and eventually counsel, have to decide exactly how to use that evidence, and whether it is likely to be believed.

Advance information

The Magistrates' Courts (Advance Information) Rules 1985 have already been mentioned (see page 68 above). The lack of advance information was one reason why the case could not proceed at the first hearing. Without knowledge of the prosecution case, it would be impossible for Jane to advise Steven properly as to whether he should choose to be tried in the magistrates' court or Crown Court on the burglary matter.

Rule 4 of the Advance Information Rules states that the prosecutor shall, if requested, before the mode of trial decision, supply either:

(a) a copy of those parts of every written statement which contains information as to the facts and matters of which the prosecutor proposes to adduce evidence in the proceedings, or
(b) a summary ...

Although the rules permit a summary, it is now generally the policy of the CPS to provide copies of the statements. The court must adjourn until the request is complied with unless the defendant would not be prejudiced (r. 7).

Note that the right to advance information does not apply to summary only matters, such as the driving disqualified charge. However, Jane could also ask the CPS for disclosure of the information in relation to this charge on a voluntary basis. Since Steven is going to plead guilty, this is not necessary in this case.

Jane therefore writes to the CPS to confirm the request which she made to the CPS representative at the previous court appearance.

Document 24

Watkins & O'Dwyer
Solicitors

17, Sycamore Avenue,
Oldcastle OL10 1BR.
Tel. 011-111-1111
Fax 011-111-1111
DX Oldcastle 1000

Partners: J. Watkins
A. O'Dwyer

Crown Prosecution Service,
Oldcastle Chambers,
Derry Street,
Oldcastle OL2 1CP.

Your ref:
Our ref: JW/Rushkin

7 May 1997

Dear Sir/Madam,

R v Steven Rushkin

We act for Mr Rushkin, who is charged with attempted burglary and driving whilst disqualified. Both matters are adjourned to the Central Magistrates' Court on 8 May.

Please will you supply advance information in relation to the attempted burglary in accordance with Advance Information Rules 1985?

Please also supply details of the following:

(a) edited extracts of any statements made by Mr Rushkin on which the prosecution wish to rely,

(b) the record of the identity parade,

(c) any original description made by the witness Ms Paling, and

(d) any convictions of any prosecution witnesses.

Yours faithfully,

Watkins & O'Dwyer

Unused material

You will note that Jane's letter to the CPS appears to go further than the strict letter of r. 4. Jane is entitled to the record of the identity parade (Code D, Annex A, para. 19: the defence have a right to a copy of any photographs or video of the parade) and to Ms Paling's original description (para. 2A of Annex A). But what about the request for details of convictions of any prosecution witnesses?

At common law, there has in the past been a duty on the prosecution to disclose the convictions of any prosecution witnesses, since these would clearly go to the issue of the witness's credibility. However, under the new Criminal Procedure and Investigations Act 1996, such old common law rules on the disclosure of 'unused material' — i.e., material which (in contrast to the advance information) the prosecutor does not intend to use — have now been abolished.

Under the Criminal Procedure and Investigations Act 1996, the prosecution will make 'primary prosecution disclosure' of unused material 'as soon as practicable' after committal (if the case is sent to Crown Court) or after a 'Not Guilty' plea is entered (if the matter remains in the magistrates' court): s. 13. At the 'primary disclosure' stage, the prosecution are only under a duty to reveal information which, in the prosecutor's opinion, might undermine the prosecution case: s. 3.

What material might undermine the prosecution case? Clearly, if the prosecution here had a statement from another eye witness who said she had seen two teenagers climbing the wall at MegaWin at the time in question, the prosecution would not be using this statement as part of their case against Steven (so it would not be material that they would disclose under the Advance Information Rules); and since the statement clearly does undermine the identification evidence from Ms Paling, it will presumably be disclosed as part of the primary disclosure. (Note that if Steven had decided to plead guilty in order to get a reduced sentence, neither he nor Jane would ever be told about this unused statement.)

So are the prosecution still under a duty to reveal any previous convictions of their witnesses? Possibly, if those convictions would damage the credibility of the witness sufficiently to undermine the prosecution case. A minor and old conviction may well be irrelevant; a more recent, or more serious conviction, may well have a greater impact. Thus if Ms Paling had been convicted of a dishonesty offence, arguably this would always have the effect of undermining her credibility and any reasonable prosecutor would disclose it. Certainly, however, under the Criminal Procedure and Investigations Act 1996, it is no longer a clear-cut decision.

You will note, however, that Jane makes the request for the information anyway. She may not get it, and even if it should be disclosed, it will not be disclosable until after committal or a not guilty plea, but the CPS may well be prepared to confirm at this stage whether there are any such convictions. It is worth asking.

Other material

Jane is also going to need a copy of the custody record and of the tapes of interview. These she requests from the police. (A copy of this letter has not been included.) Both of these are essential and should be requested in almost every case.

The Second Hearing: Central Magistrates' Court: Thursday 8 May 1997: 9.40 a.m.

Jane arrives at court and immediately goes to look for the CPS representative who will be dealing with the matter at today's hearing. Mr Cairns is dealing with the matter again. He confirms (as Jane expects) that the advance information is still not ready, so that the matter will have to be adjourned again. He has a copy of Steven's antecedents form (Document 25) and his previous convictions (Document 26). He confirms that he will again be objecting to bail.

Document 25

R v RUSHKIN

NORTHUMBRIA POLICE
Defendant Details   [date compiled   ]

Form MG 3
/ tick appropriate box

Ref. No. ☐☐☐☐
Surname (and maiden name)) RUSHKIN
Forename(s) STEVEN
Age 43   Date and place of birth 12.1.53 OLDCASTLE
Address 12 PARK VIEW, LONGFIELD
         OLDCASTLE

Male	☐	Female	☑
Married	☑	Separated	☐
Single	☐	Co-habiting	☐
Divorced	☐	Dependants	☐
White	☑	Black	☐
Asian	☐	Other	☐

Occupation UNEMPLOYED   Nationality BRITISH   Date 1st entry into U.K

Youth
Full name(s) of parent(s)/guardian(s)
Address (if different from above)
Driver No. ABCD 1234   DQ1 Yes ☐ No ☑   Date sent
Previous Convictions   Yes ☑ No ☐
Previous Cautions   Yes ☐ No ☑   C.R.O. No. (show if no trace) R 1234
Currently on bail for other offences   Yes ☐ No ☑ Not known ☐   if 'Yes', give details
and/or other proceedings pending

SPECIMEN

Defence Solicitor (name, firm and address) J WATKINS, WATKINS & O'DWYER
12 SYCAMORE AVENUE, OLDCASTLE OL10 2BR

Education He received a Secondary Modern education until age 16, obtaining no qualifications.
Home conditions—domestic circumstances—financial commitments.

Lives at above address with wife. Council accommodation, rent paid direct. No other dependants except 16-year-old daughter

Main employments during last 5 years—current wage

Decorator, self-employed until 2 years ago. Injured, unable to work except casually. Receives income support and child benefit totalling approximately £115

Any other useful antecedent information Previous convictions for assault, absconding and
2.5.97

R v RUSHKIN

Document 26

THIS PERSONAL DATA IS PROVIDED TO YOU FOR THE AGREED SPECIFIED PURPOSE(S). KEEP THE DATA SECURE AND PROTECT IT AGAINST LOSS OR UNAUTHORISED ACCESS.

CRO NO: R1234   DOB 12.1.53

FILENAME: RUSHKIN, STEVEN

1. 24/8/95 CENTRAL MAGISTRATES
   ASSAULT OCCASIONING ACTUAL BODILY   FINE £100
   HARM   COSTS £25

Neighbour dispute over parking of car; guilty plea; some provocation by victim.

2. 19/8/96 CENTRAL MAGISTRATES
   BREACH BAIL   FINE £50

Failed to attend sentencing hearing after two previous failures to attend.

3. CENTRAL MAGISTRATES
   19/8/96 BURGLARY   FINE £200
                                                          COSTS £50

Committed with another, daylight, no tools used, unoccupied derelict premises, guilty plea.

4. CENTRAL MAGISTRATES
   7/2/97 EXCESS ALCOHOL   FINE £200
                                                          DISQUALIFICATION
                                                          FROM DRIVING
                                                          12 MONTHS

Blood alcohol 42 mg, pleaded guilty.

Jane checks both forms carefully. It is always necessary to get a list of the client's own convictions. Some clients 'forget' to tell their solicitor about convictions; many cannot remember the exact details (for instance, how long a matter was suspended for; when the probation order expired). The antecedents form will have been prepared while Steven was in police custody. It is necessary to check both since the court will be referred to them during the bail application. Jane notes that the records coincide with Steven's instructions, but she also checks with Steven when he is brought up from the cells to make sure there are no errors.

As the advance information is not yet ready, the matter will have to adjourned again. Jane makes a second application for bail; under sch. 1, part IIA, para. 2, Bail Act 1976 which provides that:

At the first hearing after that at which the court decided not to grant the defendant bail he may support an application for bail with any argument as to fact or law that he desires (whether or not he has advanced that argument previously).

You will see from Jane's attendance note (Document 27 below) that Jane applies on the same grounds as at the first hearing. Again however bail is refused. This time, since it is a second remand, the court remands Steven in custody for 14 days. (On a second or subsequent remand the court can adjourn and remand for up to 28 days, even if the accused is in custody, and even if he does not consent: s. 128, Magistrates' Courts Act 1980. The court must have fixed a date when they expect the next 'effective hearing' to take place. Here the court has fixed 22 May as the date they expect the mode of trial hearing to take place.)

Because there have now been two fully argued applications for bail, Steven can now only argue for bail on arguments as to fact or law that have not previously been put forward: sch. 1, part IIA, para. 3, Bail Act 1976. The court is required to issue a certificate that they have heard the full argument, and Jane keeps this as she will now need it for the appeal to the Crown Court (see Document 28 below).

Document 27

Attendance Note

Your name   JW   Date   8 May 1997

Client's name   S. Rushkin   Person attended   Central Magistrates' Court

Time start   9.50   Time finish 10.14

Advance Information still not ready, both matters adjourned to 22 May 1997.

Applied again for bail. Prosecution objections the same. I applied as before: good community ties, wishes to fight his case, absconding caused by circumstances no longer existing, sureties available, here in court, willingness to report to police or accept other conditions.

Bail again refused. Obtained full argument certificate.

Saw client after he was taken down, said I would apply immediately to the Crown Court for bail. Asked him about the missing screwdriver, if he could recall what had happened. Said he had spoken to his wife, and now remembered quite clearly how it had been used for painting, and how annoyed he had been.

Travel: 9.30 – 9.50   5 miles

Client in cells: 9.50 – 10.00

In court: 10.10 – 10.14

R v RUSHKIN

Document 28

Central Magistrates' Court

Date: 8 May 1997

Accused: Steven Rushkin

Date of Birth: 12.1.53

Alleged offence(s): Attempted burglary

Driving whilst disqualified

I hereby certify that, at a hearing this day, the court heard full argument on an application for bail made (by) (on behalf of) the accused, before refusing the application and remanding the accused in custody under Section 10 of the Magistrates' Courts Act 1980.

(The court has not previously heard full argument on an application for bail by or on behalf of the accused in these proceedings.)

~~(The court has previously heard full argument from the accused on an application for bail, but is satisfied~~

(that there has been the following change in his circumstances;)

~~(that the following new considerations have been placed before it;)~~

By order of the Court

A. Clerk

Clerk of the court

Form 151A

Certificate as to hearing
of full argument on application
for bail (criminal cases)
(Bail Act 1976, s. 5;
M.C. Rules 1981, rr. 66, 90)

(In case you were wondering why the times on the attendance note show gaps, Jane was also in court on other matters and so was not involved in waiting on Steven's case. The return mileage and travel time are also allocated to another file.)

After the Second Hearing — Appeal Against the Refusal of Bail

The court has now heard two argued bail applications and has issued the certificate of full argument. This triggers the right of the defendant to apply to the Crown Court for bail: s. 81, Supreme Court Act 1981. Jane does not need to apply for legal aid as her current order will cover a Crown Court application: s. 19(2), Legal Aid Act 1988.

Note that at any time after a refusal of bail (or a grant of bail but on conditions which are unacceptable) a defendant also has the right to apply to a High Court judge: s. 22(1), Criminal Justice Act 1967. This is the only way to challenge bail on conditions, except to return to the magistrates' court and apply for a variation. Steven could apply to the High Court as well as or instead of applying to the Crown Court. But the major disadvantage is that the application is not covered by the criminal legal aid order. Steven would either have to pay privately or apply for civil legal aid (which even if successful is likely to take some time). High Court applications are therefore uncommon and the procedure is not illustrated here.

Jane has assured Steven she will arrange the application as soon as possible. The CPS must be given at least 24 hours notice, and in practice, once the Crown Court listing officer has been contacted and the forms completed and faxed to the court and the CPS, the first available hearing date will be on the following Monday. Making the application as soon as possible is often critical. Steven is very unhappy about being in custody when he says he has done nothing wrong. If he feels Jane is not making every effort to get bail, he will change solicitors.

For the Crown Court application, Jane completes the Notice of Application form (Document 29), and attaches her written grounds for the application (Document 30), along with a copy of the certificate of full argument (required by virtue of *Practice Direction* [1983] 2 All ER 261).

R v RUSHKIN

Document 29

NOTICE OF APPLICATION RELATING TO BAIL TO BE MADE TO THE CROWN COURT

AT OLDCASTLE

CROWN COURT NO.

(OR)

SERIAL NO. AND

NAME AND LOCATION OF MAGISTRATES COURT   CENTRAL MAGISTRATES', OLDCASTLE

Note: The appropriate office of the Crown Court should be consulted about the time and place of the hearing before this notice is sent to the other party to the application

A copy of this notice should be sent to the Crown Court

In the case of an application for bail in the course of proceedings being held before Magistrates the certificate prescribed by Section 5(6)A of the Bail Act 1976 (as amended) should accompany this notice when it is lodged at the Crown Court office

TAKE NOTICE that an application relating to bail will be made to the Crown Court

at OLDCASTLE

on 12th May 1997

at 10:00 a.m./p.m.

on behalf of the defendant/~~appellant/prosecutor/respondent~~

1. Defendant/~~appellant~~ (block letters please)

   Surname RUSHKIN   Date of birth 12.1.53
   Forename STEVEN
   Home Address 12 PARKVIEW, LONGFIELD, OLDCASTLE OL10 2NB

2. Solicitor for the applicant

   Name JANE WATKINS
   Address WATKINS & O'DWYER
            17 SYCAMORE AVENUE, OLDCASTLE OL10 2BR

3. If defendant/appellant is in custody state:

   place of detention HMP RIVERSDALE
   prison number (if applicable) SR 1234
   length of time in custody SINCE 2.5.97
   date of last remand 8.5.97

5023 Bail: Notice of application relating to bail to be made to the Crown Court

R v RUSHKIN

4. State the particulars of proceedings during which the defendant/appellant was committed to custody or bailed (un)conditionally including:

   (a) the stage reached in the proceedings as at the date of this application:

   AWAITING MODE OF TRIAL DECISION

   (b) the offences alleged:

   ATTEMPTED BURGLARY

   DRIVING WHILST DISQUALIFIED

   (c) (If the application relates to a case pending before Magistrates) Give details of next appearance:

   Place: CENTRAL MAGISTRATES' OLDCASTLE
   Date: 22.5.97
   Time: 10.00 AM

5. Give details of any relevant previous applications for bail or variation of conditions of bail:

   3.5.97 and 8.5.97 at OLDCASTLE MAGISTRATES

6. Nature and grounds of application:

   (a) State fully the grounds relied on and list previous convictions (if any):

   PLEASE REFER TO ACCOMPANYING STATEMENT

   (b) Give details of any proposed sureties and answer any objections raised previously:

   PLEASE REFER TO ACCOMPANYING STATEMENT

SPECIMEN

Document 30

Steven Rushkin

Grounds of Application to the Crown Court for Bail

1. The Defendant is remanded in custody by the Central Magistrates' Court on the grounds that if granted bail he would abscond.

2. The factors put to the court in support of this refusal were that he failed to attend court three times while before the court in 1996 resulting in a conviction for absconding in August 1996; that the offence of attempted burglary is a serious offence, and Mr Rushkin has a conviction for a similar offence in August 1996. Mr Rushkin also has a conviction for assault causing actual bodily harm in August 1995, which the prosecution did not rely on.

3. Mr Rushkin makes the following observations on these factors:

(1) In the present proceedings he was released on police bail on 19 April 1997, and answered his bail as required on 2 May 1997.

(2) He admits the absconding in 1996. At the time he was suffering from serious depression as a result of a car accident nine months previously, a depression which led to the committal of the burglary and to his uncharacteristic behaviour in not answering bail. He has always answered bail when before the court apart from the three occasions in 1996.

(3) He admits the previous offence of burglary. This was not a particularly serious offence, in that it was tried summarily, and he was fined £100. The offence was committed on the spur of the moment, at the suggestion of the co-accused, and the premises concerned were derelict. Nothing was taken and Mr Rushkin co-operated fully with the police. It contains no aspects that make the present alleged offence so serious that custody must be the result.

(4) Mr Rushkin is unlikely to contemplate absconding. He has strong community ties. He lives with his wife, who is available as a surety. He has casual employment as a barman, and his employer is willing to be a surety. He has lived in the Longfield area of Oldcastle all his life and has an extended family there.

(5) Mr Rushkin intends to contest the case. The prosecution evidence consists only of identification evidence, which will be challenged, the possible evidence of a co-accused which (if adduced at all) the court must treat with caution, and the finding of a screwdriver similar to tools found in his car, of a type commonly available. He will adduce independent evidence of alibi.

(6) The likely disposal of the case, if he is convicted, may not be custodial, given that nothing was taken, and the matter does not appear to have been professionally carried out.

(7) If refused bail and eventually tried by the Crown Court Mr Rushkin will be likely to be on remand in custody for some four months, which is equivalent to an eight month sentence. If found guilty of these offences, he is unlikely to receive a sentence of this length.

(8) While contending that he is entitled to unconditional bail, Mr Rushkin is able to offer sureties (see paragraph 4) and would agree to a residence condition and, if required, would report to his local police station.

Watkins & O'Dwyer
Solicitors to the Defendant
17, Sycamore Avenue,
Oldcastle OL10 2BR.

8 May 1997

Note that in this application the defence is giving the prosecution details of the basis on which the defence will be conducted. This has been the strategy from the police station interview onwards. In some cases, the defence may not want to reveal their approach in this way, and it would therefore be harder for them to comment fully on the strength of prosecution evidence. However, the Criminal Procedure and Investigations Act 1996 now imposes a requirement on the defence in any Crown Court matter to serve a 'defence statement' once the primary prosecution disclosure of unused material is complete. As we will see, this will happen shortly after the case is committed, and defence solicitors will therefore find themselves revealing, at least in outline, their case at that point.

Once the prosecution has been served with the notice, they may, according to the Crown Court Rules 1982 (r. 19), decide not to object, or to submit written reasons for objecting to bail, or (which is normal) to appear at the Crown Court hearing.

The 'appeal' is listed for 10.00 a.m. on Monday 12 May 1997 (the court generally tries to hear these applications before the day's trials begin). Jane will attend, since the application is in chambers and there is therefore no need to brief counsel. Steven, however, will not be present: r. 19, Crown Court Rules 1982.

The Crown Court Bail Application: Oldcastle Crown Court: Monday 12 May 1997: 10.00 a.m.

The application is a hearing 'de novo' rather than simply an appeal against the magistrates' decision. Jane recognises, however, that the court's main concern will be the issue of absconding. Again, therefore, she puts forward the proposals for sureties and residence and reporting conditions. This time the application is successful and bail is granted subject to two sureties of £500, and a condition of residence at Steven's home address. Since neither surety was at court, the sureties are asked to attend the police station so that the surety can be entered there.

Document 31

Attendance Note

Your name   JW   Date   12 May 1997

Client's name   S. Rushkin   Person attended   Oldcastle Crown Court

Time start   9.55   Time finish 10.21

Crown court bail application: Judge Fairbairn.

Applications as before. CPS (Joanne Capstan) object. Bail granted — surety £500 Jocelyn Rushkin, £500 Philip Gramsci. To reside at 12 Park View.

Travel: 9.30 – 9.55
        10.22 – 10.40   12 miles ret.

Waiting: 9.55 – 10.08

In court: 10.08 – 10.21

R v RUSHKIN

Advance Information Received: 20 May 1997

Jane receives the advance information from the CPS.

Document 32

> *Crown Prosecution Service,*
> *Oldcastle Chambers,*
> *Derry Street,*
> *Oldcastle OL2 1CP.*

Watkins & O'Dwyer,
17, Sycamore Avenue,
Oldcastle OL10 2BR.

Your ref: JW/Rushkin
Our ref: MB/0217

19 May 1997

Dear Sirs,

Re: Regina v S. Rushkin and R. Chapman
      Central Magistrates' Court

In response to your request under rule 4, Magistrates' Courts (Advance Information) Rules 1985 I enclose copies of the following documents:

(a)   ~~copy summary of the prosecution case~~
(b)   copy record of tape recorded interview
(c)   statements of witnesses
(d)   ~~other relevant information~~

Please confirm that the record of interview is acceptable by your client. Tape playing facilities are not available in court unless specifically required.

Yours faithfully,

M. Bottomley
CROWN PROSECUTION SERVICE

Document 33

Witness Statement

(CJ Act 1967, s. 9, MC Act 1980, ss. 5A(3)(a) and 5B, MC Rules 1981, r. 70)

Statement of Rachel Paling

Age if under 18   over 18 (if over 18 insert 'over 18')

Occupation Architect

This statement (consisting of 1 page(s) each signed by me) is true to the best of my knowledge and belief and I make it knowing that, if it is tendered in evidence, I shall be liable to prosecution if I have wilfully stated in it anything which I know to be false or do not believe to be true.

Dated the 19th day of April 1997

Signature R. Paling   Signature witnessed by P. Stubbs

I live at an address known to the police*, which is a block of flats. My flat is on the first floor and my bedroom looks out onto Burn Street. From my bedroom I can clearly see into the rear yard of MegaWin Amusement Arcade. The entrance to MegaWin is on Castle Street.

On 18 April 1997 at approximately 11.55 p.m. I was awoken by a sound of breaking glass followed by a burglar alarm going off somewhere outside. I opened the curtain and looked out. I saw two men in the rear yard of MegaWin. One was standing on an upturned dustbin and appeared to be trying to prise open a window. It looked as if he was using a screwdriver, or something similar. The other man was standing on the ground and looking around, while occasionally talking to the man on the dustbin.

I obtained a good view of both men. My view was uninterrupted and the scene was brightly lit by a security light mounted on the wall above where the men were. I estimate the distance from my window to where they were standing as about 40 yards.

The man on the dustbin was about 5 feet 6 inches and I would estimate his age at around 40. He was of slim build, with dark hair brushed straight back from the front. I think he had a moustache. He was wearing dark trousers and a dark anorak.

The other man was about six feet tall, with dark hair, almost completely bald, and also of slim build. He was wearing blue jeans, trainers and a blue and green anorak. He was wearing glasses.

I observed the two men for about 30 seconds before they appeared to take fright, I think because they noticed me watching them. They ran to the wall adjoining Burn Street, almost directly in front of my window, climbed over and disappeared eastwards up Burn Street. I noticed as he ran past that the taller man had a scar on one of his cheeks.

I then telephoned the police.

Signature R. Paling   Signature witnessed by P. Stubbs

---

*It is common practice to withhold the address of a witness from the statements supplied to the defence. However, the exact place from which Ms Paling says she viewed the person she later identified as Steven is relevant, and Jane asks, and obtains this information from the CPS.

R v RUSHKIN

Document 34

Witness Statement

(CJ Act 1967, s. 9, MC Act 1980, ss. 5A(3)(a) and 5B, MC Rules 1981, r. 70)

Statement of Rachel Paling

Age if under 18   over 18 (if over 18 insert 'over 18')

Occupation Architect

This statement (consisting of 1 page(s) each signed by me) is true to the best of my knowledge and belief and I make it knowing that, if it is tendered in evidence, I shall be liable to prosecution if I have wilfully stated in it anything which I know to be false or do not believe to be true.

Dated the 2nd day of May 1997

Signature R. Paling   Signature witnessed by P. Stubbs

On 2 May 1997 at 2.30 p.m. I attended an identification parade at Central Police Station. I spoke to Inspector Edmonds who showed me a parade of nine men. I identified number seven as one of the two men I saw on 18 April at the back of MegaWin Amusement Arcade. The man I identified was the one who was not standing on the dustbin.

I wish to add to my first statement that I am sure the time of the attempted break in was 11.55 because I looked at my watch as soon as I woke up.

Signature R. Paling   Signature witnessed by P. Stubbs

Document 35

Witness Statement

(CJ Act 1967, s. 9, MC Act 1980, ss. 5A(3)(a) and 5B, MC Rules 1981, r. 70)

Statement of William Jones

Age if under 18   over 18 (if over 18 insert 'over 18)

Occupation Security Officer

This statement (consisting of 1 page(s) each signed by me) is true to the best of my knowledge and belief and I make it knowing that, if it is tendered in evidence, I shall be liable to prosecution if I have wilfully stated in it anything which I know to be false or do not believe to be true.

Dated the 19th day of April 1997

Signature W. Jones   Signature witnessed by P. Stubbs

I am a security officer at MegaWin Amusement Arcade, Castle Street, Oldcastle. On 18 April 1997 I was on duty until the premises closed at 11.00. As is my usual routine I checked inside the premises, by securing and checking all external doors and windows from the inside, locking all doors and setting the burglar alarm, and then made an inspection of the exterior of the premises. There were no signs of any damage at that time to the downstairs toilet window leading onto the rear yard.

At about 12.05 the next morning I received a phone call from the police that there had been an attempted break in at the rear of the premises. [I told the police there had been couple of suspicious looking men seen there earlier that evening, according to one of my staff.]

I attended the premises where I met PC Abrahams at 0.30. I then inspected the outside of the premises, and observed that the downstairs toilet window adjacent to the rear yard had been forced using a screwdriver or similar object. A window had been broken and the wood of the frame was damaged. I estimate the cost of repair at £200, and if a conviction is obtained I seek compensation in that sum.

I noticed that there was an upturned dustbin underneath the window. Beside it I saw a yellow handled screwdriver [and a green woollen hat]. These items were seized by PC Abraham. The whole area is brightly illuminated when anyone is in the yard because of a security light which is illuminated when there is any movement.

No-one had permission to be in the yard at the time and no-one had permission to attempt to enter the building through a window or at all.

Signature W. Jones   Signature witnessed by P. Stubbs

R v RUSHKIN

Document 36

Witness Statement

(CJ Act 1967, s. 9, MC Act 1980, ss. 5A(3)(a) and 5B, MC Rules 1981, r. 70)

Statement of PC Mark Patel

Age if under 18 over 18 (if over 18 insert 'over 18')

Occupation Police Constable

This statement (consisting of 1 page(s) each signed by me) is true to the best of my knowledge and belief and I make it knowing that, if it is tendered in evidence, I shall be liable to prosecution if I have wilfully stated in it anything which I know to be false or do not believe to be true.

Dated the 19th day of April 1997

Signature Mark Patel   Signature witnessed by P. Stubbs

On 19 April 1997, accompanied by PC Walker, I was on duty in a marked police vehicle in the central area of Oldcastle. At 00.07 acting on information received I noticed two men driving a Ford Sierra registration number G123 ABC. I now know those men to be Robert Chapman and Steven Rushkin. The car was driven by Rushkin.

I followed the vehicle as it drove northwards out of the central area, before overtaking and stopping it on the North Road. PC Walker and I asked the men to get out of the car. I asked both men to identify themselves, which they did. PC Walker told Chapman and Rushkin that he had stopped them because they were suspected of having tried to break into an amusement arcade earlier that evening. Neither man made any reply. With the consent of Rushkin I searched his car and removed a screwdriver set bearing a label Woolford which I produce as exhibit RP1. There is one screwdriver missing from this set.

I asked both men where they had just come from. Mr Chapman said 'it's none of your bloody business, I've been minding my own business'. Mr Rushkin said he had come from the pub.

I informed Rushkin and Chapman that I was arresting them on suspicion of attempted burglary and cautioned them. Neither made any reply and I conveyed them to Central Police Station.

Signature Mark Patel   Signature witnessed by P. Stubbs

Document 37

Witness Statement

(CJ Act 1967, s. 9, MC Act 1980, ss. 5A(3)(a) and 5B, MC Rules 1981, r. 70)

Statement of PC Hugh Walker

Age if under 18   over 18 (if over 18 insert 'over 18')

Occupation Police Constable

This statement (consisting of 1 page~~(s)~~ each signed by me) is true to the best of my knowledge and belief and I make it knowing that, if it is tendered in evidence, I shall be liable to prosecution if I have wilfully stated in it anything which I know to be false or do not believe to be true.

Dated the 19th day of April 1997

Signature Hugh Walker   Signature witnessed by P. Stubbs

In the early morning of 19 April 1997 I was on mobile patrol in the Oldcastle central area in a marked police vehicle in the company of PC Patel. At 00.07 acting on information received I had cause to observe two men who I now know to be Robert Chapman and Steven Rushkin driving a Ford Sierra G123 ABC in North View. PC Patel drove behind them out of the central area and stopped their vehicle on the North Road. The driver of the vehicle was the man I now know to be Mr Rushkin.

PC Patel and I asked Chapman and Rushkin to get out of their car and to identify themselves, which they did. I said to them that we had stopped them because they fitted the description of two men who had been seen trying to break into an amusement arcade. I asked each of them if they could account for their movements before they were in North View. Chapman replied: 'it's none of your bloody business'. Rushkin said he had been in a pub called the King's Arms.

With the consent of Rushkin PC Patel searched the Sierra and removed a 'Woolford's' screwdriver set from the boot of the car. I observed that the set had one screwdriver missing.

PC Patel informed the two men that he was arresting them on suspicion of attempted burglary and cautioned them. Neither made any reply. We then conveyed them to Central Police Station.

Signature Hugh Walker   Signature witnessed by P. Stubbs

Document 38

Witness Statement

(CJ Act 1967, s. 9, MC Act 1980, ss. 5A(3)(a) and 5B, MC Rules 1981, r. 70)

Statement of PC W. Abrahams

Age if under 18 over 18 (if over 18 insert 'over 18')

Occupation Police Constable

This statement (consisting of 1 page(s) each signed by me) is true to the best of my knowledge and belief and I make it knowing that, if it is tendered in evidence, I shall be liable to prosecution if I have wilfully stated in it anything which I know to be false or do not believe to be true.

Dated the 19th day of April 1997

Signature W. Abrahams   Signature witnessed by P. Stubbs

On 19 April 1997 at 00.05 a.m. I was on duty at Central Police Station. Acting on information received, and in the company of Mr William Jones, security officer at MegaWin Amusement Arcade in Castle Street, I attended the rear yard at MegaWin.

I arrived there at 00.30 a.m. and inspected the outside of the premises. I saw that a ground floor lavatory window at the rear of the premises had been smashed and attempts had been made to prise loose the window frame.

I found an upturned dustbin underneath this window, and on the ground nearby I found a yellow handled 'Woolford's' screwdriver which I produce as exhibit WA1.

[I also found a green woollen hat which I produce as exhibit WA2.]

Signature W. Abrahams   Signature witnessed by P. Stubbs

Document 39

Witness Statement

(CJ Act 1967, s. 9, MC Act 1980, ss. 5A(3)(a) and 5B, MC Rules 1981, r. 70)

Statement of DC Peter Stubbs

Age if under 18   over 18 (if over 18 insert 'over 18')

Occupation Detective constable

This statement (consisting of 1 page(s) each signed by me) is true to the best of my knowledge and belief and I make it knowing that, if it is tendered in evidence, I shall be liable to prosecution if I have wilfully stated in it anything which I know to be false or do not believe to be true.

Dated the 2nd day of May 1997

Signature Peter Stubbs   Signature witnessed by H. Lessways

On 19 April 1997 I was on duty in Central Police Station. I took custody of a screwdriver set exhibit RP1 from PC Patel and a screwdriver exhibit WA1 from PC Abraham. Both screwdriver and screwdriver set bear the name 'Woolford' and are of the same type and construction. [I also took custody of a woollen hat exhibit WA2 from PC Abraham.]

At 2.05 a.m. in the company of DC Grieveson I interviewed Robert Chapman. Chapman declined legal representation. The tape recorded interview finished at 2.39 a.m. The tape reference is PS200494/1.

At 3.40 a.m. in the company of DC Grieveson I interviewed Robert Chapman again at his own request. He declined legal representation. The tape recorded interview finished at 3.55 a.m. The tape reference is PS200494/2.

At 9.20 the same morning I interviewed Steven Rushkin in the presence of his legal representative Ms Watkins. The tape recorded interview finished at 9.35 a.m. and the tape reference number is PS040594/1.

On 2 May 1997 at 15.30 p.m. in the company of legal representative Ms Watkins I interviewed Steven Rushkin. The tape recorded interview finished at 15.35 p.m. and the tape reference is PS040594/2.

I later prepared a summary of each interview. The summary relating to Steven Rushkin is produced as exhibit PS1.

Signature Peter Stubbs   Signature witnessed by H. Lessways

Document 40

OLDCASTLE POLICE

RECORD OF TAPE RECORDED INTERVIEW

Place of Interview Oldcastle Central Police Station
Times of Interview From 9.21 To 9.34 Date 19 April 1997
Tape reference number(s) PS200494/3

FULL NAME OF INTERVIEWEE Steven Rushkin
DATE OF BIRTH 12 January 1953
ADDRESS 12 Park View, Longfield, Oldcastle OL10 2AB

INTERVIEWING OFFICER(S) DC 5678 Stubbs
OTHER PERSONS PRESENT   Jane Watkins of Watkins & O'Dwyer

Tape Time/   CONTENT OF INTERVIEW

00.00   Caution and general introduction to tape system followed by a chance to explain his actions leading up to his arrest that morning in the company of Robert Chapman. Rushkin denied any involvement in the offence, but admitted that he had been in the company of Chapman when arrested. He admitted that a screwdriver set found in the boot of his car belonged to him, and that a screwdriver of the type found at the scene of the crime was missing from this set.

Rushkin admitted an offence of driving whilst disqualified.

12.30   Interview concluded, tape switched off, master seal completed

Signature of Officer Preparing Record P. Stubbs

Document 41

OLDCASTLE POLICE

Page 1 of 1

RECORD OF TAPE RECORDED INTERVIEW

Place of Interview Oldcastle Central Police Station
Times of Interview From 15.30 To 15.35 Date 2 May 1997
Tape reference number(s) PS040594/1

FULL NAME OF INTERVIEWEE Steven Rushkin
DATE OF BIRTH 12 January 1953
ADDRESS 12, Park View, Longfield, Oldcastle OL10 2AB

INTERVIEWING OFFICER(S) DC 5678 Stubbs
OTHER PERSONS PRESENT   DC 8765 Grieveson; Solicitor Jane Watkins

Tape Time/   CONTENT OF INTERVIEW
Number

00.00   Rushkin reminded of the caution and the system of tape recording interviews. It was put to him that he had been identified on a parade as one of the men who had been seen trying to gain entry to MegaWin on 18 April. Rushkin denied any involvement and stated that at the time he was working in a pub called the King's Arms.

03.30   Interview concluded, master seal completed, tape switched off

Signature of Officer Preparing Record P. Stubbs

Note that the advance information does not contain a full record of the police station interviews but only short summaries. This is one reason why Jane tried to keep good notes at the earlier interviews. She has by now also received copies of the tapes of interview from the police (along with a copy of the custody record), but her own notes are the most accessible way of checking for important omissions or errors in the summary.

Also not provided are the records of the police interviews with Steven's co-accused, Bob Chapman. Chapman's interviews are not part of the prosecution evidence against Steven, since any admissions made in those interviews are admissible in evidence only against Chapman himself. Jane therefore contacts Chapman's solicitor and they agree to exchange the summaries of interview contained in the advance information for each accused.

R v RUSHKIN

Document 42

Page 1 of 1

OLDCASTLE POLICE

RECORD OF TAPE RECORDED INTERVIEW

Place of Interview Oldcastle Central Police Station
Times of Interview From 2.05 To 2.39 Date 19 April 1997
Tape reference number(s) PS200494/1

FULL NAME OF INTERVIEWEE Robert Andrew Chapman
DATE OF BIRTH   24 October 1954
ADDRESS 78, Park View, Longfield, Oldcastle OL10 2AB

INTERVIEWING OFFICER(S) DC 5678 Stubbs
OTHER PERSONS PRESENT   DC 8765 Grieveson

Tape Time/   CONTENT OF INTERVIEW
Number

00.00   Caution and general introduction to tape system followed by a chance to explain his actions leading to his arrest that morning. Chapman refused to answer any questions beyond stating that he had not been involved in any offence.

00.34   Interview concluded, tape switched off and master seal completed.

Signature of Officer Preparing Record P. Stubbs

106

Document 43

```
                         OLDCASTLE POLICE                          Page 1 of 1

                    RECORD OF TAPE RECORDED INTERVIEW

Place of Interview Oldcastle Central Police Station
Times of Interview From 3.40 To 3.55 Date 19 April 1997
Tape reference number(s) PS200494/2

FULL NAME OF INTERVIEWEE Robert Andrew Chapman
DATE OF BIRTH 24 October 1954
ADDRESS 78, Park View, Longfield, Oldcastle OL10 2AB

INTERVIEWING OFFICER(S) DC 5678 Stubbs
OTHER PERSONS PRESENT   DC 8765 Grieveson


Tape Time/              CONTENT OF INTERVIEW
Number

00.00   Caution and reminder that he had a right to contact a solicitor. Chapman content for the
        interview to continue and stated that he wished to make a full admission to the offence. He
        explained that he had met the other man – who he did not wish to name – in a public house
        called the King's Arms earlier that evening, at about 10.00, and they had had a few drinks
        together. They had left the pub at about 11.30 and the other man had suggested he knew
        where some money could be found easily, and that they should wait until the security officer
        at MegaWin left and then it would be easy to get in through the downstairs toilet window.
        They had climbed over the wall from a back street and tried to get in through the downstairs
        window. They used a screwdriver that Chapman was carrying in his bag. It was more
        difficult to prise the window open than they had imagined, and when a burglar alarm went
        off they ran and escaped over a wall. Chapman was shown a woollen hat which he said was
        not his.

00.14   Interview concluded, tape switched off and master seal completed

Signature of Officer Preparing Record P. Stubbs
```

Preparing for Mode of Trial: Wednesday 21 May 1997: 4.30 p.m.

Jane sees Steven to go through the advance information in order to take his comments on the statements and on Chapman's interviews. (As it has turned out there is little in Chapman's interview to worry about. The only reference that may concern Steven is the meeting in the King's Arms. Steven confirms that he cannot remember seeing Chapman there, but the place was very busy that evening.)

Jane prepares Steven's comments on the prosecution evidence as a second statement, rather than trying to incorporate the comments into the body of his main statement. Such 'comments' are often laid out witness by witness, and in court they are extremely useful to an advocate as a means of ensuring that Steven's case is 'put' to each witness. (This is the rule in advocacy that an advocate must challenge a witness on each disputed point or he will be taken to have accepted that witness' account. Strictly speaking the rule does not apply in the magistrates' court: *O'Connell v Adams* [1973] Crim LR 113. However, 'putting your case' properly is always good practice. The 'comments' enables the advocate to identify which elements of this witness' testimony are disputed.)

Document 44

Additional Statement of Steven Rushkin

I have read the advance information provided by the prosecution and make the following observations:

William Jones

I make no comment, save that I was not involved in any way, and the screwdriver and woollen hat do not belong to me. Both were shown to me during interview and I have never seen the hat before. The screwdriver is similar to the ones found in my tool set. The missing screwdriver from my set is one my wife removed last autumn for use in decorating. We had an argument about it, as I do not think that is a proper use for a quality tool. She has never returned it to the car, and has now lost it.

Rachel Paling

She claims to have had a good view, and the description given to the police of one of the men does match my appearance. However, I was not there at the time; I was still clearing up at the King's Arms, and the landlord of the pub, Philip Gramsci, has been able to confirm this. I know it was after 12.00 when I left because Phil, the landlord, made a joke about it. I went straight from the pub to my car, and was never in Castle Street or Burn Street.

I am not capable of climbing the wall as alleged, because of my injury in 1996, when I was in a road traffic accident. I suffer from injury to my spine and loss of movement. At the time of the accident, and as an outpatient afterwards, I was treated at Longfield Hospital and am still on painkillers from my GP, Dr P. Khan of the Grove Surgery, Longfield Park. As a result of the injury I now receive income support as I am unable to work except casually.

Police evidence

I do not dispute the evidence. I accept that I had a screwdriver set in the car with one missing.

Taped interview with me

The part of the tape summarised is accurate but far from complete; I gave the police an account both of where I was all evening, and of why there was a screwdriver missing from my set in the car. I also made it clear that I did not see Chapman until after midnight and did not recall seeing Chapman in the pub.

Taped interview with Chapman

If Chapman was in the King's Arms at all that evening, I did not notice him and I certainly did not have a drink with him. I did not have any alcoholic drinks. If my breath had smelt of alcohol no doubt the police would have breathalysed me. Not only did I not have any involvement in the attempted break in, I have never even been in MegaWin and could not possibly know where money is kept there.

Signed S. Rushkin   Dated 21 May 1997

How to decide on mode of trial: advising Steven

Attempted burglary is triable either way. This means that the magistrates will listen to representations by the prosecution and the defence and will then decide whether they can properly agree to hear the case in the magistrates' court or whether they will decline jurisdiction. If they do accept jurisdiction, Steven will then have to decide whether he agrees with this decision or wishes to have the case heard by a jury in the Crown Court.

Jane discusses the case with Steven. On the one hand, the magistrates' court is quicker, cheaper and less stressful than the Crown Court. It also has greatly restricted sentencing powers (any sentence would be limited to a maximum of six months' custody unless, of course, the magistrates use their power to commit him to the Crown Court to be sentenced). However, speed is no longer of the essence since Steven has got bail. Indeed, some clients are happy to put matters off for as long as they can. As to the issue of cost, it may seem as if, since Steven is legally aided, cost is not a relevant factor. However, if Steven is convicted, the prosecution will certainly apply for a costs order in respect of the costs of the proceedings. This will be substantially greater if the matter has proceeded to Crown Court trial.

In Jane's opinion, however, the key factor is the likelihood of acquittal. Most defence solicitors take the view that the magistrates are more likely to convict than not, while a jury coming fresh to the case may well be more influenced by the need for the prosecution to prove the case 'beyond reasonable doubt' and are more likely to acquit. In some cases, where there was a dispute as to prosecution evidence (for example, an argument that a confession was inadmissible), Jane would also advise choosing the Crown Court in order to have a *voir dire* — in other words, a hearing on the admissibility of the evidence in the absence of the jury. Clearly this cannot occur in the magistrates' court where the magistrates are finders of law and fact. However, there does not appear to be any dispute as to admissibility in this case.

Steven follows Jane's advice. He wants to put his defence to a jury, who he feels are more likely to accept his defence, and in particular his inability to scale the wall as alleged. Jane warns him about the disadvantages of the Crown Court trial — especially the Court's greater sentencing powers and the potential costs order.

The Mode of Trial Hearing: Central Magistrates' Court: Thursday 22 May 1997: 10.00 a.m.

Jane meets Steven at court. She has a word with the CPS representative (Ms Johannes) who indicates that the CPS would be happy with summary trial. Clearly it is always a good idea to find out what the prosecution will be recommending the court does. She also talks to Bob Chapman's solicitor. Unsurprisingly, since Chapman intends to plead guilty, he is going to want to keep his case in the magistrates' court, where the sentencing options are more limited.

Procedure at a mode of trial hearing

Steven is asked to confirm his name, address and date of birth. The charge is then read and the prosecution and defence address the court as to the appropriate place for the case to be tried.

(Note that s. 49, Criminal Procedure and Investigations Act 1996, provides for the defendant to indicate his plea before the hearing starts. If the defendant indicates a guilty plea, the court then treats that guilty plea as entered and *must* accept jurisdiction of the case. This provision has, however, not yet been brought into force.

There are a number of problems with this proposed change. Many either way offences are very serious (e.g., domestic burglary, drugs importation) and the magistrates' sentencing powers will clearly be inadequate. The magistrates will therefore need to commit the defendant to the Crown Court to be sentenced, and the defendant in the meantime will lose his prima facie right to bail and will be treated as a convicted prisoner in jail (rather than getting remand privileges). Also, where a guilty plea is indicated, the prosecution will have no duty to disclose unused material. Most defendants will therefore be very reluctant to indicate a guilty plea at this stage, even if they lose some of their discount on sentence under s. 48, Criminal Justice and Public Order Act 1994, for failing to enter an early guilty plea. It therefore remains to be seen if and when this provision will be brought into force.)

After hearing the representations, the court will need to decide whether to accept the case. The magistrates must have regard to the Mode of Trial guidelines, which were originally issued as a *Practice Note* in 1990, but were reissued in 1995, having been extensively revised. Unfortunately the revised guidelines were not formally reported, but can be found in practitioner texts (such as *Blackstone's Criminal Practice*).

Under the general guidelines the court must take into account:

(a) the nature of the case;

(b) whether in the circumstances it is a serious offence;

(c) whether the magistrates have adequate powers of punishment;

(d) any other circumstances;

(e) representations made by prosecution and defence.

The prosecution's version of facts is accepted for mode of trial purposes. It is not yet clear whether Steven's previous convictions should be taken into account. The previous guidelines stated that they were irrelevant at this stage; but this has been omitted from the new guidelines. The better view, for the time being, is that they remain irrelevant. In general an offence must be tried summarily unless there are reasons not to do so. Where there are co-accused, each has a separate right of election, so the fact that Bob Chapman wishes to have his case heard in the magistrates' court should not prevent Steven from electing jury trial, or vice versa.

The guidelines also set out criteria to individual offences. In the case of non-domestic burglaries the factors which might make summary trial inappropriate are:

(a) Entry of a pharmacy or doctor's surgery.

(b) Fear caused or violence done to anyone on the premises lawfully.

(c) The offence has professional hallmarks.

(d) Vandalism on a substantial scale.

(e) Unrecovered property of high value (i.e., at least £10,000).

None of these applies to Steven's case but Jane has made representations that the case is more suitable for Crown Court trial. If the magistrates themselves decline jurisdiction, and if Steven is then later convicted in the Crown Court, the defence will then be able to argue that he should not be penalised in costs for having elected Crown Court trial in an unsuitable case. (This is a slightly double-edged sword — the Crown Court might be influenced in its sentencing by the knowledge that the magistrates had declined jurisdiction.)

However, despite Jane's arguments, the magistrates accept jurisdiction of the case.

The clerk then warns Steven that even if he accepts the jurisdiction of the magistrates' court they nonetheless have the power to commit him to the Crown Court to be sentenced if he is convicted and the court decides that its sentencing powers are inadequate: s. 38, Magistrates' Courts Act 1980.

Steven then indicates that he wishes to be tried in the Crown Court. Bob Chapman indicates that he wishes to have the matter heard in the magistrates' court.

The court now has to fix a date for the court to decide whether Steven's case should be committed to the Crown Court for trial. The prosecution will need time to serve the committal papers. The case is therefore adjourned for three weeks to Thursday 12 June 1997. Steven's bail is extended to this date.

Legal aid

Now that it is clear that the attempted burglary is going to be committed to Crown Court for trial, Jane applies for the legal aid order to be extended so that it covers work in both the magistrates' court and the Crown Court. This is known as a 'through' order, and it is not available in either way offences until after the mode of trial decision, since only then will it be known if Crown Court work is likely to be required.

Jane wants to get the through order as early as possible since she needs to start preparing parts of the Crown Court case before the committal (i.e., while the case is still in the magistrates' court). The reasons for this are clearer if you consider what will need doing immediately after committal:

(a) *Within 14 days of committal*: defence must indicate witness attendance requirements.

(b) *Within 14 days of primary prosecution disclosure (which will be 'as soon as practicable' after committal)*: defence must serve the defence statement setting out the defence case (late service will give rise to 'inferences' at trial).

(c) *Within six weeks of committal (four if the defendant is in custody)*: plea and directions hearing, with the judge now able to make binding rulings on any issues of law (e.g., admissibility of the identification evidence): s. 40, Criminal Procedure and Investigations Act 1996.

All of these matters will be discussed more fully later on. But even at this stage you can see that the case now needs to be as fully prepared as possible as soon as possible. Yet most of the work required — the defence statement, identification of legal issues for pre-trial hearings — is work that logically needs doing only once the magistrates' have decided that there is sufficient evidence against Steven to actually commit the case for trial. Provided the determining officer (in other words, the officer responsible for dealing with the legal aid claim in the Crown Court) is satisfied that the preparation done under the through order before committal was 'related directly' to the Crown Court proceedings this must be paid as part of the Crown Court work.

There is also another practical reason for this. Any committal proceedings are now dealt with as a Category 3 standard fee in the magistrates' court. Although Category 3 appears to pay at a higher rate, it is much harder to qualify for the higher standard fee and most cases will attract only the lower fee *regardless of how much work the solicitor does on the case*. Most solicitors will therefore try and do as much work as possible, even before committal, under the more generous Crown Court scheme.

Jane has now got her through order and she can therefore start preparing the case for committal and for the forthcoming trial in the crown court.

What about the driving disqualified charge?

As was discussed above the magistrates have the power to commit the summary only offence of driving while disqualified to the Crown Court under s. 41, Criminal Justice Act 1988, since the offence arises out of the same circumstances as the either way offence. If Steven is eventually convicted on the attempted burglary, he can then plead guilty to the driving offence and both matters can be sentenced together. The CPS have indicated that they intend to ask the court to commit the driving whilst disqualified, and this will therefore be dealt with at the committal hearing.

Document 45

> ## Attendance Note
>
> Your name   JW   Date   22 May 1997
>
> Client's name   S. Rushkin   Person attended   Central Magistrates' Court
>
> Time start   10.00   Time finish 10.40
>
> Prosecution suggested summary trial acceptable. Made representations that complex issues of identification and potentially evidence of accomplice make case suitable for Crown Court.
>
> Summary trial offered, Chapman willing, Rushkin declined.
>
> Through legal aid order obtained.
>
> Chapman's case severed.
>
> Took instructions on the advance information.
>
> Remanded on conditional bail for committal to 12.6.97.
>
> Travel 20 min   Mileage 10
>
> Client 20 min
>
> Court 10.35 – 10.40
>
> Waiting: 25 min

Document 46

CENTRAL MAGISTRATES' COURT

THROUGH LEGAL AID ORDER

APPLICATION NUMBER: 1011001

IN ACCORDANCE WITH THE PROVISIONS OF THE LEGAL AID ACT, 1988 THE CENTRAL MAGISTRATES' COURT HEREBY GRANTS LEGAL AID TO STEVEN RUSHKIN

FOR THE FOLLOWING PURPOSES:

(1) PROCEEDINGS BEFORE A MAGISTRATES' COURT IN CONNECTION WITH
    ATTEMPTED BURGLARY
    DRIVING WHILST DISQUALIFIED

(2) PROCEEDINGS BEFORE THE CROWN COURT IN CONNECTION WITH
    ATTEMPTED BURGLARY
    DRIVING WHILST DISQUALIFIED

EXCEPT AS PROVIDED ABOVE, THE LEGAL AID GRANTED SHALL CONSIST OF REPRESENTATION BY A SOLICITOR BEFORE A MAGISTRATES' COURT AND A SOLICITOR AND COUNSEL BEFORE THE CROWN COURT, INCLUDING ADVICE ON THE PREPARATION OF THE CASE FOR THE PROCEEDINGS.

THE SOLICITOR ASSIGNED IS AS BELOW.

DATED THE 22ND DAY OF MAY 1997

A. CLERK

CLERK TO THE JUSTICES

Preparing the Case for Committal

Committal is the process by which the magistrates ensure that there is sufficient evidence to justify sending ('committing') the defendant to the Crown Court to stand trial. It is therefore intended to be a safeguard of the liberty of the individual and an opportunity to review the prosecution case in order to ensure that the matter should properly proceed further. As you will see, all committals are now dealt with by way of 'paper evidence' (in other words, there is no provision for any live witnesses to be called) and defence challenges are likely to be become rare.

While Jane waits for the committal papers to be served, she is therefore now concerned with preparing the case for the Crown Court trial, and in particular for the plea and directions hearing which will be listed within six weeks of the committal.

R v RUSHKIN

What work needs doing?

As noted above, two of the most urgent tasks after committal will be:

(a) to decide on witness attendance; and

(b) to draft the defence disclosure statement.

Neither of these can realistically be done until Jane has seen the detail of the prosecution case. At this stage she has the advance information, but she has no way of knowing whether the prosecution will be serving additional information — for example, whether any forensic evidence will crop up.

What work does Jane therefore need to do on the defence case?

Here there are two main tasks:

(a) the defence medical report,

(b) transcripts of the police interviews.

The medical report

Jane is going to want to obtain independent evidence about Steven's mobility. It is clearly a central element of Steven's defence that, notwithstanding the identification, he could not have been the person climbing the wall as his injuries do not enable him to do this. Jane therefore needs to obtain a defence medical report. However, such a report will be expensive and will not automatically be covered by the legal aid order. To Jane it seems clear that obtaining an expert report is a 'proper step in the proceedings' but she plays it safe and ensures that the expense will be met by obtaining prior authority from the Legal Aid Board.

Jane therefore contacts an expert orthopaedic surgeon to get an estimate as to the costs of such a report. Here she intends to use a Dr Miller, who has previously treated Steven, and who she feels is therefore likely to be most persuasive about his abilities. The estimated cost of the report is £350 plus VAT and Jane then completes a form Crim 10 to apply for authority to obtain the report.

R v RUSHKIN

Document 47

Application for prior authority for expenditure in criminal proceedings

➤ Please read the notes overleaf before completing this form in block capitals.

CRIM 10

Legal Aid Order number (please copy this from the order): LA 093/97/1

LEGAL AID BOARD LEGAL AID ACT 1988

Has this application been granted over the telephone? YES ☐ NO ☑

App Type 02

Defendant's details

Surname: Mr/Mrs/Miss/Ms RUSHKIN   First Names: STEVEN
Address: 12 PARK VIEW, LONGFIELD, OLDCASTLE OL10 9AB
Date of birth: 12/1/53   Occupation: _____

Solicitor's details

Name of Solicitor: WATKINS   Initials: J   Title: MS
Name & Address of firm: WATKINS & O'DWYER, 17 SYCAMORE AVENUE, OLDFIELD OL10 2BR
Legal Aid account no: A 123 B   Reference: _____   DX No: _____
Tel No: _____   Fax No: _____

Court/charge details

Court Name: OLDCASTLE CROWN COURT
Nature of charges (including statute and section): ATTEMPT BURGLARY, CRIMINAL ATTEMPTS ACT 1981, SECTION 1
Likely plea: NOT GUILTY   Date of next hearing: _____
Purpose of next hearing: COMMITTAL

Give the full reasons for the application and state clearly the purpose of the authority sought; in the case of a medical report indicate whether as to fitness to plead and/or plea and/or disposal: ACCUSED UNABLE TO CLIMB WALL AS ALLEGED BECAUSE OF PRIOR INJURIES.

Give a brief summary of the prosecution case. You may attach the advance disclosure or extracts:
POLICE STATEMENTS (PALING AND JONES) ATTACHED

Give a summary of the defence or mitigation. Attach your client's statement and details of any previous convictions, if available in either case:
ALIBI INCAPABLE OF ESCAPE ALLEGED (RUNNING AND CLIMBING 6 FOOT WALL)

Type of Expenditure e.g. medical report: MEDICAL REPORT

Details of Charging Rates per hour: £100
(Do not include VAT) Please read the notes overleaf

Preparation: 350 —
Travel (do not include travelling expenses): _____
Total authority you are seeking: 350 —

Name and address of expert or other person you want to instruct:
DR PAUL MILLER
GENERAL HOSPITAL
OLDCASTLE

Type of expertise and qualifications:
ORTHOPAEDIC SURGEON

Only applicable to medical reports: Consultant: NO ☐ YES ☑

Are there any other defendants who would benefit from the expenditure and with whom there is no conflict of interest?
☑ NO ☐ YES: What consideration has been given to a joint instruction?

SPECIMEN

Have alternative quotes been obtained?
☑ NO ☐ YES: What were the amounts quoted?

Solicitor's signature: J. Watkins   Date: 3/6/97

115

R v RUSHKIN

Transcripts of the interviews

Jane needs to listen to the tapes of interview, which she requested from the police at the start of the case. She has received the copies of the tapes and, in the advance information, she has also received very short prosecution summaries of those interviews (see Document 40 and Document 41, pages 104 and 105). Jane checks her notes and confirms that Steven gave detailed answers about his movements up to midnight, and accounted at that stage for the missing screwdriver. He denied Chapman's allegations that they had been drinking together and he told the police he was medically incapable of climbing the six foot wall. None of this material is shown in the summary.

The previous PACE Code E contained Note for Guidance 5B, which stated:

> *The record ... shall comprise a balanced account of the interview including points in mitigation and/or defence made by the suspect.*

The current PACE Code E simply says that the record should accord with government guidelines, but none have yet been produced. However, it is clear that summaries must still provide a balanced account of what was said at the interview.

Jane now listens to the tapes of the interview in order to check her own recollection and to confirm her notes. She is satisfied that a proper transcript of the sections of the interview that deal with the explanation about the missing screwdriver, the medical conditions and the alibi is needed. She therefore writes to the prosecution to ask them to prepare the transcripts. If this cannot be sorted out, she will need to either arrange for a transcript to be prepared by the defence or for the tape of interview to be played at court (in which case *Practice Note* [1989] 2 All ER 415 sets out the requirements).

Document 48

Watkins & O'Dwyer
Solicitors

17, Sycamore Avenue,
Oldcastle OL10 1BR.
Tel. 011-111-1111
Fax 011-111-1111
DX Oldcastle 1000

Partners: J. Watkins
A. O'Dwyer

Crown Prosecution Service,
Oldcastle Chambers,
Derry Street,
Oldcastle OL2 1CP.

Your ref: MB/0217
Our ref: JW/Rushkin

3 June 1997

Dear Sir/Madam,

         R v Rushkin

We are unable to agree the record of interview supplied with the advance information in this case. Detailed questions were put to Mr Rushkin while he was in police custody and full answers were given, in particular answers relating to alibi, alleged drinking with the co-defendant and a set of screwdrivers found in Mr Rushkin's car and medical problems.

We request you to ask the police to prepare a full transcript to be served with the committal papers.

Yours faithfully,

Watkins & O'Dwyer

First Committal Hearing: Central Magistrates' Court: Thursday 12 June 1997

Jane attends court with Steven on this date, but the committal papers have still not been served. The CPS therefore request a further adjournment and Jane agrees. The new date is fixed for Thursday 3 July 1997. Steven's bail is extended to this date on the same conditions as before.

Receipt of the Committal Papers: Tuesday 17 June 1997

Shortly after the adjournment the committal bundle arrives.

The committal bundle contains:

(a) CPS letter regarding committal policy;

(b) the draft indictment;

(c) the s. 41 request;

(d) schedules of documentary evidence and of exhibits;

(e) summaries of police station interviews;

(f) warning regarding witness order notification.

We will look at these in turn.

(a) The CPS letter:

Document 49

> Crown Prosecution Service,
> Oldcastle Chambers,
> Derry Street,
> Oldcastle OL2 1CP.
>
> Watkins & O'Dwyer,
> 17, Sycamore Avenue,
> Oldcastle OL10 2BR.
>
> *(Please refer to the URN in any correspondence)*
>
> 16 June 1997
>
> Dear Sirs,
>
> R v STEVEN RUSHKIN
> OLDCASTLE MAGISTRATES' COURT
> 3RD JULY 1997
>
> I enclose by way of service in accordance with section 5B Magistrates' Courts Act 1980 committal papers for the above.
>
> Committal papers have been prepared in accordance with the Practice Direction given by the Lord Chief Justice on 3rd June 1986. I enclose one copy of the committal volumes for your client, together with a further copy for your own use.
>
> If no depositions are taken, and there are no alterations to the Crown Court case papers now served, no further copies will be served on you. It will be for you to prepare any further papers for your own counsel and your client. If there are any alterations, the Crown Prosecution Service will supply you with copies of depositions and an amended list of witnesses and/or exhibits. These arrangements will ensure that the judge and all parties at the trial will work from identically indexed volumes.
>
> The written statements contained in the committal volumes will be tendered in evidence before the magistrates unless you object to any statement being tendered under section 5B Magistrates' Courts Act 1980 and rule 70 Magistrates' Courts Rules 1981. If you object to any statement being tendered in evidence, you should inform me as soon as possible. Delay and expense may be caused if you fail to act promptly upon this letter in this regard. It is however for the prosecution to decide what evidence to bring in support of the charge at committal stage.
>
> Unless I hear to the contrary I will assume that the committal will be in accordance with the provisions of section 6(2) Magistrates' Courts Act 1980.
>
> Yours faithfully,
>
> Madeleine Bottomley,
> Principal Crown Prosecutor

Although this letter takes account of the shift to a purely paper based committal system under the Criminal Procedure and Investigations Act 1996, you will note that the CPS still need to be told whether this is to be a s. 6(2) uncontested committal, or a s. 6(1) contested committal. This is a matter that Jane will need to discuss with Steven, once they have looked at the evidence.

(b) The draft indictment:

Document 50

> Draft
>
> INDICTMENT
>
> THE CROWN COURT AT OLDCASTLE
>
> REGINA
>
> V
>
> STEVEN RUSHKIN
>
> STEVEN RUSHKIN is charged as follows:
>
> STATEMENT OF OFFENCE
>
> ATTEMPTED BURGLARY, contrary to Section 1(1) of the Criminal Attempts Act 1981.
>
> PARTICULARS OF OFFENCE
>
> STEVEN RUSHKIN together with another on the 18th day of April 1997 attempted to enter as trespassers a building, namely MegaWin Amusement Arcade in Castle Street, Oldcastle, with intent to steal therein.

Note that this is only a draft at this stage. It states the offence for which the committal is sought. The actual indictment will be drawn up and served after the committal.

(c) Section 41 request:

Document 51A

> The Crown Prosecution Service will seek committal in respect of the charge contained in this schedule pursuant to Section 41 of the Criminal Justice Act 1988.
>
> REGINA
>
> V
>
> STEVEN RUSHKIN
>
> Oldcastle Magistrates' Court
>
> Date of Hearing: 3rd July 1997
>
> Case reference number: MB/0217
>
> | **Defendant** | **Summary Offence** | **Related Either Way Offence** |
> |---|---|---|
> | Steven Rushkin | Driving while disqualified 19th April 1997 | Attempted Burglary 18th April 1997 |
>
> Signed:

Document 51B

Schedule

STEVEN RUSHKIN

That you on 19th April 1997 in the county of Oldchester did drive a motor car on a road called North Road, Oldcastle, whilst disqualified for holding or obtaining a driving licence contrary to section 103 of the Road Traffic Act 1988.

You will recall that s. 41 of the Criminal Justice Act 1988 enables the court to commit the summary only matter to the Crown Court so that a guilty plea can be taken once the related either way matter (here the attempted burglary) has been tried and Steven convicted. If either Steven is acquitted on the attempted burglary or he pleads not guilty to the driving offence, the matter will have to be sent back to the magistrates' court for trial.

(d) Schedules of documentary evidence and of exhibits:

Document 52

OLDCASTLE CROWN COURT   URN: MB/0217

R -v- Rushkin

SCHEDULE 2

List of documents containing the evidence

Witness List

NO.	NAME	DATE OF STATEMENT
1.	R. PALING	19.4.97
2.	R. PALING	2.5.97
3.	W. JONES	19.4.97
4.	M. PATEL	19.4.97
5.	H. WALKER	19.4.97
6.	W. ABRAHAMS	19.4.97
7.	P. STUBBS	2.5.97
8.	D. EDMONDS	2.5.97

PLEASE NOTE THAT THE PROSECUTION DO NOT WISH TO USE AS EVIDENCE THOSE PARTS OF STATEMENTS WHICH ARE ENCLOSED IN [ ] BRACKETS. IF COUNSEL AT THE TRIAL PROPOSES TO SEEK TO ADDUCE EVIDENCE OF THESE PARTS A NOTICE OF ADDITIONAL EVIDENCE WILL BE SERVED.

R v RUSHKIN

Exhibit List

NO.	REFERENCE	ITEM
1.	WA1	Screwdriver
2.	RP1	Screwdriver set
3.	PS2	Tape recorded interview/Rushkin Tape reference PS 200494/3
4.	PS3	Tape recorded interview/Rushkin Tape reference PS040594/1
5.	PS1	Summary of interviews*
6.	DE1	Record of identification parade*

N.B.

<u>Exhibits marked * are served with the committal papers, other exhibits may be examined on suitable appointment</u>

Please note that the statements which have been served at this stage are in fact identical to those which have been provided earlier as advance information (see Documents 32 to 39): I have not therefore set these out a second time.

(The statement of Inspector Edmonds, who conducted the identification parade, is not reproduced, nor is that of PC Grieveson. In the circumstances they do not contain anything illustrative or contentious.)

(e) Summaries of police station interviews:

Document 53

RECORD OF INTERVIEW – NOTICE TO DEFENCE

You will find included in the attached Committal Papers, copy Record(s) of Interview* relating to your client. Such Record(s) have been prepared by the interviewing officer as a true and accurate summary of what he considers to be the relevant parts of the tape recorded interview. The Record(s) will form the basis of the interviewing officer's evidence of interview at the hearing, subject to any amendments or additions which may be notified to you in writing by me.

One of the purposes of tape recording interviews is that any dispute arising out of the conduct of the interview, or of the evidence obtained thereby, can be resolved by the defence and prosecution before the case comes to trial, thus avoiding unnecessary adjournments with the risk of consequential award of costs.

In the event therefore that you wish to take issue with any part of the Record of Interview, or require additional material from the tape recorded interview to be included, you are invited to communicate such facts within seven days of the date of committal to:

The Branch Crown Prosecutor
Crown Prosecution Service,
Oldcastle Chambers,
Derry Street,
Oldcastle OL2 1CP

[*Note to the reader: as these are identical to the records disclosed in Documents 40 and 41, they are not reproduced again.]

Again, and despite Jane's letter regarding the shortcomings of the summaries, the CPS serve copies of the existing summaries of the interviews. (These have already been set out at Documents 40 and 41 and are not therefore set out again here.)

At this stage the failure to provide amended summaries or, even better, transcripts of the interviews is not a major problem but it will need to be sorted out before the trial.

The failure of the CPS to obtain a full transcript in a case like this, where the relevance of the denials to specific questions is obvious, is unusual. The case study illustrates the way the defence solicitor deals with the problem to show that it is important not to accept prosecution evidence on trust.

(f) Warning regarding witness order notification:

Document 53A

REGINA v STEVEN RUSHKIN

Form 14A

Notice to accused: right to object to written statement or deposition being read out at trial without further proof (CPIA Act 1996 sch. 2 paragraphs 1(3)(c) and 2(3)(c): MC Rules 1981, r. 8 (as amended by MC (Amendment) (No. 1) Rules 1997.

To Steven Rushkin, of 12 Park View, Longfield, Oldcastle

If you are committed for trial, the Crown Court may try you in respect of the charge or charges on which you are committed or in respect of any other charge arising out of the same transaction or set of circumstances which may, with the leave of the Court, be put to you.

Written statements have been made by the witnesses named below and copies of their statements are enclosed. Each of these statements will be read out at the trial without oral evidence being given by the witness who made the statement unless you want the witness to give oral evidence and to be cross-examined on such oral evidence. If you want any of these witnesses to give oral evidence, and be cross-examined if necessary, you should inform the Crown Court and me in writing within 14 days of being committed for trial. If you do not do so you will lose your right to prevent the statement being read out without any oral evidence being given by the witness in question and you will only be able to require the attendance of the witness with the leave of the Court, but that will not prevent the prosecutor from exercising his discretion to call the witness to give oral evidence, and be cross-examined, at the trial if the prosecutor so wishes.

If you have a solicitor acting for you in your case you should hand this notice and the statements to him at once, so that he may deal with them.

Address any reply to:

The Branch Crown Prosecutor,
Crown Prosecution Service,
Oldcastle Chambers,
Derry Street,
Oldcastle OL2 1CP

The wording of this warning letter is largely dictated by the court rules, but note how poorly it is drafted. The final sentence of the main paragraph is 78 words long. It is quite difficult to work out what the warning is about. Most unrepresented clients are unlikely to understand fully the implications of the letter.

Under the Criminal Procedure and Investigations Act 1996, an apparently minor amendment to the committal rules has meant that any statement which is produced at committal can be *read* at trial in due course and the witness need not be called. There is a power for the defence to object to this (and they must do so within 14 days of committal, which is what this letter is warning Jane about), but there is also a power for the judge to overrule that objection.

This power is potentially very worrying. Take the evidence of the identification witness, Rachel Paling; Jane has in fact seen Ms Paling at the identification parade and has a rough idea of her age and apparent health. If a solicitor had not attended the parade, however, there would be no indication from the statement as to Ms Paling's age, health, eyesight, or any other factor that might well affect the reliability of her initial identification of two men seen at a distance, and briefly, at night. Ms Paling will not give live evidence at committal as there is now no provision for live testimony at this stage. (In the past, however, concerns about identification in particular meant that the CPS would normally have required a s. 6(1) committal so that live evidence could be called and Ms Paling's credibility assessed.) Now, if Ms. Palings' s. 5B statement is simply read out at trial, as it will have been at committal, no-one will have had the chance to see this witness and to assess her credibility, let alone to test that evidence under cross-examination.

Defence Action on Receipt of the Committal Papers: Wednesday 18 June 1997

Steven must decide whether he wishes to request a s. 6(1) committal.

Under the old committal scheme, a s. 6(1) committal involved the calling of live evidence by the prosecution and (somewhat rarely) by the defence. This is no longer possible and all evidence at committals, whether ss. 6(1) or 6(2), is in the form of statements or depositions or other paper evidence within s. 5A, Magistrates' Courts Act 1980.

However, a s. 6(1) committal is still the only opportunity for Steven to argue that there is not sufficient evidence to justify committing the matter for a trial. If therefore there was a gap in the prosecution papers, Steven might want to argue at committal that an element of the offence was not made out and that the case should not therefore be committed.

Note, however, that if Steven did succeed in persuading the court not to commit the matter, there would be nothing to stop the prosecution from simply making good the defect and re-submitting the matter for committal. So if there was a gap in the case, Jane might well advise Steven to agree to a s. 6(2) committal, with no consideration of the evidence, with a view to submitting that there was no case to answer at the close of the prosecution case. A successful submission of 'no case to answer' at trial would have the effect of preventing any further proceedings against Steven on this charge.

However, in this case, there are no obvious gaps in the evidence. In the past, Jane would have requested a s. 6(1) committal (and indeed the CPS would probably have insisted upon a live committal) in order to assess the identification witness, Ms Paling. If her evidence had been very weak, Jane might have succeeded in persuading the court that they should exclude her evidence under s. 78, PACE 1984. However, under the new 1996 Act regime, it is now clear that neither s. 76 nor s. 78 can be raised at the committal stage: sch.1, part II, paras 25 and 26, Criminal Procedure and Investigations Act 1996. Since Ms Paling's statement will simply be read to the court, there seems no hope of persuading the court that the prosecution case is insufficient to justify committing the matter to trial.

Jane discusses the matter briefly with Steven at the office. She advises Steven that committal can go ahead without any consideration of the evidence, in other words under s. 6(2), and then writes to him, confirming her advice.

Document 54

Watkins & O'Dwyer
Solicitors

17, Sycamore Avenue,
Oldcastle OL10 1BR.
Tel. 011-111-1111
Fax 011-111-1111
DX Oldcastle 1000

Partners: J. Watkins
A. O'Dwyer

Steven Rushkin,
12, Park View,
Longfield,
Oldcastle OL10 2AB

Your ref:
Our ref: JW/Rushkin

18 June 1997

Dear Mr Rushkin,

I should like to confirm the discussion we had at this office today. We have received copies of the statements of the witnesses the prosecution intend to use at trial, and these are identical to the statements served earlier.

The case will not go for trial at the Crown Court unless one of two things happens. Either:

1. we agree to the case being committed for trial; or

2. we do not agree, but the magistrates' court thinks there is enough evidence against you in the police statements for a trial to take place.

We should object to committal for trial if there is no real evidence in the statements linking you to the attempted break in.

But unless we consider that there is no evidence which a jury could use to convict you, or only evidence of a very poor quality, my advice is to let the case be committed. It is very easy to show that there is some evidence, and very hard to show that there is no evidence on which a jury could convict.

On the prosecution side, there is evidence that your tool set had one screwdriver missing, which matches the screwdriver found at MegaWin. They also have a witness who claims to have seen you run away from the scene. She picked you out in a parade two weeks later. They have not provided us with any statement from Mr Chapman, which means that they do not – at least at this stage – intend to call him to give evidence against you.

> On our side we have alibi evidence from Mr Gramsci at the King's Arms, and we hope to obtain evidence from your consultant confirming that you are unfit to scale the wall as alleged by the identification witness. We have not yet received this report. We could consider getting evidence from Mr Chapman himself, but I have been in contact with his solicitor and have been told that he does not wish to co-operate any further with us. However, we cannot actually call defence evidence at the committal stage.
>
> We agreed that it would be difficult to show that no reasonable jury could possibly convict on this prosecution evidence, which is what we would have to convince the magistrates of to get the case thrown out at this stage.
>
> You asked me if there would be a court hearing for committal. There will be a hearing, but no witnesses will be called. If we object to the committal, the police statements will be read out and I will argue that they do not contain enough evidence linking you to the offence you have been accused of. I cannot present, even in writing, any evidence on your behalf.
>
> Therefore I advise you to agree to allowing the case to be committed without me putting in an objection.
>
> If you need to contact me to discuss anything before then, please do so. I will see you at court at the committal hearings on July 3rd in any case.
>
> Yours sincerely,
>
> Watkins & O'Dwyer

The Committal Hearing: Central Magistrates' Court: Thursday 3 July 1997

In the absence of any requirement from the defence, the committal takes place without the magistrates even considering the papers. The court, under s. 6(2), Magistrates' Courts Act 1980, simply checks that the prosecution statements have been served and that no defendant wishes to have the evidence in the prosecution statements considered. The committal documents are handed up to the clerk and the magistrates commit Steven to Oldcastle Crown Court for trial. (Note that in the past the court would also have made witness orders at this stage, with Jane telling the court which witnesses were required to attend for trial. This no longer takes place at committal and will generally now arise at the plea and directions hearing.)

The court does not need to deal with legal aid since Steven has a 'through order' which covers the Crown Court as well. However, the court must deal with bail. At committal, the magistrates have the full range of Bail Act powers, but Steven has attended court without problem since the Crown Court granted him conditional bail and there is no reason to vary the bail in any way. The court therefore bails Steven to attend the plea and directions hearing which is fixed for 24 July.

Document 55

> ## Attendance Note
> Your name   JW   Date   3.7.97
>
> Client's name   S. Rushkin   Person attended   Central Magistrates' Court
>
> Time start   10.50   Time finish   10.55
>
> Committal under MCA s. 6(2). Conditional bail reviewed. PDH fixed 24.7.97.
>
> Attending client 10 min
>
> Court 5 min   [No Legal Aid claim]

Note that Jane's attendance at the uncontested committal will be paid for under legal aid only if the prosecution papers were received less than two weeks in advance, or if a bail application had to be made. (See Notes for Guidance 17, para. 25, Legal Aid Handbook.) In fact neither of these conditions is satisfied. Jane was in court anyway on other cases and has therefore represented Steven, but payment is not claimed.

Document 56

COMMITTAL IN ACCORDANCE WITH THE PROVISIONS OF SECTION 6(2) OF THE MAGISTRATES' COURTS ACT 1980

OLDCASTLE CROWN COURT

REGINA
V
STEVEN RUSHKIN

DATE OF COMMITTAL	CENTRAL MAGISTRATES' COURT 3 July 1997
DATE OF PLEA AND DIRECTIONS HEARING	24 July 1997
FOR THE PROSECUTION	CROWN PROSECUTION SERVICE ADDRESS
FOR THE DEFENCE	WATKINS AND O'DWYER 17 SYCAMORE STREET OLDCASTLE OL10 1BR
CHARGES	SEE ATTACHED LIST
EXHIBITS	SEE ATTACHED LIST
WITNESSES	SEE ATTACHED LIST

The case now proceeds to the Crown Court.

Payment for Work Done So Far

Most work in the magistrates' courts is governed by the 'fixed fee' regime. In order to calculate costs, the solicitor must first work out her 'core costs' on the case. Core costs will be reasonable work actually and reasonably done in preparing the case, as well as routine letters and telephone calls, and advocacy. There are specified hourly rates of pay for preparation and advocacy, and fixed rates for each letter and phone call. (Note that travel and waiting time costs are paid on top of the core costs.)

In order to work out how much she will get paid for the work, Jane must then decide what category of case Steven's falls into. As the case involves a committal hearing, it is automatically treated as a Category 3 case: Jane's costs do not exceed the lower standard fee limit for that category (£493) and so she is only able to claim the lower standard fee for Category 3 (£290). Her travel and waiting times costs are then added to the standard fee, as are her disbursements (so far just her mileage).

Note that the fixed fee system is complicated and each case needs to be carefully checked to ensure that the appropriate core costs are identified and the appropriate standard fee claimed. The process is made more complicated by the fact that Jane can properly claim for much of the preparatory work under the Crown Court costs regime, for work done which is ascribable to preparing for the trial and which was done after the through order was issued!

Jane claims her costs on form Crim 13.

R v RUSHKIN

Document 57

Legal aid in criminal proceedings
Claim for lower standard fee
CRIM 13

→ Please refer to the Cost Claim Checklist (CK4) before completing this form

Legal aid order number (unique reference): **LA 10 11 001**

LEGAL AID BOARD — LEGAL AID ACT 1988

Solicitor's details
Firm's name & address or DX number: **OLDCASTLE 1000**
Legal aid account no.: **A123B**
Tel no.: **011-111-1111**
Solicitor's reference: **JW/Rushkin**

Type of case - category of fee

Category 1
- Guilty plea ☐
- Uncontested breach ☐
- Discontinuance / withdrawal ☐
- Bind over ☐
- Deferred sentence hearing ☐
- Change of solicitor ☐
- Warrant of arrest ☐

Category 2
- Not guilty plea ☐
- Cracked trial ☐
- Please state date guilty plea indicated to solicitor ___/___/___
- Discontinuance/withdrawal/bind over/ no evidence offered, after case fully prepared ☐
- Contested breach ☐
- Mixed pleas ☐

Category 3
- s6(2) committal (including discontinuance/withdrawal) ☑
- Committal proceedings discontinued/withdrawn before date of 6(1) committal hearing fixed ☐
- Transfer : s4 CJA 1987 ☐
- Transfer : s53 CJA 1991 ☐

Initials and surname of main defendant: **S. RUSHKIN**
Number of defendants: **1**
Name of court: **OLDCASTLE CENTRAL**
Date of order: **3/5/97**
Date commenced work: **21/4/97**
Date of final hearing: **13/7/97**

1. Did the case involve a prosecution bail application to a Judge in chambers in the Crown Court? Yes ☑ No ☐
2. Was a Wasted Costs Order made against your firm and/or counsel? Yes ☐ No ☑
   If you have ticked 'Yes', please attach a copy of the order(s)/relevant correspondence
3. Were any of the defendant(s) for whom you acted ordered to pay a contribution? Yes ☐ No ☑
   If you have ticked 'Yes', please attach a copy of the contribution order(s), unless the legal aid order states the name of each defendant ordered to pay
4. Was counsel instructed? Yes ☐ No ☑
   If you have ticked 'Yes', please tell us how many counsel were instructed ☐

Relevant case information
Information given here may expedite payment (refer to Cost Claim Check List). Please give details of any relevant factors in support of time spent in travelling and waiting. ~~If you have attended a section 6(2) committal please give your reasons for attending~~. Please also give details in support of any claim for more than one "case".

Four visits to court, including appeal to Crown Court against refusal of bail. Alibi witness interviewed while events fresh in his mind and one other witness for same reason.
Attended committal.

SPECIMEN

R v RUSHKIN

Claim for costs

Schedule of time spent	TRAVEL Hrs Mins	WAITING Hrs Mins
Time old rate	:	:
Costs old rate	£ :	£ :
Time current rate	2 : 10	0 : 55
Costs current rate	£ 53 : 62	£ 22 : 69
Total costs	£ 53 : 62	£ 22 : 69

			ATTENDANCES Hrs Mins	PREPARATION Hrs Mins	ADVOCACY Hrs Mins
A	Total time (solicitor)		:	:	:
B	Total time (unassigned counsel)				
	Total time (A + B)	2 : 10	0 : 55	3 : 20	2 : 20	0 : 29

Total number of letters	17
Total number of telephone calls	8
Total number of hearings	4
Total number of attendances	12

Solicitor's costs

1	Standard fee or core costs claimed	290	50
2	Travel time costs	53	
3	Waiting time costs	22	69
4	Total of 1, 2 & 3	366	81
5	IF COUNSEL UNASSIGNED: Less counsel's fees (excluding VAT)		
6	Solicitor's costs (4 - 5)	366	81
7	VAT (on 6)	64	19
	Total solicitor's costs	431	00

Disbursements

Travel	14	40
VAT on travel	2	52
Disbursements subject to VAT		
VAT thereon		
Disbursements not subject to VAT		
Total disbursements	16	92

Details (if car state mileage)

40 miles

Counsel's fees

Agreed fee for work done		
Agreed fee for travel & waiting		
Agreed fee for travel costs		
Total		
VAT thereon		
Total payment to counsel		

SPECIMEN

Declaration

(1) I certify that all the information given in this claim is correct.
(2) I have not claimed and will not otherwise claim for the same items from the Legal Aid Fund.
(3) I have held a valid Practising Certificate throughout the conduct of this matter.
I have read and complied with (1), (2) and (3) above.

Signed (Nominated or conducting solicitor) __J. Watkin__ Date __4 / 7 / 97__

Name (Please type or use block capitals) __J. WATKINS__

Official use only

Assessor's initials _____ Date _____

October 1994

PART C — THE CROWN COURT

Post-committal Tasks

Jane now needs to ensure that the case if fully prepared for the plea and directions hearing on 24 July 1997. While this hearing is primarily a housekeeping provision to sort out the procedural elements of the trial (witnesses, admissions, time estimates etc.), there is now a power to make binding rulings on any disputed legal arguments at this stage. Counsel therefore needs to be fully instructed and the case fully prepared.

What needs doing?

(a) *Witness requirements*: notification to the Crown Court and CPS.

(b) *Defence medical evidence*: Jane has applied for Legal Aid Board authorisation to obtain a medical report. This will need to be chased up so that the report can be obtained.

(c) *Transcripts of interview*: Jane needs to arrange for transcripts to be prepared as the CPS have failed to do this. Again this will require Legal Aid Board authorisation.

(d) *Disclosure*: primary prosecution disclosure of unused material will be made as soon as practicable. A defence disclosure statement must then be submitted within 14 days. This will trigger the secondary prosecution disclosure.

(a) Witness requirements:

As we have seen, there is one critical task that Jane must complete as soon as practicable after committal, and that is to notify the Crown Court and the CPS that she objects to committal statements being used at trial. She must do this within *14 days* of committal or the statements will simply be read and the witness not called.

In fact, looking at the statements, it is clear that the evidence of some witnesses (especially Rachel Paling, the identification witness) is highly contentious; but other witnesses (for example, William Jones, the security officer) appear to be largely irrelevant. At this stage, however, Jane is reluctant to bind the hands of the advocate who will be conducting the trial. Jane does not want to write to the CPS and say that William Jones is not needed at trial, when the trial advocate may decide that he could usefully cross-examine Jones on the fact that there was a substantial gap between his last attendance at MegaWin and his attendance after the attempted burglary, so that there is no way of telling when the screwdriver was left on the premises.

Jane therefore writes to the CPS and the Crown Court to inform them that all the committal witnesses are required to give live evidence at trial.

Document 58A

Watkins & O'Dwyer
Solicitors

17, Sycamore Avenue,
Oldcastle OL10 1BR.
Tel. 011-111-1111
Fax 011-111-1111
DX Oldcastle 1000

Partners: J. Watkins
A. O'Dwyer

Crown Prosecution Service,
Oldcastle Chambers,
Derry Street,
Oldcastle OL2 1CP.

Your ref: MB/0217
Our ref: JW/Rushkin

4 July 1997

Dear Sirs,

R v Rushkin, attempted burglary

Please find attached notification of our requirements in respect of the evidence tendered at the committal proceedings of 3rd July 1997.

Yours faithfully,

Watkins & O'Dwyer

Document 58B

NOTIFICATION OF WITNESS REQUIREMENTS

REGINA v RUSHKIN

TAKE NOTICE that we Watkins & O'Dwyer, on behalf of Steven Rushkin, in accordance with Rule 2 of the Crown Court Rules 1982 (as amended) **hereby notify you** that, in respect of the evidence tendered at the committal proceedings, we

- do not require any prosecution witness in the above case to attend the trial at the Crown Court to give oral evidence;
- require all prosecution witnesses in the above case to attend the trial at the Crown Court and give oral evidence;
- require the following named witnesses only to attend the Crown Court trial to give oral evidence:

Signed: Watkins & O'Dwyer   Date: 4th July 1997

To: Crown Prosecution Service
      Oldcastle Crown Court

The notice is sent to both the CPS and the Crown Court. I have only shown one of the cover letters (the other is in identical terms).

(b) Defence medical evidence

Jane rings the Legal Aid Board who confirm that the authorisation aleady requested (see p. 115) has now been granted to obtain a medical report from Dr Miller. Jane therefore writes to Dr Miller to ask him to prepare the report, and she also writes to Steven to ask him to contact Dr Miller's secretary as soon as possible to arrange an appointment.

(c) Transcripts of interviews

Jane needs to obtain Legal Aid Board authorisation. Again form Crim 10 is used.

(d) Disclosure

R v RUSHKIN

Document 59

Application for prior authority for expenditure in criminal proceedings
➤ Please read the notes overleaf before completing this form in block capitals.

CRIM 10

LEGAL AID BOARD LEGAL AID ACT 1988

Legal Aid Order number (please copy this from the order) LA 098194

Has this application been granted over the telephone? ☐ YES ☑ NO

App Type 02

Defendant's details
- Surname: Mr/~~Mrs/Miss/Ms~~ RUSHKIN — First Names: STEVEN
- Address: 12 PARK VIEW, LONGFIELD, OLDCASTLE OL10 2AB
- Date of birth: 12/1/53 Occupation: UNEMPLOYED

Solicitor's details
- Name of Solicitor: WATKINS — Initials: J — Title: MS
- Name & Address of firm: WATKINS & O'DWYER, 17 SYCAMORE AVENUE, OLDFIELD OL10 2BR
- Legal Aid account no: A1238 — Reference: JW/RUSHKIN — DX No:
- Tel No: — Fax No:

Court/charge details
Court Name: OLDCASTLE CROWN COURT

Nature of charges (including statute and section): ATTEMPTED BURGLARY, CRIMINAL ATTEMPTS ACT 1981, SECTION 1

Likely plea: NOT GUILTY — Date of next hearing:

Purpose of next hearing: PLEA AND DIRECTIONS

Give the full reasons for the application and state clearly the purpose of the authority sought; in the case of a medical report indicate whether as to fitness to plead and/or plea and/or disposal:

THE ACCUSED GAVE FULL EXPLANATION OF ALIBI AND ACCOUNTED FOR OWNERSHIP OF CERTAIN TOOLS DURING POLICE INTERVIEW; HE ALSO GAVE NOTICE OF A RELEVANT MEDICAL CONDITION. PROSECUTION SUMMARIES OF THE TAPE DO NOT SHOW THIS. REQUEST FOR TRANSCRIPT IGNORED BY CPS.

Give a brief summary of the prosecution case. You may attach the advance disclosure or extracts:

PERSON MATCHING RUSHKIN'S DESCRIPTION SEEN TRYING TO BREAK INTO AMUSEMENT ARCADE. RUSHKIN STOPPED IN CAR SHORTLY AFTER TRAVELLING WITH A PERSON WHO HAS CONFESSED THE OFFENCE, BUT NOT IMPLICATED MR RUSHKIN.

Give a summary of the defence or mitigation. Attach your client's statement and details of any previous convictions, if available in either case:

ALIBI; MEDICALLY INCAPABLE OF THE ESCAPE ALLEGED (RUNNING AND CLIMBING A SIX FOOT WALL).

Type of Expenditure e.g. medical report	TRANSCRIBE TAPE (£2.50 PER MINUTE OF TAPED INTERVIEW)	
Details of Charging Rates per hour (Do not include VAT)		
Preparation	30	00
Travel (do not include travelling expenses)		
Total authority you are seeking	30	00

Name and address of expert or other person you want to instruct: LEGAL TRANSCRIPTS LTD, 5 HIGH ROAD, OLDCASTLE OL11

Type of expertise and qualifications: LEGAL TRANSCRIBERS

Only applicable to medical reports: Consultant: ☐ NO ☐ YES

Are there any other defendants who would benefit from the expenditure and with whom there is no conflict of interest?
☑ NO ☐ YES: What consideration has been given to a joint instruction?

SPECIMEN

Have alternative quotes been obtained?
☑ NO ☐ YES: What were the amounts quoted?

Solicitor's signature: J. Watkins — Date: 4/7/97

Specific information required

1. Court attendance fees of expert witnesses cannot be authorised - these are payable from Central Funds in the absence of a court direction to the contrary. Solicitors should consider what fee is likely to be allowed (if necessary, by asking the court) so that instructions are not given to an expert whose full court attendance fee is unlikely to be allowed by the court. The costs of medical reports ordered by the court to assist in sentencing are also payable from Central Funds and will not be authorised.
2. In Intoximeter or excess alcohol cases, include the reading or blood level, the nature or amount of alcohol consumed before and after driving with the times of consumption and the times of the test. In "hip flask" cases, also give details of any corroborative evidence.
3. The absence of alternative quotes will not, in itself, lead to a refusal to incur expenditure.
4. Check that the application has been sent to the appropriate area office and that a legal aid order is held which covers the proceedings. The Board will deal with applications on the basis of the information sent by the solicitor and an Area Committee only has jurisdiction where it is the correct Area Committee and there is the appropriate legal aid cover.
5. Send applications to the Area Office in whose area the court is situated. A covering letter is not needed but you can continue on a separate sheet of paper if necessary.

For area office use only

COURT CODE: DATE:

DECISION:

RF2	Request further information	
G10	Granted - Delegated	
G12	Granted - Committee	
R21	Refused - Committee	

CL4	Out of Time	
W10	Withdrawn	
CL5	No Jurisdiction	

DOCUMENT CODES AND STANDARD WORDINGS CODES REQUIRED:

SPECIMEN

SUMMARY FOR COMMITTEE:

September 1993

R v RUSHKIN

Document 60A

> *Crown Prosecution Service,*
> *Oldcastle Chambers,*
> *Derry Street,*
> *Oldcastle OL2 1CP.*

Watkins & O'Dwyer,
17, Sycamore Avenue,
Oldcastle OL10 2BR.
(Please refer to the URN in any correspondence)

7 July 1997

Dear Sirs,

R v STEVEN RUSHKIN
OLDCASTLE CROWN COURT   PDH: 24 JULY 1997
Disclosure of Prosecution Material under section 3 Criminal Procedure and Investigations Act 1996

I am required by section 3 Criminal Procedure and Investigations Act 1996 (CPIA) to disclose to you any prosecution material which has not previously been disclosed and which in my opinion might undermine the case for the prosecution against you.

Attached to this letter is a copy of a schedule of non-sensitive unused material prepared by the police in compliance with their duty under Part II CPIA and the provisions of the Code of Practice. The schedule has been prepared by the police Disclosure Officer, who in this case is DS Peters.

Unless the word 'evidence' appears alongside any item, all the items listed on the schedule are not intended to be used as part of the prosecution case. You will receive a written notice should the position change.

Where indicated, copies of the items listed are attached. Material marked as available for inspection can be viewed by arrangement with myself.

This material is disclosed to you in accordance with the provisions of the CPIA, and you must not use or disclose it, or any information recorded in it, for any purpose other than in connection with these criminal proceedings. If you do so without permission of the court, you may commit an offence.

If you supply a written defence statement to me and to the court within 14 days of the date of receipt of this letter, material which has not been disclosed at this stage will be further reviewed in the light of that statement.

A defence statement is required by section 5 CPIA in Crown Court cases. In magistrates' court cases, section 6 CPIA makes a defence statement optional. Please bear in mind that we will rely upon the information you provide in the statement to identify any remaining material which has not already been disclosed but which might reasonably assist the defence case as you have described it. The statement will also be relied on by the court if you later make an application under section 8 CPIA.

If you do not make a defence statement where one is required, or provide one late, the court may permit comment and/or draw an adverse inference.

If you request access to any item which marked for disclosure by inspection, it is essential that you preserve this schedule in its present form, as access will only be granted upon production of the schedule to the person supervising access.

If you have a query in connection with this letter, please contact myself.

Yours faithfully,

Maureen Docherty,
Reviewing Lawyer
Crown Prosecution Service

R v RUSHKIN

Document 60B

Form **MG 6C**

POLICE SCHEDULE OF NON-SENSITIVE UNUSED MATERIAL

Page No.

R v ..... STEVEN RUSHKIN .....

The Disclosure Officer believes that the following material which does not form part of the prosecution case is **NOT SENSITIVE**

Item No.	DESCRIPTION	LOCATION	*	FOR CPS USE COMMENT
1	Officers' pocketbooks — PATEL — WALKER — STUBBS	Oldcastle Police Station		
2	Statement: — HATTERSLEY	Oldcastle Police Station	D	
3	Statement: — GRAMSCI	Oldcastle Police Station		
4	Custody record — RUSHKIN	Oldcastle Police Station		Disclosed
5	Custody record — CHAPMAN	Oldcastle Police Station		
6	Tape of interview — CHAPMAN	Oldcastle Police Station		**SPECIMEN**
7	Telephone log — 18/19th April 1997	Oldcastle Police Station		

Date: 12.5.97

Continuation Sheet: Yes ☐ No ☑

Reviewing Lawyer: Maureen Docherty

* Enter
D = Disclose to defence
I = Defence may inspect

April 97

CPS Disclosure Notice

Document 60C

CRIMINAL PROCEDURE AND INVESTIGATIONS ACT 1996
PART I: DISCLOSURE

RIGHTS AND DUTIES OF ACCUSED PERSONS

1. The Criminal Procedure and Investigations Act 1996 makes important changes to the law on prosecution and defence disclosure in criminal cases. This notice sets out your rights and duties under the relevant provisions. Please read it carefully and show it to your solicitor if you have one.

2. Although this notice is sent to you by the prosecutor, he cannot advise you on its contents and you should not approach him for advice.

Disclosure by the accused

3. Before the trial begins, the prosecutor must disclose to you prosecution material which he thinks might undermine the case against you. If there is no such material, he must write to you to say so. In either case, he must also send you a schedule of non-sensitive material at the same time.

4. If your case is to be tried in the Crown Court, you must give the prosecutor and the court a 'defence statement' containing certain information about your defence. This must —

   (a) set out in general terms the nature of your defence, i.e., the reasons for your intention to plead not guilty,
   (b) state the matters on which you disagree with the prosecution, and
   (c) state in each case the reason why you disagree.

5. If you have an alibi, you must give details of the alibi in the defence statement, including —

   (a) if you know it, the name and address of any witness you believe is able to give evidence in support of the alibi, or
   (b) any information you have which might be useful in finding any such witness.

'Evidence in support of an alibi' means 'evidence tending to show that by reason of the presence of the accused at a particular place or in a particular area at a particular time he was not, or was unlikely, to have been at the place where the offence is alleged to have been committed at the time of its alleged commission.'

6. You must give the defence statement within **14 days** of the prosecutor making disclosure to you. The 14-day period starts on the date when the prosecutor writes to you, not the date when you receive his letter. If you cannot give a defence statement within 14 days, you may ask the court for more time. The court will want to know why you cannot do so, and how much more time you need. If you apply for more time, you must —

   (a) do so before the 14 days are up, and
   (b) give the prosecutor a copy of your application.

7. Section 11 of the Act says that if you fail to comply with these requirements, certain consequences follow. You fail to comply with the requirements if you:

(a) do not give a defence statement, or
(b) give a defence statement after the end of the 14-day period, or after the end of any longer period of time allowed by the court, or
(c) set out inconsistent defences in the defence statement, or
(d) put forward a defence at trial which is different from any defence set out in the defence statement, or
(e) put forward evidence in support of an alibi at trial, without giving details of the alibi in the defence statement, or
(f) call a witness in support of an alibi at trial without giving details of the witness in the defence statement.

8. If you fail to comply with these requirements, the court (or, if the court allows, any other party) may comment on the failure to comply, and the jury may draw such inferences as appear proper in deciding whether you are guilty.

9. If you put forward a defence at trial which is different from any defence set out in the defence statement, then (when deciding whether to comment on the failure to comply) the court must consider the extent of the difference in the defences, and whether there is any justification for it.

10. You cannot be convicted solely on the basis of an inference drawn from a failure to comply with these requirements.

11. If your case is to be tried in the magistrates' court, you may give a defence statement if you wish (for example, to get further prosecution disclosure) but you are not required to do so. If you do not give a defence statement, no inference may be drawn. If you do give a defence statement, the same procedures apply as if you case was being tried in the Crown Court (paragraphs 4–10 above), except that there is no jury but the court may draw inferences from a failure to comply with the relevant requirements.

12. If you decide not to give a defence statement, your case may come to court more quickly if you tell the court and the prosecutor before the end of the 14-day period.

Right of accused person to apply for additional prosecution disclosure

13. If you give a defence statement, the prosecutor must then disclose to you any additional prosecution material which might reasonably be expected to assist the defence which you disclosed in your defence statement. If there is no such material he must write to you to say so.

14. After this, if you have reason to believe that there is more prosecution material which has been not disclosed to you and which might reasonably be expected to assist the defence which you disclosed in your defence statement, you may apply to the court for an order to disclose it. You must —

(a) identify the material you need, and
(b) tell the court why you think it might assist your defence.

If you apply to the court, you must give the prosecutor a copy of your application. If you contact the prosecutor first, you may be able to obtain the material you need without having to apply to the court.

Right of accused person to apply for review of a non-disclosure ruling

15. If the prosecutor has material which he ought to disclose to you, but which is sensitive for some reason, he may apply to the court for a ruling that on balance it is not in the public interest to disclose it.

16. If the court rules against disclosure, you may ask the court to review its ruling. If you do so, you must —

(a) say why you think the ruling should be reviewed, and
(b) give the prosecutor a copy of your application.

Duty to treat disclosed material in confidence

17. You may use material disclosed to you for the purposes of your trial, or (if you are convicted) in connection with any appeal. If you want to use the material for any other purpose, you must first apply to the court for permission to do so, and say why you want to use it. You must also give a copy of your application to the prosecutor.

18. If you use the material for any other purpose without getting the permission of the court, you may be liable to proceedings for contempt of court. If the court finds you guilty of contempt, it may commit you to custody for a specified period or fine you or both.

Document 60D

Witness Statement

(CJAct 1967, s. 9, MC Act 1980, s. 5A(3)(a) and 5B, MC Rules 1981, r. 70)

Statement of Dr J R Hattersley

Age if under 18   over 18   (if over 18 insert 'over 18')

Occupation   General Practitioner

This statement (consisting of 1 page(s) each signed by me) is true to the best of my knowledge and belief and I make it knowing that, if it is tendered in evidence, I shall be liable to prosecution if I have wilfully stated in it anything which I know to be false or do not believe to be true.

Dated the 5th day of May 1997

I am a medical practitioner. On the evening of 18 April 1997 at around midnight I was called to an address in Burn Street, Oldcastle, for an emergency home visit.

As I was parking my car on the north side of Burn Street, opposite to Court Street, my attention was drawn to two people who I noticed running fast along the north side of Burn Street. As I could hear a burglar alarm in the direction they were coming from, and as they appeared to be looking around anxiously behind them, I decided to contact the police on my car telephone.

One of the men was about five feet six inches tall and appeared to be middle aged. He had a moustache. The other was a little taller and looked to be in his twenties. He had a scar on the side of his face, and wore glasses.

I am not sure if I would recognise either of them again, as I did not obtain a very clear view from inside my car, and they ran past quickly. I cannot recall what clothing they were wearing.

I saw the men continue to run in the direction of North View, before they disappeared from my view about 100 yards on.

Signed Joseph Hattersley   Signature witnessed by DC Turnbull

R v RUSHKIN

The prosecution are under a duty at this stage to disclose unused material which has not previously been disclosed and which, in the prosecutor's opinion, might undermine the prosecution case. You will see from the schedule that amidst the unused material listed are some officers' pocketbooks, the tapes of the interview relating to Chapman and a telephone log, which might reveal exactly when the burglary was called in. Also listed is Phil Gramsci's statement to the police. Note that at this stage none of these has been disclosed since the prosecutor is of the opinion that they do not undermine the prosecution case. You will also note that there is no mention of any evidence relating to the forensic analysis.

What has been disclosed is a statement from Dr Hattersley. This statement is potentially useful since, on Steven's instructions, the younger of the two men would be Chapman, while the description of the other man is different in age to Steven, although the details of height, glasses and scar are all accurate.

Defence statement

This must be served within 14 days of prosecution disclosure being made. But do the 14 days run from the date the CPS send out the letter (as the Home Office pro forma (Document 60C) suggests) or from the receipt of the documents (as the CPS letter (Document 60A) suggests)? The statute speaks only of the period running from the date when disclosure is made, so that the better view is that disclosure is not made until the defence receive the documents. However, in view of the adverse inferences that can be drawn if the defence statement is served late, Jane will want to provide the statement as soon as she can.

The only new evidence is the statement of Dr Hattersley, and this does not affect Steven's basic account, which is that he was not present at the scene and he has an alibi. Jane has already drafted a defence statement, and she now sees Steven briefly to go through the details. He approves of the statement and she asks him to sign the draft to this effect. (Since inferences will arise at trial where clients have earlier failed to put forward defence facts or have given contradictory defence statements, among other things, it is a good idea, where possible, for solicitors to get clients to sign their instructions to prevent any later confusion!)

Jane is then in a position to send off a finalised copy of the defence statement. This is sent to the CPS and to the Crown Court.

Document 61A

Watkins & O'Dwyer
Solicitors

17, Sycamore Avenue,
Oldcastle OL10 1BR.
Tel. 011-111-1111
Fax 011-111-1111
DX Oldcastle 1000

Partners: J. Watkins
A. O'Dwyer

Crown Prosecution Service,
Oldcastle Chambers,
Derry Street,
Oldcastle OL2 1CP

Your ref: MB/0217
Our ref: JW/Rushkin

14 July 1997

Dear Sir/Madam

R v Rushkin, attempted burglary

Please find attached the defence statement under s. 5, Criminal Procedure and Investigations Act 1996 in respect of Steven Rushkin.

We look forward to receiving secondary prosecution disclosure. In particular, we note that we have still not received disclosure of the outstanding forensic evidence in this matter. Moreover, we trust that the disclosure of the defence case will now trigger the appropriate disclosure of the officers' notebooks, the statement of Philip Gramsci, and the interview tapes of Robert Chapman — all of which are listed in the original disclosure schedule.

May we also have details of the exact address of the witness Paling, as this is critical to her evidence of identification?

We wish to examine the screwdriver, exhibit WA1. In view of the imminent hearing of this matter, it would seem simplest to request that this exhibit is brought to court on 24 July 1997 for examination.

We look forward to hearing from you accordingly.

Yours faithfully,

Watkins & O'Dwyer

(Note that this letter and the enclosed defence statement are also sent to the Crown Court.)

Document 61B

> # DEFENCE STATEMENT
>
> s. 5, Criminal Procedure and Investigations Act 1996
>
> ## REGINA v RUSHKIN
>
> I, Steven Rushkin, will be raising in my general defence the fact that I was not one of the two persons allegedly attempting to burgle MegaWin Amusement Arcade on 20 April 1997 and that I have an alibi.
>
> I take issue with those prosecution statements which suggest that I was one of the two men as aforesaid as I was not present at that place at that time and was not in any way involved with any alleged burglary.
>
> I intend to adduce evidence of alibi at trial: namely, that at the time of the offence I was at the King's Arms Public House, North View. In support of my alibi the defence intend to call the publican Mr Philip Gramsci of this address and also myself.
>
> Signed: Steven Rushkin   Date: 14 July 1997
>
> To: Crown Prosecution Service
>   Oldcastle Crown Court

The requirement for a defence statement of this kind is entirely new. It was introduced by the Criminal Procedure and Investigations Act 1996 in respect of investigations into offences which commenced on or after 1 April 1997. Section 5(6) of the Act provides the only definition of a defence statement, while s. 5(7) replaces the old disclosure rules in respect of alibi evidence:

(6) *For the purposes of this section a defence statement is a written statement—*

    (a) setting out in general terms the nature of the accused's defence,
    (b) indicating the matters on which he takes issue with the prosecution, and
    (c) setting out, in the case of each such matter, the reason why he takes issue with the prosecution.

(7) *If the defence statement discloses an alibi the accused must give particulars of the alibi in the statement, including —*

    (a) the name and address of any witness the accused believes is able to give evidence in support of the alibi, if the name and address are known to the accused when the statement is given;
    (b) any information in the accused's possession which might be of material assistance in finding any such witness, if his name or address is not known to the accused when the statement is given.

There is no guidance as to the level of disclosure required beyond the wording of s. 5(6). On the one hand practitioners will be concerned that inadequate disclosure will lead to inferences being drawn from a failure to comply with s. 5; on the other hand, the defence will often want to reveal as little of the detail of its defence as possible, especially where it may wish to cross-examine prosecution witnesses on a particular point or an inconsistency and will be worried that the witnesses would be forewarned by any prior disclosure.

In this case, however, Steven has always been consistent in his defence. He has put forward all the main details in his interviews in the police station. It is therefore relatively easy for Jane to draft a defence disclosure statement. However, while I believe that the disclosure in Document 61B is more than sufficient, ultimately we will have to wait for guidance from the Court of Appeal before we can be sure.

Note that there is no prescribed form for the defence disclosure statement. Here Jane has drafted it in a fairly formal manner, conscious that the statement may in due course become part of the documentation at trial. Please note that Jane has in fact sent copies of the defence statement to both the Crown Court and the CPS, although only the covering letter to the CPS is illustrated.

Secondary prosecution disclosure

Once the defence disclosure is made, the prosecution is under a duty to review the unused material in order to disclose material which assists the defence which has been disclosed. Thus in Steven's case, the prosecution will disclose any material which might support his contention that it was not him at the scene and that he was elsewhere.

You will note from Jane's covering letter (Document 61A) that she is still concerned that she has heard nothing about the forensic evidence. She also wants to see the statement which Phil Gramsci gave to the police and she wants to check what, if anything, Bob Chapman said in interview (she has only seen the summary of this interview). Under the old common law system of disclosure, Jane would not have been entitled to either of these, but under the new 1996 Act regime, they will be disclosable provided they support Steven's defence in some respect.

Jane is also asking for disclosure of the police notebooks. This is a standard request by most advocates, since the notebooks may often contain telling errors, corrections or discrepancies which can be exploited in cross-examination. The notebooks were clearly disclosable under the old common law regime, but again they will only fall to be disclosed under the 1996 Act if they are thought to support the defence which has been disclosed. This is a matter of concern, since it is hard to see how the prosecutor will be in a position to identify the detail of the notebooks which may prove invaluable to the defence in cross-examination. Jane therefore requests disclosure of the notebooks anyway.

Plea and Directions Hearings

Jane was careful to obtain a through legal aid order, covering Crown Court preparation, as soon as mode of trial was determined. This enables her to begin preparations for the plea and directions hearing before the committal. Many of the preparations for plea and directions hearing have already started, and in the commentary I indicated why.

Plea and directions hearing – the theory

The plea and directions hearing is created not by statute or court rules, but under practice rules issued by the Lord Chief Justice. The present rules are dated 25.7.95. The purpose of the plea and directions hearing is to ensure that guilty pleas can be identified at an early stage, and where appropriate pre-sentence reports ordered; those cases that will be going to a contested trial can be properly prepared, because the issues on both sides have been identified. The length of trial can be more accurately predicted, and therefore there should be less listing problems.

The plea and directions hearing system has been found to work better than the old system in reducing the number of cracked trials (change of plea to guilty at the last minute) and has enabled the courts to fix more trial dates, rather than putting cases into a floating list.

There are a lot of reasons for the courts, and the judge who presides at the plea and directions hearing, to want co-operation at the plea and directions hearing. The system only works if the issues in the case, including decisions on which witnesses will be used, which of the prosecution witnesses are to be cross examined, what other directions are needed, are all worked out in time for the plea and directions hearing. For the system to work at its best, the same barrister should attend both the plea and directions hearing and the trial itself, especially now that the judge at plea and directions hearings has the power to make a binding ruling on any questions of law.

Timetable

It is the magistrates who fix the date for the plea and directions hearing, which they do (in liaison with Crown Court listing officers of course) at the time of the committal. The defence is entitled to at least two weeks' notice of the plea and directions hearing. Two weeks is inadequate to prepare the issues in the case. Preparation in a case where there will be a not guilty plea includes: taking a full story from the accused; interviewing witnesses; preparing proofs of evidence; instructing experts; seeking undisclosed prosecution material etc. It takes far longer, which is why some of these steps have, in this case study, been taken as soon as the through legal aid order was granted. Even when the defence have completed these steps, there should be a conference with counsel in time to make the decision about which prosecution witnesses the defence wish to cross examine, as well as to look at the overall defence strategy. At the plea and directions hearing the court will try to fix a date for the trial, and therefore the availability of witnesses must already be known then.

Working back from this, the prosecution need to know which witnesses they must call for cross examination, which is mainly dependent on the defence indicating which prosecution statements contain material the defence would challenge rather than allow to be read out. The defence must tell this to the prosecution within 14 days of committal.

Since Jane wants counsel to have the opportunity to advise on this issue of which prosecution witnesses are required at trial, the conference must be at least two weeks before the plea and directions hearing. Therefore the brief to counsel must be even sooner. It is necessary to be in a position to start writing the brief shortly after the committal itself. Law Society guidelines suggest the defence brief counsel within 21 days of committal, or seven if the accused is in custody (*Gazette*, 8 March 1995). If Jane had wanted counsel's advice on the defence disclosure statement, a conference would need to be arranged almost immediately after committal.

A failure to prepare each and every aspect of the case in time for briefing counsel to appear at the plea and directions hearing is inevitable. In the present case study, Jane could not request unused material from the prosecution until she knew what the prosecution were in fact disclosing. She could not organise the tape transcripts until she knew the CPS were not prepared to organise this. Had she wanted forensic evidence, she could not have obtained this until she knew what the prosecution forensic evidence consisted of and then obtained legal aid authority. Therefore the exhortation to prepare the case before the plea and directions hearing does not mean that preparations cease afterwards.

At the plea and directions hearing itself the court requires the two sides to complete one questionnaire to be submitted to the judge before the hearing starts. To indicate what this looks like, I have had Jane complete this questionnaire in draft for counsel's use before the conference (Document 62).

It will help you to understand what is expected to happen at the plea and directions hearing before reading the brief. The points below are taken from the Lord Chief Justice's Rules of 25.7.95. The numbering follows that in the rules, and some points are not covered here.

8. Arraignment (i.e., submitting to the court's jurisdiction — no preparation needed except surrender to bail);

9. Plea and sentencing if appropriate (where there is to be a guilty plea the defence must tell the CPS and the probation service in advance, so that sentencing can take place immediately);

10. Each side then informs the judge of the following:

   (a) the issues in the case (subject as mentioned already to confidentiality considerations by the defence);
   (b) any problems with witnesses' fitness to attend;
   (c) numbers of witnesses, including those whose evidence can be given by statement rather than orally;

(d) any defence witnesses whose written statements have been served and accepted;
(e) additional witnesses who may be called by the prosecution, and the evidence they will give (see below, Document 72A);
(f) facts which are admitted, and witnesses whose attendance at trial is not required;
(g) details of any exhibits and schedules which either side will adduce;
(h) details of how the prosecution documents will be numbered; the order the prosecution witnesses will be called in;
(i) the defence alibi (which, as shown above, has already had to be disclosed);
(j) points of law and admissibility that are anticipated, and any authorities that will be cited;
((k) and (l) deal with trials where closed circuit television links will be needed;)
(m) any need for technical equipment, such as tape recorder to play back interview tapes (this will be needed in Steven's case if the prosecution and defence cannot agree the transcripts);
(n) details of further work the parties need to do, and of any other relevant matter;
(o) estimated length of the trial;
(p) when those witnesses who are to give oral evidence are unavailable;
(q) when the trial advocate is unavailable;
(r) any directions that any party wants the court to give (this might, for example, include a direction to disclose prosecution evidence).

12. No later than 14 days before the trial all parties must write to the court and confirm that they have complied with the order made at plea and directions hearing.

The Judge's Questionnaire

The plea and directions hearing rules require all parties to submit to the judge just before the hearing agreed responses to a standard questionnaire, which the judge can then use as an agenda for the plea and directions hearing. The defence answers to the standard questions need to be anticipated, as counsel for the two sides will only meet at the plea and directions hearing, not before. Jane assists counsel by sending with the brief for the plea and directions hearing her draft replies for the defence. Document 62 shows this.

R v RUSHKIN

Document 62

Plea and Directions Hearing

Judge's Questionnaire

(In accordance with the practice rules issued by the Lord Chief Justice)

A copy of this questionnaire, completed as far as possible with the agreement of both advocates, is to be handed in to the court prior to the commencement of the Plea and Directions Hearing.

The Crown Court at OLDCASTLE

Case No. ~~FH~~ OL2000

PTI URN MB 0217

R v RUSHKIN

Date of PDH 24 July 1997

Name of Prosecution Advocate at PDH

Name of Defence Advocate at PDH

SPECIMEN

---

1   a   Are the actual/proposed not guilty pleas definitely to be maintained through to a jury trial?   Yes ✓   No

   b   Has the defence advocate advised his client of section 48 of CJPOA 1994? *(Reductions in sentence for guilty pleas)*   Yes ✓   No

   c   Will the prosecution accept part guilty or alternative pleas?   Yes   No

---

2   How long is the trial likely to take?

3   What are the issues in the case?   IDENTIFICATION, ALIBI AND POSSIBLY FORENSIC EVIDENCE

---

4   Issues as to the mental or medical condition of any defendant or witness.   DEFENDANT ALLEGED TO HAVE CLIMBED WALL. MEDICAL EVIDENCE MAY BE CALLED AS TO CAPACITY.

---

5   Prosecution witnesses whose evidence will be given.

   Can any statement be read instead of calling the witnesses?

   To be read (number)
   To be called (number)
   Names:
   PC WALKER
   DC STUBBS
   INSP EDMONDS

Form 5122 Plea and Directions Hearings in the Crown Court Practice Rules 1995   1

R v RUSHKIN

6	a	Number of Defence witnesses whose evidence will be placed before the Court.	Defendant + 3
	b	Any whose statements have been served which can be agreed and accepted in writing.	
7		Is the prosecution intending to serve any further evidence?	Yes No
		If **Yes**, what area(s) will it cover?	
		What are the witnesses' names?	SPECIMEN
8		Facts which are admitted and can be reduced into writing. (s10(2)(b) CJA 1967)	
9		Exhibits and schedules which are to be admitted.	
10		Is the order and pagination of the prosecution papers agreed?	
11		Any alibi which should have been disclosed in accordance with CJA 1967?	Yes ✓ No
12	a	Any points of law likely to arise at trial?	DIRECTIONS ON IDENTIFICATION EVIDENCE
	b	Any questions of admissibility of evidence together with any authorities it is intended to rely upon.	
13	a	Has the defence notified the prosecution of any issue arising out of the record of interview? *(Practice Direction Crime: Tape Recording of police interview 26 May 1989)*	Yes ✓ No
	b	What efforts have been made to agree verbatim records or summaries and have they been successful?	THESE HAVE BEEN TRANSCRIBED AND PROVIDED TO THE PROSECUTION.

Form 5122 Plea and Directions Hearings in the Crown Court Practice Rules 1995

R v RUSHKIN

14	Any applications granted / pending for:		
	(i) evidence to be given through live television links?	Yes	No ✓
	(ii) evidence to be given by pre-recorded video interviews with children?	Yes	No ✓
	(iii) screens?	Yes	No ✓
	(iv) the use of video equipment during the trial?	Yes	No ✓
	(v) use of tape playback equipment?	Yes ✓	No

SPECIMEN

15	Any other significant matter which might affect the proper and convenient trial of the case? (e.g. expert witnesses or other cases outstanding against the defendant)	No

16	Any other work which needs to be done. Orders of the Court with time limits should be noted on page 4.	Prosecution
		Defence OBTAIN EXPERT EVIDENCE OBTAIN DISCLOSURE OF FORENSIC EVIDENCE AND IF NECESSARY SEEK INDEPENDENT EXPERT EVIDENCE

17 a	Witness availability and approximate length of witness evidence.	Prosecution
		Defence NO PROBLEMS AT PRESENT, BUT MEDICAL REPORT STILL AWAITED
b	Can any witness attendance be staggered?	Yes No
c	If **Yes**, have any arrangements been agreed?	Yes No

18	Advocates' availability?	Prosecution
		Defence

Form 5122 *Plea and Directions Hearings in the Crown Court Practice Rules 1995*   3

Proofs of evidence

It is a solicitor's task to prepare for counsel's use both in preparing for the plea and directions hearing and at trial (and for his or her own use if not instructing counsel) a proof of evidence for each witness called. This proof is based on the original statement obtained, but updated to incorporate all relevant evidence which it is intended the witness will give, and eliminating all evidence the witness is not to adduce. The proof will be very similar to witness statements exchanged under Order 38 in civil proceedings, except that it is not necessarily seen by the other side or the court. (A specially prepared version could be disclosed under s. 9, Criminal Justice Act 1967 in an attempt to have it agreed by the prosecution. See Document 76 page 176 for an example.) It is tempting merely to provide counsel with the existing statements, but better to prepare the proofs of evidence (and therefore to spot problems in the evidence) before sending the brief.

Some of the information in the proofs was, up to now, contained in attendance notes, not all of which are reproduced in this case study.

The proofs are set out below as Documents 63, 64 and 65.

Document 63

Proof of evidence of Steven Rushkin, 12, Park View, Longfield, Oldcastle OL10 2AB

I am 44, and was born on 12 January 1953.

I live at the above property with my wife Jocelyn.

I am unable to follow my usual trade of painter and decorator at present because of an injury I sustained in October 1996, in a road accident. I work from time to time in the King's Arms public house in North View, Oldcastle. In April 1997 I was working about two evenings a week. The manager of the pub is Philip Gramsci.

My work consisted of general serving and cleaning up duties, and the start and finishing times would vary according to staff absences, and how busy things were.

On 18 April I went to work at about 5.30. It was a very busy evening, and I went in earlier than usual because of the expected pressure. As well as the usual numbers in the downstairs bars, we had a private function with buffet food in the upstairs function room. As well as the manager and myself, there were five other staff on duty. I estimate that at the busiest time that evening the pub had over 100 people in it.

I was at work either behind the bar or, when opportunities allowed, collecting glasses, emptying ash trays etc., throughout the evening. After last orders at 11.00 we all cleaned up the downstairs bars, finishing at about 11.30. Usually we can all go home then, but on this occasion there was still the remains of the private function to clear up. I agreed to stay, and Phil and I tackled it together.

We finally finished clearing up at midnight. I know it was no earlier because once we had finished Phil made a joke about my carriage turning into a pumpkin. I also knew what time it was, because I am paid by the hour, and receive my pay in cash at the end of every evening. That evening I worked 6½ hours and received £32.50. The rate of pay is £5 per hour.

As I left shortly after midnight I went to the pub car park to drive home. As I was driving out of the car park towards North View I saw Bob Chapman approaching from the Burn Street direction. I asked him where he was going, and he said he was looking for a taxi. Bob lives in the same street as me – I do not know the number, and I do not know him at all well. I offered him a lift, and he got in.

About five minutes later, as we travelled up North Road, we were pulled in by a police car. Two officers asked us to get out and we did so. They searched the car and removed a screwdriver set. They then arrested us.

The screwdriver set is one I bought from Woolford's about two years ago. It should contain six screwdrivers ranging from very small to big. My particular set was bought for use in the car. The largest screwdriver had been missing for some time, since the previous autumn, but it had not been necessary to replace it because the other screwdrivers were adequate for my purposes. The screwdriver had been taken by my wife Jocelyn who was decorating the hall and front bedroom at the time. I saw that she had used it to prise off paint lids, and for mixing the paint. We had an argument about this. After that I never saw the screwdriver again.

I have been shown a screwdriver apparently found in the rear yard of MegaWin on 19 April. It is of the same type as my set but it is not my screwdriver, which is still lost.

I have visited Burn Street and looked at the wall dividing the rear yard of MegaWin from the street. t is six feet tall. Because of my injuries I could not climb over it, even with time and even with assistance. My injuries are such that I cannot run, and I walk with a limp. I can work in the bar, but could not maintain a full time job.

I make the following comments on the statements of the prosecution witnesses.

R. Paling

The description appears to be accurate, but I was not the second man. I do not have a blue and green anorak, and on the evening of my arrest I was wearing a blue and yellow anorak.

PC Patel and PC Walker

Their account is accurate as far as I can remember.

PC Abrahams

Neither the screwdriver or the hat could have been mine as I was not present at the scene. I note that my fingerprints and my hair do not match these items.

W. Jones

I was not in MegaWin that evening, or indeed ever. If any suspicious characters were there that evening, I was not one of them. I cannot comment on his statement as I have no knowledge at all of the matters he describes.

Signed S. Rushkin

Dated 14 July 1997

Document 64

Proof of evidence of Philip Gramsci, of the King's Arms, North View, Oldcastle, who will say as follows:

I am the landlord of the King's Arms and have been employed in this capacity by Northern Breweries for five years.

I am aged 32 and have no criminal convictions.

I can remember the evening of 18 April 1997. We were open as usual, and I was serving all evening in the bar, which serves the lounge and the public bar. We also had a private function in the upstairs room, where we served a buffet and drinks to about 50 people.

One of my casual staff is Steven Rushkin, who works in the pub on an ad hoc basis when I need extra staff. I would estimate he works for me about two or three evenings a week, and I pay him cash in hand. During the week of 18–25 April I had asked Steven to come in every evening from 7.00 p.m. to whenever we finished clearing up, as one of the regular staff was sick. On Friday 18 April in fact I asked him to start earlier, at 5.30.

On that day Steven was on duty in the pub to my knowledge until midnight. He was the last of the staff to leave. I know he did not leave until midnight because when we had finally finished clearing up, a good deal later than usual because of the buffet, I remarked to him: 'look, it's midnight, hope your coach doesn't turn into a pumpkin on the way home', or words to that effect. He remarked that he was pleased he had the car as he did not want to have to wait for a taxi. I remember looking at the clock. I also remember because I pay Steven at the end of every night according to the hours worked, so I have to check the time when he is finished.

The clock I keep in the bar is accurate. I need to have exact times because of licensing laws and the need to pay staff by their hours worked.

Steven suffers from injuries caused by an accident before I knew him. He walks with a limp, but his work is not otherwise affected.

Signed P. Gramsci   Dated 14 July 1997

Document 65

> Proof of evidence of Jocelyn Rushkin, of 12, Park View, Longfield, Oldcastle OL10 2AB, who will say as follows:
>
> I am the wife of Steven Rushkin, to whom I have been married for 24 years. I have lived with him at the above address for about 13 years. Our daughter Claire lives there and our other two children left home some two or three years ago.
>
> I am asked to recall a screwdriver set kept in the back of our Ford Sierra. I can remember the set, as one Steve bought about 2 years ago. It is a Woolford's own brand set, and as far as I can remember, it has about 6 screwdrivers in it, ranging from very small (I presume for electrical use) to large (over 12 inches). The handles are all made of yellow plastic.
>
> The largest screwdriver has been missing from the set since last autumn. I took it out of the car and used it to lever off paint tin lids when I redecorated the hall and front room of our house last autumn. I remember Steve being angry with me for removing it from the car, and ridiculing me for getting it covered in paint, as I had used it to stir the paint. When I finished the painting I intended to put it back in the car, but I never got round to it, and now I cannot find it.
>
> I am sure that the screwdriver was not in the car on 18 April or at any time during that month.
>
> Steven was injured in a car crash in January 1996. He still suffers from the effects. He can only walk with a limp, cannot run, and has been unable to undertake heavy domestic work like gardening or painting since then.
>
> Signed J. Rushkin   Dated 14 July 1997

Brief to counsel to appear at the plea and directions hearing

Jane has completed the tasks following committal: the alibi notice; the bill of costs. She has continued with as many aspects of case preparation as possible — getting tape transcripts organised, medical evidence, and seeking further unused material. She cannot wait however until all these points are sorted; she must get on with the brief to counsel. (See 'timescale', above for reasons.)

The brief set out below is modelled on the guidance provided by the Law Society in its letter to local societies. It should be received by counsel within 21 days of committal in a bail case, or seven days in a custody case. This gives time for a conference with counsel no later than seven days after the brief is received, while still allowing a further 14 days before the plea and directions hearing.

I have taken the risk, in this brief, of using informal language. 'Instructing solicitors' becomes 'I', and 'Counsel' becomes 'you'. The second brief, Document 77, uses the old traditions. Readers are free to choose.

The front sheet for this brief is not reproduced here. It is marked LEGAL AID.

Document 66

IN THE OLDCASTLE CROWN COURT
Plea and Directions Hearing
24 July 1997

REGINA

-V-

STEVEN RUSHKIN

BRIEF TO COUNSEL TO ATTEND AT PDH

I enclose copies of the following:

1. Draft indictment
2. Notice under Criminal Justice Act 1988, s. 41
3. Through legal aid order
4. Prosecution statements consisting of
   - 4(i) R. Paling × 2
   - 4(ii) W. Jones
   - 4(iii) PC Patel
   - 4(iv) PC Walker
   - 4(v) Insp Edmonds (not reproduced in case study)
   - 4(vi) PC Abrahams
   - 4(vii) DC Stubbs.
5. Prosecution list of exhibits
6. Primary prosecution disclosure
7. Attendance note of conversation with Dr Hattersley (not reproduced)
8. Advance information and defendant's comments
9. Summary of police interviews with defendant and Mr R. Chapman
10. Attendance note for identification parade 2 May 1997
11. Initial statement of defendant
12. Proof of evidence of defendant
13. Statement of witness P. Gramsci
14. Proof of evidence of P. Gramsci
15. Statement of J. Rushkin
16. Proof of evidence of J. Rushkin
17. Defence disclosure statement
18. Police list of previous convictions of defendant
19. Police antecedents form
20. Extracts of correspondence with CPS
21. Draft plea and directions hearing judge's questionnaire

1. The defendant is indicted on a count of attempted burglary. It is alleged that he, together with Robert Chapman, attempted to break in to an amusement arcade called MegaWin at 11.55 on Friday 18th April 1997. Mr Chapman consented to summary trial and has been dealt with following a guilty plea in Oldcastle Central Magistrates' Court.

2. Mr Rushkin's instructions are that he is not guilty.

3. Mr Rushkin is also charged with a summary matter, driving whilst disqualified. He will plead guilty to this matter. He will appear before the Crown Court under s. 41, Criminal Justice Act 1988 for sentencing if convicted of the attempted burglary.

4. The matter was committed for trial on 3rd July 1997. No objection to committal was made under s. 6, Magistrates' Courts Act 1980, as I believe there to be a prima facie case.

5. The plea and directions hearing is listed for 24th July 1997 at 10.20 a.m. You are requested to advise in conference on a date to be arranged shortly, and to appear on behalf of the defendant at the plea and directions hearing. I intend to brief you for the trial itself, and please take this into account in considering listing arrangements.

6. Mr Rushkin is currently on conditional bail, subject to two sureties, each in the sum of £500. The sureties are Mr P. Gramsci and Mrs J. Rushkin, both of whom are potential defence witnesses.

7. Please advise in conference on all issues likely to arise at the plea and directions hearing, and generally on preparation for trial. A draft judge's questionnaire is enclosed indicating my current thinking on issues which will arise at the plea and directions hearing. [Note to the reader: by drafting these replies to the questionnaire, Jane has covered most of the issues which instructions to counsel should cover; you could equally well put the same material into the brief. One way or the other, make sure counsel has the benefit of your responses on each point in the questionnaire.]

8. Issues on which I am not yet able to complete the questionnaire are as follows.

Tapes of interview

9. The police interviews with the defendant show that the defendant's story has been virtually the same throughout, and consistent with the proof of evidence enclosed. I believe the balanced summary provided by the prosecution is inadequate; legal aid authority has been obtained for a full transcript, and this is expected within the next week. As soon as this is received, I will send a copy to the CPS for their agreement. If no agreement is forthcoming please request facilities for playing the tapes of interview at trial.

Medical evidence

10. The prosecution allege (evidence of R. Paling) that the defendant scaled a six foot wall. A report from Mr Rushkin's consultant orthopaedic surgeon has been commissioned, which, it is anticipated, will confirm that Mr Rushkin is unable to carry out such a feat because of pre-existing injuries. Until you have seen this report, it is not possible to inform the court of the witness's dates, as this particular witness may not be called and another report commissioned. You may prefer not to allude to this at the plea and directions hearing, as the prosecution could be assisted by knowing that a report was commissioned but then not used. The consultant, Dr Miller, is aware of the need to complete the report as soon as possible, and I will have attempted to speak to him if the report is not available at the plea and directions hearing.

Unused material

11. Primary prosecution disclosure has been made and a defence statement served. The prosecution have supplied a statement from Dr J. Hattersley, which does not form part of their case. I have spoken on the telephone to Dr Hattersley, and a copy of an attendance note is supplied with these instructions. You will see that Dr Hattersley's evidence of identification is vague, although supportive of the defence case that it was Chapman and another who carried out the attempt. Please advise in conference of the desirability of interviewing and calling Dr Hattersley, so that his availability can be checked before plea and directions hearing, and the questionnaire answered accordingly.

12. I have requested records of telephone conversations at Oldcastle Police Station, relating to the alleged break in attempt. Precise timings are crucial to the issue of alibi, in particular the time R. Paling made her call. If these details are not supplied before the plea and directions hearing please ask for a direction from the judge.

13. The outcome of forensic tests on a hair sample found on a hat at the scene, and tests for fingerprints on a screwdriver found at the scene, is not known to the defence. A request has been sent to the prosecution. Again, if responses have not been received please deal with this at the plea and directions hearing, and advise in conference on the possibility of obtaining forensic analysis for the defence, should this be necessary in light of the results of prosecution analysis.

14. The police have interviewed the alibi witness, Mr Gramsci. I am waiting for a copy of this which I believe should be available by way of secondary prosecution disclosure.

Admissions

15. Depending on the results of the forensic examinations referred to in paragraph 13, it may be possible to seek formal admissions under s. 10, Criminal Justice Act 1988, that the hair sample and fingerprints do not match the defendant (and if appropriate, do not match Mr Chapman). Such an admission can be sought at the plea and directions hearing if the forensic results are available in time and favour such a course.

16. Please advise in conference in respect of other admissions which can be sought or, if requested, granted. An admission that the wall at the back of MegaWin is six feet high is a possibility, and if this is not admitted, I will, if you advise, prepare formal evidence on the point, and this will increase the number of defence witnesses by one.

Other investigation

17. Draft replies to the judge's questionnaire are based on the assumption that there will be three defence witnesses including the defendant himself. Please consider whether further investigations should be carried out; the witness Jones, an employee of the victim company, mentions that two characters had been seen in the premises earlier that evening. If a description can be obtained, this will potentially assist in casting doubt on Ms Paling's testimony, especially if the second man is similar to the second man seen by Dr Hattersely with (presumably) Chapman. It is also possible that witnesses could be traced who saw Mr Chapman in the King's Arms with another man. If you advise, I will carry out investigations. This will mean the precise number of witnesses cannot be identified at the plea and directions hearing.

18. I understand from the CPS that a plan of the area is being prepared. I do not propose to duplicate this work, unless you advise, and any plan received may be admissible under s. 9, CJA 1967. Any plan and witness statment will be forwarded to you on receipt.

19. Please advise in conference on the possibility of calling Mr Chapman for the defence. Before he was sentenced, his solicitors provided an exchange of advance information, but since then there has been a refusal of any assistance. I suspect that Mr Chapman may wish to avoid revealing the identity of his accomplice. Given Chapman's refusal to co-operate, please consider the possibility of calling him as a witness for the defence.

Issues of law and admissibility

20. I have identified no point of legal argument or admissibility of evidence relevant to the plea and directions hearing. Of course you will need to remind the court at trial of the need to treat identification evidence with caution, but this will require no legal argument. Please consider whether other issues of law or admissibility of evidence arise which should be mentioned at the plea and directions hearing.

21. You are instructed to appear on behalf of the defendant at the plea and directions hearing on 24th July 1997 at 10.20.

JW

Conference with Counsel: New Square Chambers, Oldcastle: 21 July 1997:

Jane has arranged with counsel's clerk for a conference with counsel. This will be the first meeting between Steven and the barrister who will be conducting the trial. The earlier brief (Document 66) sets out the issues that are discussed. You will note from the brief that Jane has managed to contact Dr Hattersley. In the attendance note (which is not reproduced) she notes that he has little to add to his previous statement to the police and that he does not wish to attend court.

As a result of the conference, counsel advises that:

(a) Dr Hattersley must be asked to attend at trial, with a witness summons if necessary;

(b) Jane should try to interview MegaWin employees;

(c) the chances of success in finding drinkers at the King's Arms who would be able to help are too small to bother with;

(d) counsel will try to obtain the forensic evidence at the plea and directions hearing or an order for its disclosure;

(e) counsel will request at the plea and directions hearing that the CPS provide a plan of the area for use at trial;

(f) Paling, Patel, Walker and Abrahams are required to give oral testimony; the remaining statements can be read.

The Transcripts of Interviews: Tuesday 22 July 1997

The request for legal aid authorisation to obtain transcripts was granted earlier. Jane commissioned the transcripts, which she forwards to counsel so that these can be agreed with the prosecution, if possible, at the plea and directions hearing.

Relevant extracts from the transcript are set out below.

Document 67

R v Rushkin

Transcript of tape recorded interview, exhibit PS1 tape ref PS200494/3, prepared by Legal Transcripts Ltd, 5, High Road, Oldcastle OL11.

The transcript starts by identifying the parties present: DC Stubbs, Steven Rushkin and Jane Watkins. The caution is read out, and for the first few minutes [not reproduced here] Mr Rushkin is questioned about the driving offence, which he fully admits. [This extract we show commences at 7 min 30 sec.]

Question: You know why you are here, Mr Rushkin, do you, apart from the driving? Something a little more serious.

Answer: Yes.

Q: Well then, tell us what you have to say about it. Take your time, I want to hear everything.

A: There isn't much to say. I had nothing to do with a break in.

Q: Well, there's a number of points I'm going to need to put to you. You'd better think extremely carefully how you answer these questions. All the evidence we have points a finger at you. Shall we take them one by one?

A: Mmm mm.

Q: O.K., here's the first. Take a look at this screwdriver I'm now holding, exhibit WA1. It's in a bag, I know, but you can see it quite clearly, can you? Do you recognise it?

A: No I don't.

Q: Read the name on it. Go on.

8 min 00 sec

A: Woolford's.

Q: Woolford, that's it. Now, I've got some more screwdrivers. These ones aren't in a bag, because we know exactly where they come from, don't we?

A: Does not reply.

Q: Don't we? Do you know where this set came from? Where we found it? Just a few hours ago? In someone's car?

A: Yes, I know. My car.

Q: What's the name on the box, and on each of the screwdrivers?

A: Woolford's.

Q: Good, we're getting there fast. Do you see the connection?

A: No.

Q: I had hoped you would. Perhaps you do, or you will when I spell it out. This screwdriver was found at the amusement arcade tonight, where someone who was trying to break into the place had dropped it. And this screwdriver fits your set. See? It's not just the same type. It's the one that is actually missing from your set. See? A perfect match. Ever so neat. Come on, Steven, you were there, weren't you. Bob has admitted he was there. We found him in your car. We found your screwdriver at the scene of the crime. Come on.

8 min 30 sec

A: That missing screwdriver has been missing for ages. The one you've got is not from my set.

Q: I find that very hard to believe. Tell us where you bought the screwdrivers.

A: A couple of years ago, at Woolfords in Longfield. I keep them in the car all the time.

Q: With one missing?

A: I don't know what happened to it; it went missing a long time ago, and I still had enough to do any jobs on the car that I might have to. I didn't need the big one.

Q: Lost it a while ago. I'm afraid I'm not convinced. But let's move on. Oh, but before I do, we think there may be some fingerprints on this screwdriver. Would you let us have a sample of your fingerprints so we can compare? Or is that something you'd rather we didn't do.

Solicitor: I was not aware that you were planning to raise this matter during the taped interview, and I should like to speak to my client in private for a couple of minutes.

Q: Go ahead. Do you want to take a break?

Tape switched off. Resumption at tape counter 9 min 04 secs.

Q: I'm now resuming the tape after an interval of three minutes thirty seconds. You understand that you are still under caution, Mr Rushkin?

A: Yes.

Q: Are you ready to continue?

A: Yes.

Q: Right, about the fingerprints?

A: Yes, you can take them.

Q: Good. Wearing gloves were you? Is that why you agree?

Solicitor: Officer, I must object to that question. My client agrees to provide a sample of fingerprints on my advice.

Q: O.K. We'll move on. The screwdriver isn't the most important evidence, you know. You were found in the company of a man who admits the offence. And you were seen by a witness who describes you and Chapman exactly. So you're going to need to tell me exactly where you were, when, who with and all of that, if you expect us to believe your story at all.

Solicitor: Officer, I must advise my client not to attempt to answer that question, as you are asking more than one question at a time. If you want to know where my client was, will you please tell him exactly what time it is that you need to know about?

9 min 30 sec

Q: Thank you, that's very helpful. Mr Rushkin, we know that Mr Chapman and one other person was seen at 5 to 12 trying to hack open a window at MegaWin. Where were you at that time if it wasn't you?

A: In the King's Arms.

Q: Really? At five to 12? Shouldn't it have been shut by then? Come on.

A: I work there.

Q: We thought you were unemployed. What do you mean you work there?

A: I was working there tonight. I work there sometimes, when they need help.

Q: O.K. When did you leave?

A: Just after midnight.

Q: That's handy. But how do you know? Who saw you leave?

A: I left then because that's when I finished working. Phil can tell you. He was there. He paid me off.

Q: Phil who? How much did he pay you?

A: I don't know his surname. He runs the King's Arms.

10 mins 00 secs

Q: Well, we can check that. How much do you earn?

A: Five pounds an hour.

Q: When we picked you up, you didn't have a wage slip or a pay packet on you. How do you account for that?

A: I just get cash. By the hour, paid in hand. You know.

Q: I know, avoids nasty things like tax, and losing your benefits. Very handy. But is it true? I think you were in the pub alright, because that's where Mr Chapman says he was before he went off to do the Amusement Arcade. You were drinking with him.

A: No I wasn't, I didn't see him all evening until I was leaving the car park after I left work.

Q: After midnight?

A: Yes.

Q: You seem very sure of that. How come?

A: Because I don't usually work that late, and we were very busy, so we had to work out how much extra time I had done before Phil could pay me.

Q: You know the witness who saw you gave a very good description of you and Bob?

A: Well, she's wrong. It wasn't me, I wasn't there.

Q: So there you are, it's your screwdriver, you're picked up with a man who confesses the whole thing, a witness describes the two of you...

A: What is Bob saying?

10 min 30 sec

Q: I see you are worried. He admits he did it. He admits another man was with him. But he won't name that other man. Honour among thieves, no doubt you know what I mean. Anyway, we'll get a parade if you're insisting on saying it wasn't you. I think when the witness picks you out, you may decide to think again. Will you go on a parade?

A: Should I?

Solicitor: I will just confer with my client.

The tape is stopped and resumes with the counter at 11 min 06 sec.

Q: I'm now resuming the taping after a break of 1 minute 10 seconds. As before, Mr Rushkin, you're under caution, are you ready to proceed?

Solicitor: Mr Rushkin is happy to attend a parade, and I will want to be notified when it takes place.

Q: I think we can't get much further at the moment, can we?

Solicitor: I understand that there is an allegation from the identification witness that my client ran off from the scene of the attempted break in and climbed over a six foot wall. I would ask you to put that allegation at this early opportunity.

Q: Right. Let's see. The witness says she's looking out, there's the two men, one of them hacking away at the window with a screwdriver, and the other, who fits your description, standing on the ground. Suddenly you see her, or maybe the burglar alarm frightens you, it doesn't matter. You don't want to be seen around. You head for the wall and over into Burn Street as quick as you can. What do you want to say to that?

12 min 00 sec

A: I couldn't climb a wall that's six foot high. I got badly smashed up in a car crash two years back, I have permanent pain in my legs and back, I'm unable to work, and there's no way I could climb a wall, no way.

Q: Are you quite sure of what you are saying Mr Rushkin? You can't work. And yet you are giving us an alibi that if we are expected to believe it means you were at work at the very time we say you were out trying to get into MegaWin with Bob. I don't think you are doing all that well at the moment.

A: I can't do my proper job is what I meant. I used to be a painter and decorator like. I had to stop that. All I can do is the odd bit of casual work.

Document 68

Second interview: 2 May 1997

1 min 06 sec

Q: Well, as I expected, she picked you out Mr Rushkin. You've got to hand it to me, that's what I said she would do. Well, what do you say now? I know your solicitor will want me to put everything clearly to you, so here we go. One, we find you in the company of Bob Chapman, who admits the offence. Two, a witness gives a description of the two people she saw, and she describes Bob accurately, and we know that's accurate because he has admitted it. And she gives a good description of you. Three, she picks you out in a parade. Four, we have your screwdriver set and you can't deny that the one we found at the scene fits it perfectly where you say yours is missing. Have I missed anything out? I think four is pretty strong.

1 min 30 sec

A: All I wish to say is that it was not me. I was in the King's Arms up till midnight, and then I went straight to my car, drove out of the car park, stopped to pick up Bob, drove off towards home and then got arrested. I didn't commit any offence.

Q: You tried to break into MegaWin with Bob.

A: No. Anyway, I know you've talked to Phil and he's told you where I was.

Q: How do you know that?

A: I've talked to him, I've been back at work a few nights, and he told me you'd been to visit him.

Q: And what do you think he told us?

A: The same.

2 min 00 sec

Q: A man who helps you to commit a social security fraud and seems to be a good friend of yours is not likely to carry much weight with the court. He certainly didn't persuade me that all my other evidence is wrong. I think it's time to have you charged. Is there anything else you want to say?

A: I know I was at the pub till midnight. I know it wasn't me. Why don't you get Bob to tell you that it wasn't me, even if he won't tell you who it was.

2 min 30 sec

Q: Thank you for that suggestion. I'll do my job, and talk to who I think I need to, thank you. And don't you go telling Bob what to say, now will you?

Solicitor intervenes to assure Rushkin he does not have to answer that question.

Interview terminates at 3 min 20 sec.

Plea and Directions Hearing: Oldcastle Crown Court: 24 July 1997

There are no matters of law on which binding rulings are required before the trial (for example, although the defence will wish to challenge Ms Paling's evidence, there is no suggestion that it is so manifestly unreliable or irrelevant as to have an adverse effect of the fairness of the proceedings, so that it should be excluded under s. 78, PACE 1984). The plea and directions hearing is therefore primarily concerned with identifying matters that need to be dealt with before trial.

Thus witness attendance is confirmed. Counsel for the prosecution and defence agree a time estimate of three days for the trial, and the court is provided with details as to witness and counsel's availability. The defence barrister successfully argues that since it is likely that the defence will wish to call medical evidence, as well as factual evidence from a doctor (Dr Hattersley), and in view of the large number of witnesses, the trial should be given a fixed date rather than being listed as a 'floater' (i.e., a case which will be placed in a warned list and which will come on for trial at very little notice).

A number of very useful discussions take place with the prosecution:

(a) The transcripts: the prosecution confirm that they will accept the transcripts as accurate records of the interviews.

(b) The forensic evidence: the prosecution also states that the forensic analysts have confirmed that there is no match between hairs recovered from the hat and Steven's hair sample. Only partial prints were recovered from the screwdriver, but these do not match Steven's fingerprints.

(c) The unused material: the prosecution have looked at the notebooks, telephone log and the interview with Chapman, but these are consistent with material already served and do not support the defence account. They confirm that Gramsci's statement will be served by way of secondary prosecution disclosure.

(d) Address of the witness: Ms. Paling's address is disclosed.

The trial is fixed to start on Friday 12 September 1997.

After the Plea and Directions Hearing: Preparing for Trial

There seems to now be a long(ish) gap between the plea and directions hearing and trial date. This has arisen in this case because the court has agreed to fix a trial date, but obviously it has been difficult to find four clear days when all prosecution and defence witnesses can attend. (In the normal course of events, cases are not listed for a fixed date but are placed in a 'warned list'. Every week the local solicitors will receive a list from the Crown Court stating which cases are 'warned' for the next week or fortnight. Once notified, the solicitors are on notice that the court may ring on any afternoon during this 'warned' period to tell them that the case will start on the next morning. The solicitors must therefore ask their clients to ring them after five every afternoon, starting on the Friday before the warned list starts, to check to see if the case has been listed for the following day.)

Jane has a fair amount of work to complete before the trial. Secondary prosecution disclosure will have to be considered, once it has been received. She will need to chase up the defence medical report, which will have to be served on the prosecution. Steps need to be taken to confirm the lack of forensic evidence linking Steven to the offence, and the CPS have agreed to serve a plan of the vicinity for use at trial.

Secondary Prosecution Disclosure: 29 July 1997:

Document 69

Crown Prosecution Service,
Oldcastle Chambers,
Derry Street,
Oldcastle OL2 1CP.

Watkins & O'Dwyer,
17, Sycamore Avenue,
Oldcastle OL10 2BR.
(Please refer to the URN in any correspondence)

29 July 1997

Dear Sirs,

R v STEVEN RUSHKIN
OLDCASTLE CROWN COURT   PLEA AND DIRECTIONS HEARING: 24 JULY 1997
Disclosure of Prosecution Material under section 3, Criminal Procedure and Investigations Act 1996

I have considered your defence statement dated 14 July 1997 provided under section 5, Criminal Procedure and Investigations Act 1996. Under section 7, Criminal Procedure and Investigations Act 1996 I am required to disclose to you any prosecution material which has not previously been disclosed and which might reasonably be expected to assist your defence, as described in your statement.

A copy of a schedule of non-sensitive unused material prepared by the police has already been sent to you. The items listed below are those which I consider might reasonably be expected to assist your defence, as described in your statement. The numbers refer to the numbers on the schedule previously provided. Where indicated, copies of the items listed are attached. Material marked as available for inspection can be viewed by arrangement with myself.

Item	Description	Copy	Insp.
3	Statement: Gramsci	Yes	N/a

This material is disclosed to you in accordance with the provisions of the Criminal Procedure and Investigations Act 1996, and you must not use or disclose it, or any information recorded in it for any purpose other than in connection with these criminal proceedings. If you do so without the permission of the court, you may commit an offence.

If you consider that there is other prosecution material which might assist your defence and which has not already been disclosed, please let me know and I will reconsider my decision in the light of any further information that you provide. Alternatively, you may apply to the court under section 8, Criminal Procedure and Investigations Act 1996. The court will assess your application in the light of your defence statement.

If you request access to any item which has been marked for disclosure by inspection, it is essential that you preserve this letter in its present form, as access will only be granted upon production of this letter and the schedule previously provided to the person supervising access.

If you have a query in connection with this letter, please contact myself.

Yours faithfully,

Maureen Docherty,
Reviewing Lawyer
Crown Prosecution Service

The statement of Philip Gramsci, the publican, is enclosed with the letter. It is very short and adds nothing to the statement which Jane took from him at the start of the case.

The prosecution have already assured the defence at the plea and directions hearing that there is no disclosable material within the remaining items on the disclosure schedule. The police notebooks will doubtless be seen at trial, since many officers use them in the witness box when giving evidence, thereby entitling the defence advocate to have a look at the notebooks. Jane already knows the basic content of the Chapman's interview, and although she would like to listen to the tape just to make sure there is nothing useful on it, she decides to accept the prosecution assurance that it does not support her client's account and she therefore lets sleeping dogs lie.

On the other hand, the lack of any forensic evidence is potentially useful. Indeed, on the basis of what the prosecution said at the plea and directions hearing the evidence appears to rule out Steven's involvement, at least to the extent that it indicates that any hairs found in the hat and any fingerprints on the screwdriver are not his.

Jane contacts the CPS to discuss the failure to disclose the formal statements from the forensic scientists and is told that the statements have still not been received. It is agreed that Jane will therefore draft formal admissions which the CPS will agree; these will then be used at trial to the same effect as the missing forensic statements. During the discussion with the CPS, Jane learns that there is no forensic link between Chapman and the fingerprints or the hair. Her proposed admissions are drafted to include this fact.

It is helpful to obtain one or more of these admissions, since they can partially damage the inference the prosecution are seeking to draw: Rushkin must have been involved because the screwdriver must have been his. Someone's fingerprints and someone's hat were found – but not Rushkin's. To prove this point would be difficult for the defence. It would mean calling a police fingerprint analyst. The defence could not be sure to establish the point in cross-examination of any prosecution witnesses, as the police witnesses called may not have first hand knowledge of any fingerprinting.

Similar inferences could be drawn in relation to the woollen hat, and the hair sample. Also, the defence could write to the CPS and ask whose hair, if any, was identified on the hat, and whose fingerprints on the screwdriver. If the answer is: not Chapman, there is a glimpse of light in that the defence can argue that someone else must have been there. If any of the material, admissions and requests for information are not dealt with, Counsel could be asked to bring these up at the plea and directions hearing.

Formal Admissions

Defence solicitors should be aware of the potential uses of s. 10, Criminal Justice Act 1967, which operates in a similar way to the better known Notice to Admit Facts in the civil courts. It carries no automatic cost consequences, however, if the recipient refuses to make an admission. But it enables the defence to concentrate their preparation on issues which are disputed, and to avoid preparation on issues which may be more thorough than the Legal Aid Board will pay for.

If the defence do not obtain an admission, the alternative is to put the matter to a particular witness in cross-examination (never guaranteed to work; the witness may say 'I don't know') or to call such evidence as they need themselves (which is the expensive part, and many of the witnesses will be potential prosecution witnesses.)

With the implementation of plea and directions hearings in all Crown Court cases, the normal place to seek a formal admission is at the plea and directions hearing. However, it can be sought in writing after the plea and directions hearing, as here, or in the magistrates' court, where there is no plea and directions hearing.

Document 70

> # Watkins & O'Dwyer
> ## Solicitors
>
> *17, Sycamore Avenue,*
> *Oldcastle OL10 1BR.*
> *Tel. 011-111-1111*
> *Fax 011-111-1111*
> *DX Oldcastle 1000*
>
> Partners: J. Watkins
> A. O'Dwyer
>
> Crown Prosecution Service,
> Oldcastle Chambers,
> Derry Street,
> Oldcastle OL2 1CP.
>
> Your ref: MB/0217
> Our ref: JW/Rushkin
>
> 1 August 1997
>
> Dear Sir/Madam,
>
> R v Rushkin
>
> We enclose a draft formal admission under s. 10 of the Criminal Justice Act 1967. If the prosecution is in a position to make the admissions, we should be pleased to hear from you as soon as possible in order to avoid the necessity of calling evidence on these matters.
>
> Yours faithfully.
>
> Watkins & O'Dwyer
>
> Enclosure

The admission shown below is returned by the CPS after the plea and directions hearing, but before trial.

Document 71

> <u>IN THE OLDCASTLE CROWN COURT</u>   Case No. OL2000
>
> R v RUSHKIN
>
> The Crown Prosecution Service for the purpose of proceedings against Steven Rushkin for attempted burglary make the following admission(s):
>
> 1. Fingerprint samples taken from a screwdriver (exhibit WA1) are not those of the defendant Steven Rushkin.
>
> 2. Fingerprint samples taken from screwdriver exhibit WA1 are not those of Robert Chapman.
>
> 3. No hair sample taken from a woollen hat found in the yard of MegaWin on 19 April 1997 matched the hair of Steven Rushkin.
>
> 4. No hair sample taken from a woollen hat found in the yard of MegaWin on 19 April 1997 matched the hair of Robert Chapman.
>
> Signed on behalf of CPS
>
> Dated 8 August 1997

The CPS duly sign and return the admissions.

Additional Evidence: 11 August 1997

Shortly after the plea and directions hearing, the defence receive a notice of additional evidence. It is served under the Criminal Justice Act 1967, s. 9 which means that the defence must object within seven days if they do not want the evidence adduced in the absence of the maker of the statement.

Document 72A

IN THE CROWN COURT AT OLDCASTLE   Indictment No. OL2000

NOTICE OF INTENTION TO ADDUCE ADDITIONAL EVIDENCE

R v S RUSHKIN

TAKE NOTICE that upon the trial of the above named it is proposed under the provisions of Section 9 of the Criminal Justice Act 1967 to adduce the evidence of the following witnesses contained in the attached statements.

Additional statement	Page number	Documents
P. PLUMBER		Plan annexed (PP1)

Would you confirm that you accept service of the notice and accompanying statements on behalf of your client?

Please note that unless you inform the Crown Prosecution Service within 7 days of receipt of this Notice that you require the witness to attend to give evidence you will lose your right to prevent the statements being tendered in evidence and you will not be able to require the attendance of the witnesses without the leave of the Court.

Dated this 11th day of August 1997

Crown Prosecution Service

Document 72B

Witness Statement

(CJ Act 1967, s. 9, MC Act 1980, ss. 5A(3)(a) and 5B, MC Rules 1981, r. 70)

Statement of Philip Plumber

Age if under 18   over 18 (if over 18 insert 'over 18')

Occupation Plan Drawer

This statement (consisting of 1 page(s) each signed by me) is true to the best of my knowledge and belief and I make it knowing that, if it is tendered in evidence, I shall be liable to prosecution if I have wilfully stated in it anything which I know to be false or do not believe to be true.

Dated the 4th day of August 1997

Signature P. Plumber

I am a detective constable employed by Oldcastle Police. My duties include drawing plans.

On Monday 4 August 1997 as a result of a request by the Crown Prosecution Service I prepared a pencil drawn plan of the layout of the scene of the alleged crime at MegaWin Amusement Arcade on 18 April 1997. As requested, I have marked the following locations: MegaWin, MegaWin rear yard, and downstairs toilet window; security light above rear yard; position of Ms Paling's window on Burn Street; King's Arms public house and car park. I now produce this plan, which is not to strict scale, as exhibit PP1.

Signed P. Plumber   Signature witnessed by P. Stubbs

R v RUSHKIN

Document 72C

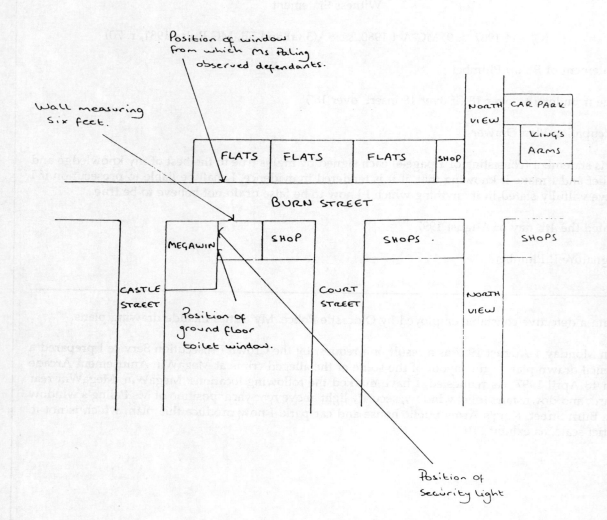

The plan at first appears to be innocuous, and is certainly useful in preparing the case. However, Jane does not like one aspect of it, and therefore objects to the evidence of the witness being tendered as presented.

Document 73

Watkins & O'Dwyer
Solicitors

17, Sycamore Avenue,
Oldcastle OL10 1BR.
Tel. 011-111-1111
Fax 011-111-1111
DX Oldcastle 1000

Partners: J. Watkins
A. O'Dwyer

Crown Prosecution Service,
Oldcastle Chambers,
Derry Street,
Oldcastle OL2 1CP.

Your ref: MB/0217
Our ref: JW/Rushkin

14 August 1997

Dear Sir/Madam,

R v Steven Rushkin
Criminal Justice Act 1967, s. 9

Thank you for the notice of additional evidence received on 13.8.97. We would have no objection to the tendering of this evidence, if the reference to what the witness saw is removed from the plan, since this is a matter which can only be established, if at all, by her own evidence.

If you will kindly re-serve the statement and exhibit with that alteration, we shall have no objection to the plan being submitted in the absence of DC Plumber.

Yours faithfully,

Watkins & O'Dwyer

The plan is duly amended and becomes part of the evidence. (Not reproduced here.)

The Expert Evidence

Steven stated in his first interview with the police that he was medically incapable of the feat of running or climbing a six foot wall. Immediately after mode of trial was decided Jane sought legal aid authority to incur the cost of obtaining a medical report.

The report is now obtained, with a covering letter.

Document 74A

Dr P. Miller FRCS,
Orthopaedic Surgeon,
General Hospital,
Oldcastle.

Tel: 011-111-2222

8, Grange Street,
Gosfield,
Oldcastle.

Tel: 011-555-6666

14 August 1997

Dear Ms Watkins,

I have pleasure in enclosing my report on Steven Rushkin, and I have taken the opportunity of enclosing my fee note for your kind attention.

You have asked me specifically whether in my opinion Mr Rushkin is capable of climbing over a six foot wall. It is my opinion that in view of his injuries this is very unlikely. Having seen Mr Rushkin several times since his accident I can confirm that I would have no reason to expect him to be able to achieve this on 18 April.

However, I must point out that there are no physical signs of the injuries, which will be obvious to any orthopaedic surgeon reading my report. This in no way detracts from my conviction that Mr Rushkin's complaints are entirely genuine.

If I can assist further will you kindly let me know. Please note that I am unavailable for attending court between 22 and 26 August 1997 and again on 14 to 18 October 1997.

Yours sincerely,

Paul Miller

Document 74B

Paul Miller FRCS

Medical Report on Steven Rushkin

Date of birth 12 January 1953

Date of examination 1 August 1997

History

On 28 January 1996 this man was driving with his wife when his car was involved in a head on crash with the side of a taxi which had apparently turned across its path.

He and his wife were both taken to the Casualty Department at Oldfield General Hospital by ambulance. He was suffering from shock and severe pains in his neck and upper back. He was examined and found to be tender over the cervical, thoracic and upper lumbar spine, and all movement of his spine was limited by pain. X rays of his cervical spine showed some degenerative changes in the 4th and 6th vertebrae, but there was no evidence of bony injury. X rays of the thoracic and lumbar spines were normal.

He was provided with a cervical collar and some anti-inflammatory analgesics and sent home to rest. The next day he called his general practitioner as he was in so much pain that he could barely get out of bed. He was prescribed stronger pain killers and some muscle relaxants and advised to rest.

Over the course of the next two months he consulted his GP eight times with continuing pain, although with the help of pain killers he was able to move around with some difficulty. He was referred for physiotherapy, and had six treatments in the physiotherapy department. At the end of this time he was able to walk short distances and his back and neck pain were slightly improved.

He has not worked since the accident.

Present Complaints

At the time of the examination he had the following complaints:

1. He has continuous pain in his neck and shoulders, aggravated by any movement of his head, particularly looking up and turning from side to side.

2. He has intermittent pain in his back. This is aggravated by bending and sudden movement. He can only walk a quarter of a mile before he has to stop because of pain.

3. He has tingling in his left hand and tends to drop things.

4. He gets shooting pains down the outer part of both legs, particularly the left. These are made much worse by bending, and by having to stand for long periods.

5. He continues to be prescribed analgesics by his general practitioner.

On Examination

He is 6' 0" tall and of slim build. He looks healthy but walks slowly with a pronounced limp.

All his back movements were limited by pain in the lumbar region. He could forward flex only until his finger tips reached his kneecaps. Extension was negligible and he had only 10 degrees of lateral flexion on either side. Straight leg raising was 30 degrees on the left and 50 degrees on the right. Reflexes and sensation in his legs were normal, but power in both legs was reduced by pain.

His spine was tender over the 2nd and 3rd lumbar vertebrae and over both sacro-iliac joints. He also had tenderness over the 4th – 6th cervical vertebrae and to both sides of the cervical spine, particularly the left.

Forward neck flexion was reduced to half the expected range, and extension was almost non-existent. Lateral flexion and rotation were reduced by about 50% to the right and 70% to the left.

Arm reflexes and sensation were normal, but the power of his grip was reduced on the left.

Opinion

This man appears to be significantly disabled by the problems in his back and neck. His mobility is significantly restricted and even slow walking produces obvious pain. His inability to look upwards (because of the restricted movement of his neck), the reduced grip in his left hand, and the pain and limited movement of his back would all make it extremely unlikely that he would be able to either run or climb over a six foot wall.

Paul Miller
2 August 1997

In order to try to obtain agreement on this report, and because of the need in any event to disclose expert evidence in Crown Court cases as soon as possible after committal, a common approach is to draft a short statement for the expert to sign, and to send this to the prosecution under Criminal Justice Act 1967, s. 9.

Document 75

Watkins & O'Dwyer
Solicitors

17, Sycamore Avenue,
Oldcastle OL10 1BR.
Tel. 011-111-1111
Fax 011-111-1111
DX Oldcastle 1000

Partners: J. Watkins
A. O'Dwyer

Crown Prosecution Service,
Oldcastle Chambers,
Derry Street,
Oldcastle OL2 1CP.

Your ref: MB/0217
Our ref: JW/Rushkin

15 August 1997

Dear Sir/Madam,

We enclose, in accordance with the Crown Court (Advance Notice of Expert Evidence) Rules 1987 a copy of a report dated 2 August 1997 and covering letter from Dr P. Miller, Orthopaedic Surgeon at the Oldfield General Hospital. Please note that Dr Miller's report is served with a statement under Criminal Justice Act 1967, s. 9. The defence will call Dr Miller unless his report can be agreed.

Yours faithfully.

Watkins & O'Dwyer

The statement exhibiting the report and signed by Dr Miller is enclosed.

Document 76

| IN THE OLDCASTLE CROWN COURT | Case No. OL2000 |

R v Rushkin

Witness Statement

Criminal Justice Act 1967, s. 9

Statement of Dr Paul Miller FRCS

Age over 18

Occupation Orthopaedic Surgeon

This statement (consisting of 1 page signed by me) is true to the best of my knowledge and belief and I make it knowing that, if it is tendered in evidence, I shall be liable to prosecution if I have wilfully stated in it anything which I know to be false or do not believe to be true.

Dated the 14th day of August 1997

Signature P. Miller

On 2 August 1997 I prepared a report of my findings and conclusions in respect of Mr Steven Rushkin's medical condition. This report is produced by me as exhibit PM1.

Signed Paul Miller   Witnessed Jonathan Shaw

The s. 9 format is not strictly necessary, since if the prosecution are prepared to agree the medical evidence, they will indicate this. Also, under s. 30, Criminal Justice Act 1988, the report is admissible in the absence of Dr Miller with the leave of the court. In any event, if the medical evidence is disputed, Dr Miller is likely to have to attend if the jury is to be persuaded.

Witness Summons

Jane has spoken with Dr Hattersley over the telephone. He does not wish to attend court. She decides, having conferred with counsel, that his attendance at trial should be compelled. A witness summons can be obtained from the Crown Court office on request, and must be served on the witness (the rules surprisingly do not state a time limit for doing this). The form is taken from the White Book, and is laid down by r. 10, RSC Ord. 79.

Under the Criminal Procedure and Investigations Act 1996 it will be necessary to have a reason for compelling a witness to attend. However, this provision has not yet been implemented. Until this comes into force no reason is needed.

R v RUSHKIN

Document 77

Witness summons

OLDCASTLE CROWN COURT   Case No. OL2000

[Royal arms]

To Dr Joseph Hattersley of 15, Water Down Mansions, Glanville Road, Oldcastle OL12

You are hereby summonsed to attend before the Crown Court at Oldcastle at the Court House, Court Street, Oldcastle OL1 on the 12th day of September 1997 at 10.00 o'clock to give evidence on behalf of Steven Rushkin on an indictment for attempted burglary and to attend from day to day until the said indictment is tried.

Issued on the 20th day of August 1997 by Watkins & O'Dwyer, solicitors for the defendant.

Briefing Counsel for Trial

At the plea and directions hearing counsel will already have needed to understand the issues in the case. The brief for trial could, therefore, be just that: brief. However, even under the new system of plea and directions hearings, during the trial period at least, returned briefs were far from eliminated. A returned brief arises where counsel of choice — or his/her clerk, more probably — rings the solicitor shortly before the trial and says 'Awfully sorry old chap, part heard in another case'. A last minute substitute becomes necessary, so a good set of instructions will help that new barrister get on top of the issues in a short time. For this reason I have included a full evidential analysis in this brief – but there is a school of thought that putting a piece of ribbon round the papers and asking counsel to do his/her best is sufficient instructions.

The following brief is drafted in the old style, using the third person rather than 'I' and 'you'.

Document 78

IN THE OLDCASTLE CROWN COURT   Indictment No. OL2000

Trial fixed for 12 September 1997

REGINA

v

STEVEN RUSHKIN

BRIEF TO COUNSEL TO APPEAR AT TRIAL

Documents provided with these instructions are copies of the following:

All papers previously before counsel and the following additional documents:
22. Transcripts of telephone calls at Central Police Station (not supplied with this case study)
23. Transcripts of police interviews with defendant
24. Formal admission
25. Photographs of scene of alleged crime (not supplied with this case study)
26. Report of Dr P. Miller with covering letter
27. Additional prosecution witness statement and plan

1. Counsel will be aware of the issues in this case as a result of advising in conference and representing Mr Rushkin at plea and directions hearing on 24 July 1997.

2. Mr Rushkin has entered a plea of not guilty, and remains on bail to attend trial on 12 September 1997.

3. Of the prosecution witnesses, Paling, Patel, Walker, and Abrahams were required, on counsel's advice, to attend trial. Their statements are shown in enclosure 4. The oral evidence of Stubbs, Edmonds and Jones was not required. The evidence of PC Plumber (enclosure 27) has been accepted by the defence under s. 9, CJA 1967. The exhibits listed in the prosecution schedule (enclosure 5) will all be produced at trial.

4. The defence witnesses will be the defendant (encl 12), the alibi witness Mr Gramsci (encl 14), Mrs Rushkin (encl 16), Dr Hattersley (encl 6), and the medical witness Dr Miller (encl 26). The alibi evidence was disclosed after transfer (see encl 20), and the medical evidence was disclosed on 15 August 1997. The prosecution have been unable to agree this evidence and the witness has agreed to attend without a witness summons. The witness Dr Hattersley, for whom a proof of evidence is not available and who was reluctantly interviewed on the telephone (encl 7), has been summonsed to attend trial. On counsel's advice, Mr Chapman has not been approached. Counsel will recall advising instructing solicitors to interview employees at MegaWin who might give a description of suspicious characters seen earlier that evening (as reported by Mr Jones, enclosure 4(vii)). Attempts to find any such person have proved futile.

5. A formal admission (enclosure 24) has been obtained in respect of forensic evidence. Transcripts of interview (enclosure 24) were agreed at the plea and directions hearing.

6. Trial length is estimated at two days, and instructing solicitors believe this estimate remains accurate. Instructing solicitors intend, unless counsel advises otherwise, to inform the court as is required by the plea and directions hearing rules that all directions have now been complied with.

The Prosecution Case

7. The details of the circumstances leading to Mr Rushkin's arrest will be found in the prosecution statements. In summary, the prosecution allege that on 18 April 1997 Mr Rushkin met up with Mr Robert Chapman, a man who lives in the same street as Mr Rushkin, and together they attempted a break in at MegaWin Amusement Arcade, which is situated at the junction of Castle Street and Burn Street. Evidence has been disclosed in Mr Jones' statement (with an indication that the prosecution do not intend to rely on it) that an employee told Mr Jones there were two suspicious men in the arcade earlier in the evening. Enquiries by instructing solicitors, on counsel's advice, were unsuccessful in identifying this employee.

8. The break in was attempted by two men at 11.55 p.m. They were seen at a downstairs window in the enclosed rear yard of MegaWin. A description fitting Chapman has him standing on an upturned dustbin, and the man alleged to be Rushkin standing keeping watch.

9. An alarm went off, the exact time unknown. This woke a witness, R. Paling, who watched from a flat in Burn Street about 40 yards away. When the two men saw they were being watched, they ran off quickly, climbing over the wall dividing MegaWin's yard from Burn Street. The witness phoned the police with descriptions.

10. Presumably the prosecution allege that Chapman and Rushkin then went on foot to the car park at the Kings Arms, which is about 300 yards away (see map, enclosure 27). As they left there, they were observed by two police officers on mobile patrol, who followed, overtook, and arrested them. The defence are unsure what the prosecution may allege took place between 11.56, when the men escaped down Burn Street, and 12.07, when the defendant was first seen with Mr Chapman.

11. A screwdriver found at the scene of the crime was found to match a set in Mr Rushkin's car, and that set had a screwdriver missing of exactly that size. Instructing solicitors have inspected this evidence and confirm that the screwdriver found at MegaWin matches the set in Mr Rushkin's car boot. The prosecution accept that there is no fingerprint evidence linking either Mr Rushkin or Mr Chapman to this screwdriver.

12. Mr Chapman confessed to the police before Mr Rushkin was interviewed. In the summary of his interview (enclosure 9) Mr Chapman states that he was with another man, but declines to name him. He was drinking with this man in the King's Arms before the attempt. However, no notice of intention to call Chapman as a witness has been served by the prosecution, even though Mr Chapman has been dealt with in the Central Magistrates' Court already, having elected summary trial and pleaded guilty.

13. The prosecution supplied details of an unused witness, Dr J. R. Hattersley (enclosure 6). Instructing solicitors were able to contact this witness by telephone and he confirmed the information given to the police, but said he was unsure of the details of the descriptions of the two men. He declined to be interviewed further. On counsel's advice this witness has been served with a witness order.

The Defence Case

14. The defence case is simple. Mr Rushkin was not involved at all, and met Mr Chapman by chance as Mr Rushkin was leaving work as a barman at the King's Arms and offered Mr Chapman a lift, as they both live in the same street. The screwdriver is acknowledged to match the one missing from Mr Rushkin's set, but he and his wife Mrs J. Rushkin offer another explanation. Counsel should note that the exact details of how the screwdriver came to be used for opening tins of paint were not given in police interview, and indeed not given to instructing solicitors until the information was volunteered by Mrs Rushkin. This could cause problems in cross-examination on this point.

15. Mr Rushkin has served a defence disclosure statement. He recalls being in the King's Arms until after midnight, and is confident of his recollection because his pay is based on the time actually worked, and that night was unusually long. The alibi is supported by one witness, Mr Gramsci, who is the landlord of the pub. This witness has also been interviewed by the police and apparently gave a consistent story – but this was not sufficient to persuade the police not to charge Mr Rushkin.

16. Neither of the defence witnesses, Mrs Rushkin or Mr Gramsci, say they have any previous criminal record.

Evidential Issues

17. The police found a screwdriver bearing fingerprints. When analysed these bore the mark of neither Chapman nor Rushkin. Similarly a hair sample taken from a hat found at the scene did not match either man. The identification witness does not mention either man wearing a hat. Counsel may wish to cross examine PC Abrahams to establish that a hat was found which could not have been Mr Rushkin's, and to cross examine the identification witness Ms Paling on whether one of the men she saw had a hat. Admissions have been obtained under s. 10, Criminal Justice Act 1967, that the hair samples and fingerprints were not those of either Rushkin or Chapman (enclosure 24).

18. A description given by Dr Hattersley to the police in a phone call at exactly the relevant time and place (and confirmed in the police telephone transcripts (enclosure 22) as arriving within seconds of that of the witness in the overlooking flat) describes Chapman but describes a second person clearly different to Rushkin in age, but more like him in height, glasses and the presence of a scar. Ms Paling said the man was bald, which indeed Mr Rushkin is, but Dr Hattersley does not mention this.

20. The identification witness Ms Paling claims to have had a good view of Mr Rushkin. The distance was 40 yards, by her own estimate and confirmed by the map drawn by DC Plumber (enclosure 27). Instructing solicitors, who attended the parade, believe she is a woman in her fifties, and she was wearing glasses. Counsel will wish to consider cross-examining her about her eyesight, and whether she wore glasses at the relevant time (having been woken from sleep). Mr Rushkin accepts that the description given to the police fits him, save that he was not wearing a green and blue anorak, but a yellow and blue one. Given that the light is said to be a good one, this could be put to the witness as an error of observation not merely caused by the lighting. Counsel will also refer to the medical report (enclosure 26) and the proof of Mr Rushkin, both of which confirm that he walks with a pronounced limp. The witness Ms Paling makes no mention of the person she saw limping, and again counsel may consider this in cross examination. Your instructing solicitor has met Mr Rushkin on a number of occasions and has never seen him walk without a limp, and this is confirmed by Mr Gramsci and Mrs Rushkin.

21. A further medical aspect of the defence case, confirmed by the medical evidence of Dr Miller, is that Mr Rushkin suffers from an injury sustained in a road accident some 22 months ago. Mr Rushkin states categorically that he could not clear the six foot wall he is alleged to have climbed to escape from the yard at MegaWin. The opinion of the consultant is that such a feat is extremely unlikely. The prosecution agreed the height of this wall, and the photograph showing it (enclosure 25) at the plea and directions hearing. Counsel will, of course, note that the medical report, while helpful, does not reveal any present physical symptoms, and Dr Miller has helpfully pointed out in his covering letter (with enclosure 23) that this will be a matter obvious to any orthopaedic surgeon. Aggressive cross-examination of Dr Miller is therefore likely. The medical report has been disclosed to the prosecution under s. 9, Criminal Justice Act 1967 and a letter was received stating that the prosecution will not accept this evidence without the witness attending.

22. The defence case is clearly a difficult one in relation to the screwdriver, the parade, and being apprehended with Mr Chapman. Other matters which counsel will please consider in preparing the case are that Mr Rushkin has a recent conviction for a similar offence (burglary – see enclosure 18). Instructing solicitors believe there is no risk of him being cross-examined on his character, as there is no aspect of the defence case that would amount to an imputation on a prosecution witness. Will counsel please advise if she anticipates problems in this area? Additionally, Mr Rushkin can anticipate unpleasant cross examination when it comes to his medical condition. He says he is unable to work, and is drawing unemployment benefit, while at the same time engaging in what the prosecution may suggest are relatively strenuous duties in his casual work. Although not relevant to any fact in issue, the jury will become aware that he is claiming a means tested benefit without declaring his casual earnings. Counsel will please consider whether any tactics can be used to minimise any prejudical conclusion, and will no doubt ensure that no inadmissible questions are put to him in relation to this matter. Instructing solicitors have discussed these matters with Mr Rushkin.

Mitigation

23. If Mr Rushkin is found guilty, counsel will please mitigate in relation to this offence, and that of driving whilst disqualified, to which he will then plead guilty in accordance with s. 41, Criminal Justice Act 1988.

24. The offence of driving whilst disqualified is, as counsel is aware, treated by the Magistrates' Association as attracting an initial custodial sentence, and no doubt the judge will take a similar view. In mitigation it can be said that this was the only time he took the decision to use the vehicle, and that Mr Rushkin has been a driver for over 20 years, with no previous blemish on his record. The offence of driving whilst over the limit for alcohol was freely admitted, and Mr Rushkin points out that the excess of blood alcohol over the limit of 35 mg was small – his reading was 42. On the present occasion he took the car on the spur of the moment. He was late for work because of a surprise visit from his daughter, who lives in London, and the early start on that day. Although he does not offer any excuses, he hopes the court will recognise that this offence was not premeditated nor part of a series of offences. If Mr Rushkin is convicted of the attempted burglary, however, the court may take the view that the use of his car to commit an offence, during a period of disqualification, makes the offence considerably more serious. Mr Rushkin has an otherwise clean licence, which is of course currently surrendered.

25. In respect of the attempted burglary, counsel will be aware that the previous offence of burglary only a year ago is likely to be taken into account in increasing the seriousness of the present offence, both for purposes of a possible custodial sentence, and for a community sentence. Instructing solicitors take the view that the court will be considering either a community sentence or a custodial sentence, in view of the earlier offending, and the not guilty plea. In that case, the court will order a pre-sentence report. Mr Rushkin will consent to any appropriate community sentence, for example community service. Counsel will please consider the pre-sentence report and any instructions received from Mr Rushkin after trial and seek to mitigate accordingly in relation to both offences.

26. Mr and Mrs Rushkin's financial position is as follows (all figures are weekly):

income support:	£104.05
child benefit:	£10.80
average weekly earnings from pub:	£40

Rent and council tax are met directly.

> | Outgoings: | catalogue debt repayments: | £5 |
> |---|---|---|
> | | T.V. licence: | £1.50 |
> | | Car (tax, insurance, repair, depreciation, fuel) | £20 |
>
> | Food | £25 |
> |---|---|
> | Gas | £10 |
> | Electricity | £5 |
> | Water | £7.50 |
> | Telephone | £5.00 |
>
> The family have debts of £350 to Benwicks Department Store.
>
> Instructing solicitors have asked Mr Rushkin to produce documentary evidence of these items before trial.
>
> 27. Instructing solicitors have advised Mr Rushkin that at sentencing the court may take an unsympathetic view of the fact that he has continued to claim unemployment benefit and income support during a period when he has been in employment which may well disqualify him.
>
> 28. Counsel is requested to advise generally in conference; to attend on Mr Rushkin's behalf at pre-trial review, and to represent him on a not guilty plea. If necessary will counsel please mitigate on sentence if he is convicted, and advise orally and if requested in writing on any appeal.
>
> JW 21 August 1997

Before trial Steven informs Jane that, following discussions with her and counsel at the conference, he has decided to notify the Department of Social Security that he has casual employment, and as a result he no longer receives income support. His wife has obtained part time work.

The family are financially no better off, but Jane must nevertheless inform the court of the new situation. The change in financial status means that Steven may have to pay a contribution towards legal aid – withdrawal is most unlikely. She helps Steven complete a fresh means form, taking into account both his own earnings and those of his wife. Because he no longer receives income support, he must also declare his outgoings in detail.

Trial: Oldcastle Crown Court: 12 September 1997

Trial takes place – the most important part of the case, and we skip right over it! That is not what the case study is about. But any reader who has not watched a few trials should stop reading and get down to the courts now.

As it turns out, counsel's lack of optimism was justified. Steven was convicted. Clearly the jury believed that Steven was identified accurately, that he could climb a six foot fence if necessary, that Dr Hattersley was right in saying he could not remember events that well, that the screwdriver going missing for painting was just too improbable (overlooking the problem of just whose prints were on it), and that Steven was stretching credulity too far by suggesting that he picked up Mr Chapman only afterwards. Mr Chapman was never called for either side, so his admission to committing the offence was not in fact in evidence at all.

The medical evidence of Dr Miller did not assist greatly, as in cross-examination he had to admit that had he known that Steven was working in a pub he would not have been so certain of his conclusions about his ability to run and climb.

Sentencing: Oldcastle Crown Court: Monday 6 October 1997

So there remains nothing but the sentencing. After a three week remand in custody, the case returns to court with the following pre-sentence report now available to the court, and to counsel.

Document 79

Confidential

Northern Probation Service

This is a pre-sentence report as defined in s. 3(5) of the Criminal Justice Act 1991. It has been prepared in accordance with the requirements of the Probation Service National Standards for pre-sentence reports.

Court Oldcastle Crown Court   Date 6th October

Full name Steven Rushkin   DOB 53 Age 44 years

Offence(s)   Driving whilst disqualified 19 April 1997

               Attempted burglary 18 April 1997

Basis of the Report

I base this report on an interview with Mr Rushkin while in custody on 23 September, an interview with his occasional employer, Philip Gramsci on 26 September, and a discussion with Mr Rushkin's wife at her home on 26 September.

1. Sources of information
Attempted burglary. Following conviction for this offence Mr Rushkin continues to deny the offence. It has therefore been impossible to discuss with him his attitude to the causes of the offending. I have not had access to CPS information.

Driving whilst disqualified. This occurred when he drove to work on 18 April instead of catching a bus, which was his normal practice. He acknowledges that he knew he was driving in breach of the disqualification imposed on 7 February 1997, and he states that this was and remains the only occasion when he has succumbed to the temptation of using the car. He says that he had missed the bus, and his employer had asked him to report early to his work as a barman because of the expected pressure of work that evening.

2. Relevant information about the offender
Mr Rushkin has appeared before the Central Magistrates' Court on two previous occasions. In August 1995 he appeared before the court for an offence of causing actual bodily harm, and in August 1996 for an offence of burglary. In both instances he pleaded guilty and was fined. I understand that all fines were paid off promptly.

3. Personal information
   (1) Steven Rushkin is a man of 44 who had not been any trouble until reaching the age of 42. Mr Rushkin informs me that the first offence was committed as a result of a dispute with a neighbour who was persistently blocking his driveway. Tempers rose on both sides, and Mr Rushkin accepts that he responded to what he saw as threats in an excessive fashion. This offence

was committed on the spur of the moment, and both Mr Rushkin's other history, his manner, and the comments made by his wife and Mr Gramsci indicate that he is not normally a violent or even hot-tempered man.

(2) In January 1996 Mr Rushkin was a passenger in a car which was involved in a road accident. He has been left with permanent injuries to his back. He was, until that time, a self-employed painter and decorator with a successful business. The accident and the resulting incapacity have changed his life. When he came out of hospital he says he was very depressed. His inability to work, or even to carry out simple household tasks like decorating his own home, caused him to become very moody and unpredictable. His wife comments that the changes were very marked, and are still very evident. In my opinion he has suffered a serious loss of self esteem, and it is apparent to Mr Rushkin, and I accept what he says on this, that this unpredictability of mood led directly to the burglary in 1996.

(3) The burglary in 1996 was a spur of the moment decision, carried out on a derelict house, with no resulting gain to Mr Rushkin or his companion. Mr Rushkin informs me that it was not planned, and that he was not the one who suggested it. Again he tells me, and I accept, that he was behaving out of character through the depression.

(4) The breach of bail while awaiting a hearing on this burglary charge similarly appears to have been a direct result of the depression Mr Rushkin suffered at the time.

(5) Despite the difficulties resulting from the accident, Mr Rushkin presents as a man with a positive outlook. He has been determined to pick himself up, and has obtained casual work at a bar several nights a week. He tells me that he does this work against the advice of his doctor, and even though it now leaves him without income support and invalidity benefit.

(6) Mr Rushkin has a stable home life, and despite the depression of the past two years, it is apparent from what he and Mrs Rushkin each say independently that the marriage is a strong one and he can count on her continued support. As a result of the recent loss of State benefits to the household, Mrs Rushkin has now obtained part time work. While Mrs Rushkin does not accept that Mr Rushkin is guilty of the present offence of attempted burglary, she is supportive of his desire to stay out of any further trouble.

4. Financial circumstances

It is an indication of Mr Rushkin's determination to overcome his difficulties that he has obtained casual, but regular, work in a bar, even though he would have preferred to resume his work as a decorator. He has thereby disentitled the family from income support and lost the right to invalidity benefit. His wife has been supportive, and herself obtained part time work as a cleaner. Their net weekly income is:

Mr Rushkin (average)	£70
Mrs Rushkin	£65

Because of the low level of income, they obtain 100% assistance with rent and council tax

Outgoings are estimated at:

Food	£25
Catalogue repayments	£5
Gas	£10
Electricity	£5
Water	£7.50
Telephone	£5
Car (running and depreciation)	£20

The family has debts of £385 to Benwicks Department Store.

> 5. Conclusion and proposal
>
> Mr Rushkin's problems seem to start from an obvious cause, the injuries in 1996. In my opinion, leaving out of account the present offences, he has done his utmost recently to pull himself out of the despair and uncharacteristic behaviour which he fell into at first. He is a man who has, surprisingly in view of the offending in 1996, received no professional help or counselling to assist him to adjust to his changed circumstances. While talking to him to prepare this report I reached the conclusion that the opportunity for guidance, combined with his positive attitude to overcome his difficulties, could lead to a marked improvement in his personal circumstances. I believe that with professional assistance it is extremely unlikely Mr Rushkin will re-offend, particularly in view of his age and previous record. I recommend a period of probation for one year, a recommendation with which Mr Rushkin has indicated he is willing to comply. He would be required to report in accordance with national standards. Mr Rushkin has indicated that he will seek medical advice in relation to the depression. I do not believe conditions need to be attached to any order.
>
> I submit that a community sentence of this sort is appropriate not only because of Mr Rushkin's needs for support and counselling, but also because I see this as a disposal most likely to address the root cause of Mr Rushkin's offending. A custodial sentence would affect not only Mr Rushkin's attempts to re-establish a stable life, including regular employment, but would adversely affect his wife. If this recommendation is accepted, then it follows that a custodial sentence in relation to the road traffic offence would be counter-productive. The court may, I respectfully suggest, wish to dispose of this offence by way of a financial penalty and a further period of disqualification.
>
> Ms. Barbara Cavendish
> Probation Officer
>
> 29 September 1997

It is not necessary, nor generally possible, to send counsel a separate brief for the mitigation. The original brief contained instructions to mitigate, and counsel, having attended the trial, will know the facts of both offences. The pre-sentence report is probably not available until the sentencing hearing in any event, although there is no reason for the defence not to contact the probation service to discuss its contents in advance.

The Outcome: 6 October 1997

Steven is sentenced on 6 October to a period of imprisonment of three months in relation to the attempted burglary. An attempt to have it suspended fails, as, contrary to earlier practice of seeing a suspended sentence as another step up the tariff, it should now only be imposed in 'exceptional circumstances' (s. 22(2)(b), Powers of Criminal Courts Act 1973). A compensation order of £250 (the actual cost of repair was higher than originally estimated) was also ordered.

For the driving whilst disqualified he is sentenced to one month's prison concurrent. He also receives six penalty points to his licence (obligatory in the absence of special reasons not to endorse the licence) and discretionary disqualification of two years (which runs concurrently with the remainder of the existing disqualification).

A three month sentence actually means one and a half months in prison. (Early release for a sentence of under 12 months is half way through – s. 33, Criminal Justice Act 1991.) Taking into account 27 days already spent on remand in custody, he will serve just over two more weeks.

An order for prosecution costs of £500 is also made.

Counsel is asked to advise on the merits of an appeal against sentence. This is within the scope of the original legal aid order (Notes for Guidance 17, para. 04), although an appeal itself would require legal aid from the Crown Court or the Court of Appeal, which will not be granted until the notice of appeal has been lodged (reg. 22(5)(a), Legal Aid in Criminal and Care Proceedings (General) Regulations 1989). The application for an extension of legal aid can be made on the notice of appeal itself. The notice of appeal must be signed by the client or on the client's express instructions.

It is not strictly necessary to send formal instructions to counsel to advise, given that the original brief included instructions to advise on appeal if necessary. In fact if this causes any delay, it is best to confer with counsel by telephone – see *A Guide to Proceedings in the Court of Appeal Criminal Division* (1983) 77 Cr App Rep 138. I have drafted instructions in this case to highlight the arguments that will be relevant, but these instructions must be sent urgently to counsel.

Document 80

IN THE OLDCASTLE CROWN COURT   Case No. OL2000

R

v

Steven Rushkin

INSTRUCTIONS TO ADVISE ON APPEAL AGAINST SENTENCE

---

1. Counsel has, at the request of instructing solicitors, retained the papers in this matter, and there are no further enclosures.

2. In the brief for trial counsel was requested to advise on an appeal against conviction and/or sentence if appropriate. At the time of the sentencing the defendant was unsure if he wished to consider an appeal, and therefore instructing solicitors have sought further instructions. Mr Rushkin does indeed wish to appeal against sentence, and counsel is requested to advise accordingly.

3. Counsel is fully aware of the facts of the case. In relation to the sentence instructing solicitors make the following observations:

   1. Driving whilst disqualified: a term of immediate imprisonment for a first offence is harsh. In the absence of a Newton hearing, the court is presumed to have accepted that this was the only occasion on which he had driven since disqualification. However, counsel will recall that the judge took into account that the offence was committed in the course of committing another offence, the attempted burglary.

   2. The attempted burglary: the court stated that the seriousness of this offence was such that only custody was appropriate. The court took into account Mr Rushkin's offence of burglary a year previously in viewing the present offence as being more serious, as it is entitled to do. However, using the seriousness indicators from the Magistrates' Association for both the offence in 1996 and the attempt for which he stands convicted this time, it appears that neither offence is at the serious end: only the fact that the offence was at night, damage was caused, and the fact of a previous conviction, indicate seriousness for the present offence. The Association's guidelines make a community sentence the normal entry point. In 1996, Mr Rushkin was fined – an outcome below the seriousness threshold for custody or even a community sentence. Instructing solicitors would argue that the court was not justified in stating that the present offence was so serious that only custody was appropriate.

The court seems to have ignored all mitigating factors raised by counsel and referred to in the pre-sentence report under s. 28, Criminal Justice Act 1991. Even if the court had been minded to make a custodial disposition on the seriousness of the crime, after considering the tragic circumstances which have led Mr Rushkin into offending, and after learning of the positive effect guidance from a probation order could have on Mr Rushkin, instructing solicitors believe a community disposition to be the most sensible outcome.

Instructing solicitors are aware, of course, that the Court of Appeal can increase as well as confirm or decrease any sentence. Mr Rushkin may well have been released by the time the appeal can be heard, and he is aware that he runs the risk of being returned to custody if the sentence is increased. However, despite advising Mr Rushkin clearly of this risk, your instructing solicitors are instructed to appeal if counsel so advises. It appears that Mr Rushkin is motivated as much by his continuing protestations of innocence as by the severity of the sentence, although he recognises that there appear to be no grounds for an appeal against conviction.

Will counsel, if she advises to proceed with an appeal, draft the apropriate grounds of appeal? Counsel will be aware of the time limit for lodging an appeal, which expires on 4 November 1996. If counsel advises against an appeal, will she kindly advise in writing?

JW
13 October 1997

To Appeal or not to Appeal

The advice sought, and the notice of appeal, can all be paid for under the existing legal aid order. If the appeal goes ahead, further legal aid will be necessary, though a separate means assessment will not be required unless Mr or Mrs Rushkin's means have changed.

The notice of appeal must be served on the Crown Court's 'appropriate officer' within 28 days of sentence (or conviction if appeal relates to conviction) – rule 2, Criminal Appeal Rules 1968 and s. 18(1), Criminal Appeal Act 1968. The form of the notice is set out in Form 2 prescribed by the 1968 Rules, and must be accompanied by the grounds of appeal set out according to Form 3 of the Rules.

Counsel's advice is not set out here. In essence counsel thought that the sentence was better than it might have been. The attempted burglary might have attracted a much longer term of imprisonment (see for example *R v Dorries* (1993)14 Cr App R 608 and *R v Kyle* (1993) 14 Cr App Rep 613 – in both cases it was accepted by the defence as well as the prosecution that for a run of the mill burglary without particular aggravating features the custody threshhold from s. 1, Criminal Justice Act 1991 is reached. *R v Teteh* [1993] Crim LR 629 provides any similar facts leading to a non-custodial outcome under s. 1 – but in that case the defendant pleaded guilty, and was able to claim the crime was committed on impulse. This is not open to Mr Rushkin. (The earlier a plea of guilty is indicated, the greater the mitigation – s. 44 of the Criminal Justice and Public Order Act will make this even clearer.)

The one month for driving whilst disqualified could possibly be excessive, but against that did the client want to re-open the possibility of any increase given that it had now been served by time spent on remand? Any appeal against the additional period of disqualification is optimistic.

Notice of Appeal

If counsel had advised to go ahead with the appeal, or indeed if Mr Rushkin had appealed notwithstanding counsel's advice, it would be the solicitor's task to draft the notice (but not the grounds which I have left blank). A notice of appeal in Form 2 is set out below (Document 80).

Document 81

R v RUSHKIN

The Court of Appeal Criminal Division

Form **NG** (Forms 2 & 3)

NOTICE and GROUNDS of appeal or application for leave to appeal
(Criminal Appeal Act 1968)   CAO No. ___ / ___ / ___

● Please read the notes for guidance overleaf. Write in BLACK INK and USE BLOCK CAPITALS

ON COMPLETION PLEASE SEND THIS FORM TO THE CROWN COURT WHERE TRIED OR SENTENCED

The appellant
give full name

Surname: RUSHKIN
Forenames: STEVEN

If in custody give Prison Index Number and address where detained

Address: HM PRISON RIVERSDALE, IRONGATE, RIVERSDALE
Post code: RV1 1DT
Date of birth: 12.1.53

Prison index no.: 1 2 3 4 5 6

The Court where tried or sentenced

Give details if the case was transferred from another court

The Crown Court at: OLDCASTLE
Name of Judge: McQUEEN

Underline the dates of conviction and sentence

Dates of appearance in the Crown Court: 12.9.97   6.10.97
Total period of remand in custody prior to sentence: 29 DAYS

The conviction(s) and sentence(s)
The full Crown Court case number(s) must be given, and particulars of ALL counts, offences and sentences included.

Crown Court case number(s)	Count or charge no.	Offence	Sentence
OL 2000	1	ATTEMPT BURGLARY SECTION 1, CRIMINAL ATTEMPTS ACT 1981	3 MONTHS PRISON
	2	DRIVING WHILST DISQUALIFIED SECTION 103, ROAD TRAFFIC ACT 1988	1 MONTH PRISON CONCURRENT, 6 PENALTY POINTS, DISQUALIFIED 2 YEARS

Number of offences taken into consideration: NIL
Total sentence: 3 MONTHS

Applications SEE NOTE 5
The appellant is applying for: *Please tick as appropriate*

SPECIMEN

- [ ] Extension of time in which to apply for leave to appeal against conviction and/or sentence
- [ ] Leave to appeal against conviction
- [x] Leave to appeal against sentence
- [x] Legal aid
- [ ] Bail
- [ ] Leave to call a witness

F1457 (10/87) XBD P2295

SPECIMEN

Notes for guidance on the completion of this form

1. Everyone who is convicted or sentenced in the Crown Court in circumstances where an appeal would lie to the Court of Appeal Criminal Division should have advice or assistance on appeal. Provision for this is included in a trial legal aid order (section 30(7) Legal Aid Act 1974).

2. Solicitors and counsel are expected to be familiar with 'A Guide to Proceedings in the Court of Appeal Criminal Division' (available from any Crown Court Centre and reproduced in "Archbold Criminal Pleadings Evidence and Practice" 1992 Volume 1 at 7-173.

3. Separate forms should be submitted for convictions or sentences which do not arise in the same proceedings.

4. This notice will be treated as a notice of appeal where leave to appeal is not required.

5. **Applications**

   This should be sent to the appropriate officer of the Crown Court within 28 days of the conviction, sentence, verdict or finding appealed against. If the appellant is in custody the form should be handed to the prison authority (or other person having custody) for forwarding to the Crown Court, and the date of handing in should be recorded on the form.

   - Extension of time

     The period of 28 days cannot be extended except by leave of the Court of Appeal Criminal Division and the reasons for the delay will be required.

     NOTE that the time for applying for leave to appeal against conviction runs from the date of **conviction** even where sentence is passed on a later date.

   - Leave to appeal against conviction
   - Leave to appeal against sentence } See note 6

   - Legal aid

     A legal aid order made in the Crown Court does not provide for oral argument before the Court of Appeal. If legal aid is sought for this purpose it should be applied for.

   - Bail

     Where bail is applied for **Form B** must also be completed. If Form B accompanies Form NG it should be submitted to the Crown Court but if submitted later should be sent to: The Registrar, Criminal Appeal Office, Royal Courts of Justice, Strand, London WC2A 2LL.

   - Leave to call a witness (Conviction applicants only)

     Application made on **Form W** which should be included only where leave is sought to call a witness in support of an application for leave to appeal against **conviction**. A separate form is required for each witness. If Form W accompanies Form NG it should be sent to the Crown Court but if submitted later should be sent to: The Registrar, Criminal Appeal Office, Royal Courts of Justice, Strand, London WC2A 2LL.

6. **Grounds of appeal**

   Where grounds have been settled by counsel **they must be signed by counsel** with the name of counsel printed underneath, and attached to this form. There is no obligation to include a copy of counsel's advice although in some cases it may be helpful to do so. Grounds must be settled with sufficient detail to enable matters relied upon to be clearly identified. Wording such as "the conviction is unsafe and unsatisfactory" or "the sentence is in all circumstances too severe" will be ineffective as grounds and an extension of time may have to be applied for (see note 5). Unsigned grounds will be returned with resulting delay to the application.

7. Where a certificate that the case is fit for appeal is granted by the trial judge this should be stated and see generally paragraph 17 of 'A Guide to Proceedings in the Court of Appeal Criminal Division'.

8. Where an appellant has been **granted** leave to appeal he is entitled to be present on the hearing of his appeal. It will be assumed that an appellant in custody is applying for leave to be present at any hearing for which leave to be present is required unless he indicates to the contrary.

Grounds of appeal see notes 6 and 7

SPECIMEN

R v RUSHKIN

> I understand that if I am in custody, and the single judge and/or the court is of the opinion that the appeal is plainly without merit, an order may be made that time spent in custody as an appellant shall not count towards sentence.
>
> I also understand that whether or not I am in custody the court may make an order for payment of costs against me, including the cost of any transcript obtained.
>
> This form should be signed by the appellant but may be signed by his/her legal representative *provided* the WARNING set out above has been explained to him, and he is sent a copy of this form.

Signature of appellant

S Ruskin

Date 13.10.97

Details of any person signing on *behalf* of the appellant:

Name _____
Solicitor/Counsel*

Address _____

post code ___ DX number ___
Telephone No. ___ Reference ___

Delete as appropriate

FOR PRISON USE

This notice was handed to me by the appellant today.

Signed _____ Prison Officer

Date _____

Appellant's Index No. _____

EDR. _____

PED. _____

FOR CROWN COURT USE

Notice received:
Signed _____   Date _____

Sent to CAO:
Signed _____   Date _____

Name and full address / DX number of Prosecuting Authority:
_____
_____

This notice must be sent to the Registrar of Criminal Appeals together with trial documents **forthwith**

SPECIMEN

FOR CROWN COURT USE

Immediately upon receipt of Form NG the Crown Court must complete and send tear off slips 1-4 overleaf as applicable and record the action taken below:

tick appropriate boxes

Date sent _____

Signed _____

Slip 1 (Acknowledgement)
☐ sent to _____

Slip 3 (Monetary penalty/order)
☐ _____ Mags. Ct

Slip 2 (Sentencing remarks)
☐ Messrs _____

Slip 4 (Statements)
☐ CPS _____

R v RUSHKIN

Slip 4 Request for transcript of sentencing observations
(to be sent if application/appeal is against sentence only).

NB Please send this request by Fax Machine if possible.   From: Chief Clerk _____
                                                          Crown Court at _____
To Messrs_____ (Shorthand-   Sentencing Judge _____
Dear Sir,   Writers)   Crown Court Case Number _____
R v _____   Note taker _____
Date of sentence_____

Copies of the appropriate record sheets are attached.
Would you please supply transcript (top and one carbon) of Judges observations on passing sentence
(including any co-accused), enclosing this slip and any fax confirmation slip for reference purposes, to:

The Transcript Section, Criminal Appeal Office,   (telephone 071-936-6817   Yours faithfully,
Royal Courts of Justice,   DX:RCJ 44450 Strand
Strand, London WC2A 2LL   FAX: 071-936-6900   Date:

Slip 3 Notification to Magistrates of appeal in cases involving monetary penalty or
order (to be sent in all cases involving monetary penalty or order)

To: Clerk to the Justices   From: Chief Clerk _____
_____ Magistrates   Crown Court at _____
Dear Sir,   Date _____
R v _____   Crown Court Ref. _____

I write to inform you that in this case in which you are responsible for enforcing the monetary
penalty or order the above-named has lodged notice of appeal to the Court of Appeal Criminal
Division.

                          Yours faithfully,   SPECIMEN

Slip 2 Notification to Prosecuting Authority of receipt of Application for
leave to appeal to the Court of Appeal (to be sent in all cases)

To: _____   From: Crown Court at _____
Dear Sir/Madam   Date _____
R v _____   Crown Court Ref. _____

Please note that an application for leave to appeal has been received in the above matter. All exhibits must be retained
in safe custody pending the determination of the appeal. If the matter involves a committal for sentence, please forward
forthwith witness statements/statement of facts, enclosing this slip for reference purposes, to:

The Registrar, Criminal Appeal Office   (telephone 071 936 6011/6014)   Yours faithfully
Royal Courts of Justice,   DX: RCJ 44450 Strand
Strand, London WC2A 2LL   FAX: 071 936 6900   (on behalf of the Registrar)

Slip 1 Acknowledgement of form NG (to be sent in all cases to sender of form NG)

                                        From: Chief Clerk _____
                                        Crown Court at _____
                                        Crown Court Ref. _____
                                        Date _____

To: _____   Your Ref _____
                                        R v _____

Dear Sir,
I acknowledge receipt of forms NG (B* W*) which have been forwarded to the Registrar of Criminal Appeals for
attention. All further communications should be addressed to:
            The Registrar, Criminal Appeal Office   Yours faithfully,
            Royal Courts of Justice, Strand, London WC2A 2LL
            (Tel 071-936-6011/6014; DX: RCJ 44450 Strand; FAX: 071-936-6900)

* *Delete as appropriate*

R v RUSHKIN

In fact there is no appeal. Jane sees Steven briefly when he is released from Riversdale Prison. It remains only for Jane to advise Steven to avoid using his car until October 1999, to thank him for instructing her, and to submit her costs claim (Document 73) expeditiously.

Crown Court Costs

The payment rates, as you can see, from the claim below, are less generous than those in the magistrates' court. It is assumed that the fee earner is junior, probably not qualified, especially the attendances at court. A similar regime of standard profit costs operates. Disbursements are additional.

R v RUSHKIN

Document 82

Standard Fees

The Crown Court at OLDCASTLE
R -v- or Appeal of STEVEN RUSHKIN

Determining Officer:

Date:

To: WATKINS & O'DWYER
17 SYCAMORE AVENUE
OLDCASTLE OL10 2BR

- Boxes 2 *only* is to be completed by the solicitor

1.	Form No.	2984519
2.	Solicitor's L.A. code	A123B
3.	Record type	
4.	Court location code	A
5.	London weighting	
6.	Case number	
7.	Date of conclusion of case	
8.	Date of receipt of claim	
9.	Date of determination	
10.	Date of payment	
11.	Tape recording	
12.	Counsel alone	
13.	Class & Offence code	
14.	Type of case	
15.	Duration code	
16.	Length of case	Q
17.	Scheme year	
18.	No. of defendants	
19.	No. of cases	
20.	Amount claimed	

Legal Aid cost in the above case have been determined and a payable order is enclosed. Details of the determination are shown in the summary below. The rate codes 1, 2, 3 are as follows:

1 = basic rate, all work.
2 = more than basic rate, all or part work.
3 = less than basic, all or part work

Summary of Fees allowed			Fee Earner	Time/Items	Rate Code	Amount allowed	
STANDARD FEE FOR PREPARATION AND PERCENTAGE UPLIFTS	Principal Standard fee	SPF		—			21
	Lower Standard fee	SLF		—			22
STANDARD FEE FOR BAIL APPLICATIONS		SBA		—			23
ADVOCACY BY SOLICITOR		ADV	A				24
			B				25
				—	—		26
STANDARD FEE FOR ATTENDANCE & WAITING		SAW		—			27
SATNDARD FEE FOR TRAVELLING		STF		—			28
TRAVELLING		TRA	A				29
			B				30
			C				31
WAITING		WAI	A				32
			B				33
			C				34

SPECIMEN

HOW ORIGINALLY CLAIMED 0 0   35

SOLICITORS DISBURSEMENTS LIABLE TO VAT   DIS   36

VAT No. 123456789   TOTAL FOR VAT PURPOSES   37

VAT   38

OTHER DISBURSEMENTS (inclusive of VAT where appropnate)
Please specify, e.g. expert fees, medical reports, agency work and include receipted vouchers and accounts.

Transcript of interview tapes   34.25   39

TOTAL   34.25   40

LESS ANY PAYMENT ON ACCOUNT   41
TOTAL CLAIMED AND ALLOWED   42

Solicitor's signature J. Watkins
Ref: JW/Rushkin
011-111-1111

5144A Solicitor's claim for standard fees in Legal Aid in Criminal and Care Proceedings (Costs) Regulations 1989

R v RUSHKIN

The Crown Court at OLDCASTLE

Case No. 02 2000

Standard Fees Solicitors

Court copy

Notes for guidance may be obtained from the court

1. R-v- or Appeal **of**
   Messrs WATKINS & O'DWYER
   Address 17 SYCAMORE AVENUE
            OLDCASTLE

   Date of legal aid order 05.04.97
   Date of case disposal 10.10.97

   Date received

	Fee Claimed	For official use Fee allowed

2 STANDARD FEE FOR PREPARATION *tick where appropriate*

- Jury trial ☑
- Prepared for trial no jury sworn ☐
- Guilty plea ☐
- Appeal against conviction ☐
- Appeal against sentence ☐
- Committal for sentence/breach ☐
- Principal standard fee ☑ 312.00
- Lower standard fee ☐

Additional defendants (state number)

3 ADDITIONAL CASES (state number)
- Additional indictments
- Additional defendants
- Additional appeals
- Additional appellants
- Additional committals for sentence/breaches
- Additional defendants

SPECIMEN

4 ADDITIONAL FEES *tick where appropriate*
- Prepared for counsel to appear alone ☐
- Listened to tape of police interview ☐

5 STANDARD FEE FOR BAIL APPLICATIONS CONDUCTED BY SOLICITOR
(please give details)

Date

Additional defendants (state number)

6 ADVOCACY BY SOLICITOR (No standard fee provided)
(please give details)

	Hrs	Mins			Hrs	Mins
Waiting time						

7 STANDARD HOURLY FEES FOR ATTENDANCE AT COURT AND WAITING TIME WHERE COUNSEL ASSIGNED (please give details)

	Hrs	Mins	Date		
Attend client and counsel at Oldcastle Crown Court	6	05	12/9/97	150.56	
Attend client and counsel at Oldcastle Crown Court	2	45	15/9/97	68.06	
Attend client and counsel at Oldcastle Crown Court		45	16/10/97	18.56	

8 TRAVELLING TIME (please specify with reference to sections 2, 5, 6 and 7)

		Mins	Date		
Longfield - OCC - return - see 7		20	12/9/97	8.25	
Longfield - OCC - return - see 7		20	15/9/97	8.25	
Longfield - OCC - return - see 7		20	16/10/97	8.25	

9 SOLICITORS DISBURSEMENTS LIABLE TO VAT
(please specify journeys with reference to section 8)

	Miles	Rate	Date		Miles	Rate
Longfield - OCC - return	10	.36	12/9/97	3.60		
Longfield - OCC - return	10	.36	15/9/97	3.60		
Longfield - OCC - return	10	.36	16/10/97	3.60		

5144A Solicitors claim for standard fees in Legal Aid in Criminal and Care Proceedings (Costs) Regulations 1989

*sub-totals